LIKE A BAT OUT OF HELL

Also by Mick Wall:

LIKE A BAT OUT OF HELL

The Larger-than-life Story of Meat Loaf

MICK WALL

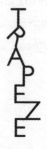

First published in Great Britain in 2017 by Trapeze,
an imprint of The Orion Publishing Group Ltd
Carmelite House, 50 Victoria Embankment,
London EC4Y 0DZ

An Hachette UK company

1 3 5 7 9 10 8 6 4 2

A CIP catalogue record for this book is
available from the British Library.

ISBN (Hardback): 978 1 4091 7352 6
ISBN (Trade Paperback): 978 1 4091 7353 3
ISBN (eBook): 978 1 4091 7354 0

Typeset by Input Data Services Ltd, Somerset

Printed and bound by CPI Group (UK) Ltd, Croydon, CR0 4YY

MIX
Paper from
responsible sources
FSC® C104740

www.orionbooks.co.uk

For Sandy Robertson, without whom . . .

CONTENTS

CONTENTS

THANK YOUS & ACKNOWLEDGEMENTS

Heartfelt thanks to all those that helped make this book a reality: Anna Valentine, Robert Kirby, Linda Wall, Jon Hotten, Marleigh Price, Kate Walsh, Jessica Purdue, Krystyna Kujawinska, Helena Caldon, Tomas Almeida, David Dickson, Steve Morant, Ian Clark, John Hawkins – and last but hardly least, Meat Loaf and Jim Steinman.

BAT ONE

The Wolf With The Red Roses

CHAPTER ONE

Lost Boy

'The object of the artist is the creation of the beautiful.
What the beautiful is, is another question.'
—*A Portrait of the Artist as a Young Man*, James Joyce

Some of this happened. All of it is true.

The guy at the restaurant table looks like late-period Howard Hughes, when the mad old billionaire was holed up at the Desert Inn in Vegas, dressed all in white and scared to touch anything because of the germs. He has long, grey hair that is so dry it might snap off in your hand if you try to grab it. His pallor is somewhere on the colour spectrum between 'haven't slept for three days' and 'haven't been outside for six years'. He is offended by the notion of fresh air. He has small beady eyes, pudgy hamster cheeks, a treble chin. He lives at night, rising at about 1am, and works feverishly through the small, lost hours in a house filled with clutter and junk, so that when he's forced into an accommodation with the rest of the world – as he has been today – and he actually goes out in daylight, he retains a vampiric quality, an otherness. He speaks in a melodious voice that is much lower than the one in which he sings, and for much of the time that he does this, a smile plays on the edges of his lips.

As if all of this isn't enough to get him noticed by the waiters who are dancing past the table – and the other diners who pretend not to notice but stare at him unblinkingly when they think he is not looking – he is wearing a black leather biker jacket that is decorated with studs and sequins in ornate patterns. On each upper arm is a death's head, hand-painted onto the leather. He is also wearing aviator sunglasses, Fat Elvis style, even though the restaurant is as dark as winter.

As a kid, an astrologist once told him he had an overwhelming desire to astonish people. But he didn't need a sign-reader to tell him that. Unable to decide what he wants to eat, he has ordered everything on the menu – *everything* – which causes the waiters to commandeer another table close by and load this and his own with dozens of silver bowls full of food. He talks and talks, and as he does, he tries a little from each of the bowls using his fingers to feed himself. His fingernails are long and white, but they quickly become stained by the different sauces he's dipping in and out of.

Talk, talk, talk.

Dip, dip, dip.

Talk, talk, talk.

Dip, dip, dip.

'I love eating . . .' he says, somewhat unnecessarily.

After ten or fifteen minutes no one else is eating, because no one else at the table can be sure which bowls have had his fingers in and which haven't. He is oblivious to this, and to all of the stares and the circling waiters. The conversation roams over his obsessions like high birds circling. One of those obsessions is wine, which he collects and drinks at night at his desk, he says. He writes about it in a journal, describing exactly how it tastes and how it makes him feel, and the journey it takes his imagination on.

'How much of this stuff have you got?' someone enquires.

'Oh, pages and pages, maybe thousands of them. If it was

published it would be the greatest book on wine ever written . . .'

Another obsession is motorcycles. He has dreams of seeing one driven wildly up the stone stairs of a church bell tower, he says, crashing through the roof down to the ground just as the bell strikes the hour. He doesn't own a motorcycle, though, or even a driver's licence, because he can't drive. A third obsession, the great obsession of his life, is music, specifically his music, which everyone agrees is like no one else's.

'Almost every song I write,' he says, 'has a line . . . A line that's explicitly, specifically sexual . . .'

Oh, yes? Can he give an example?

'Like, "*I know you belong, inside my aching heart . . . And can't you see my faded Levi's bursting apart . . .*" I'm very proud of that line. I call it the boner line. Or, "*Surf's up, surf's up, surf's up . . . and so am I . . .*" A boner line . . .'

He smiles happily at the thought.

No one at the table knows if he is married – unlikely, as he seems to live alone – or has a girlfriend, or has ever had one. He certainly has no children. He's happy to admit that he's 'a weird guy'. Maybe he's never had sex. Who knows? Who knows anything about him at all? Except his name: Jim Steinman.

Jim invented Meat Loaf. He created him in song. He tried to do it with others, but it worked best when it worked with Meat. And when it did . . . Meat Loaf was Jim, and Jim was Meat Loaf.

They existed together, or not really at all.

CHAPTER TWO

Poor Fat Marvin

Dallas, Texas, the morning of Friday, 22 November 1963. A sunny day in the Texan darklands . . .

Sixteen-year-old Marvin Aday and his pals Billy and Jimmy skipped school and drove down to the airport at Love Field to watch Air Force One, the president's plane, come in. There were hundreds of others with the same idea. Jimmy's dad worked there, and he had tipped them off about the side gate that Kennedy would use to get into his car. Many years later, Marvin would remember a conversation with one of the cops who was standing around:

'What if someone had a gun?'

'Well,' the cop said, 'if somebody was going to shoot him, they wouldn't do it here in Dallas.'

At least, that's how he remembered it. It had been a crazy kind of day, after all.

Marvin, Billy and Jimmy were in Mickey Mantle's Bowling Alley just after lunch when the receptionist said, 'The president's been shot . . .'

They drove out to Parkland Hospital, because that was where all of the people who got badly hurt in Dallas were taken – the auto accident cases and gunshot victims. They'd sometimes hang around there when they had nothing else to do; it was like a free horror movie. As they got near the emergency room, a guy with

6

a badge pulled them over and told them not to get out of the car. They saw the limousine arrive, and watched wide-eyed as Jackie Kennedy got out, still dressed in the blood-spattered pink suit she'd been wearing all day. They saw Texas Governor John Connally carried out. They sat in the parking lot for an hour or so while guys with guns ran around. Soon there were so many rubberneckers they figured it was safe to get out of the car. They wandered around, through the crowds of police and senators and a group of women who were sitting on the ground crying. The secret service guy came back and offered them money for gas, which seemed strange, but no stranger than everything else that was going on. When they got back to school they were told off for missing football practice, but that night they saw themselves on the television news.

Many years later Marvin would read that there were no secret service agents in Dallas that day. What the hell? The whole thing had been weird. Lots of people in Dallas claimed to have known that Kennedy was going to be shot. The Warren Commission report turned out to be one of the stupidest things ever written, Marvin thought. There were some odd cases in Dealey Plaza – there was the guy holding an umbrella even though the sun was shining, there was the Babushka lady in her headscarf, the three tramps they found hiding out in a box car nearby (there was a crazy story that one of them turned out to be Woody Harrelson's father . . . it wasn't, but that kind of summed up what the day had become, at least in Marvin's mind).

Marvin's father, whose name was Orvis Wesley Aday, knew Jack Ruby, who shot Kennedy's supposed assassin Lee Harvey Oswald two days later at the Dallas Police Headquarters. Jack ran a few nightclubs and strip joints in town and entertained plenty of the local cops, who got free liquor and prostitutes for favours. Marvin's dad had been a cop, and he'd always tell Marvin that the police knew what Jack Ruby was going to do to Lee, which was how come he could get so close. It turned out that Jack had been at Parkland Hospital while Marvin and his pals had been there, too.

Orvis had quit the police force to become a salesman. He could charm the birds out of the trees and he soon had a business with Marvin's mother, Wilma, and a friend of theirs. They called it the Griffin Grocery Company, but all they sold was a homemade cough remedy. Orvis travelled small-town Texas finding family-run shops, known as mom-and-pop stores, that would stock it. At first they did well, but Orvis was a drinker, and had been ever since he'd returned home from the Second World War, invalided out of the army when he was struck by shrapnel from a mortar shell. He never spoke about it, instead he drank it all away in the strip of bars between Fort Worth and Dallas, terrifying places that he'd disappear in for days until Wilma arrived in her car, with young Marvin in tow, to pull him out. Many years later, Marvin would theorise that this was where he began to learn to act, putting on a tough-kid persona among all of the rough men drinking and shooting pool, even though he was really scared to death of this half-lit adult underworld.

Orvis was a big strong guy, and so were his brothers. Little Marvin was big, too. In first grade he was bigger than all of the other kids. By seventh grade, aged just eleven, he weighed 240 pounds and shopped for his clothes in the men's store. The football coach called him 'tree trunks' because of the size of his legs. There was a TV commercial for jeans that had the tag line: 'Poor fat Marvin can't wear Levi's . . .', which made him hate his name.

Marvin = fat kid's name. Marvin the fat kid. Poor fat Marvin the fat freak.

The alternative wasn't great, but at least there was one. All his life, his daddy had called him 'ML', which was short for Meat Loaf. It was meant as a term of endearment for his plump baby son, but as the years sped by and the boy just grew, it became a horribly apt name for a kid his size. It was still better than Marvin, though – anything was better than that. Plus, you know, there were Marvins everywhere but no one else was called Meat Loaf. Or even ML. Right?

So to hell with poor fat Marvin. There are some things that a fat kid from Texas just can't be expected to take.

Marvin's mom was something different. Like the rest of the family, Wilma was a big lady. But so what? She held everything together for him, acting as the defining force of his childhood. For twenty-five years she worked as a schoolteacher. She could sing, too. She and her sister Texie were part of a gospel group called the Vo-di-o-do Girls, who got as far as appearing live on Bing Crosby's syndicated radio show.

Texie went on to marry Frank Heath, who ran a chain of furniture stores across Texas, and they lived a rich, comfortable life. Wilma scrambled along with Orvis, her daredevil drunk, and Meat Loaf, her accident-prone, outsized son. Meat Loaf was a handful, no doubt. When he was four years old, he liked running away. Then he began getting concussions, all shapes and sizes, from being hit in the head with a toy arrow, hit on the head by the back window of the car, knocked out in a collision with a kid in a football helmet, kneed in the head playing football, hit on the head by a shot put (he ended up in the hospital after that one), hit in the head by a baseball, hit in the head by a brick, running into a goal post, getting his head stuck in a Corvette steering wheel . . . that's in addition to all the fights and other scrapes he got himself into.

Between Orvis and Meat Loaf, Wilma had plenty to worry about. Yet her son was like her in one way – well, two if you count the size thing – he was a singer, a performer, a born ham. Made for the stage.

Not that Wilma saw that straight away. 'My mother was a singer,' Meat recalled, 'my grandfather played four instruments: piano, trumpet, guitar and something else weird, like violin.' But

Wilma never saw any real musical potential in big little Marvin. 'I can remember driving down the road singing some song on the radio and my mother turned to me and said, "You can't carry a tune in a bucket. One thing you won't be is a singer! You better find something else to do, boy." I think that made me very angry, at that point. So just to spite her I decided to open my mouth and scream.'

Through high school he got a part in every play he could wangle his way into – *The Bad Seed, Charley's Aunt, The Music Man, Plain and Fancy* – sometimes with a few lines to say, sometimes with more. He'd do anything – tell a joke, sing a song, improvise a laugh or a gasp somehow. When the baseball coach told him he'd have to choose between sports and the play, there was no choice: he was a ham and he knew it, but he loved it, loved to connect with the crowd and his fellow performers. 'I was shy, as a kid,' he would tell me years later, fidgeting nervously in his chair, flicking his unkempt hair and drumming his fingers. 'When I was in high school I was shy.' Going on stage was a good way of concealing that shyness, he explained. He didn't have to think up things to say, how to be. He'd stand up there like Lennie from Steinbeck's *Of Mice and Men*, a giant kid playing the sucker, playing the fool and milking every moment. Years later, even after *Bat Out of Hell* had been such a success, he was still happier, he confessed, being onstage as someone called Meat Loaf than he was off it being Marvin the Fat Kid. Offstage, back in the so-called real world, was where all ML's troubles lay: the father who terrorised him, the kids at school who despised and bullied him. The disgusted looks of strangers as he came walking down the street with his heavy sailor's gait, avoiding his own glutinous reflection in store windows. He would watch movies on TV – cowboys and Indians – and imagine himself the white-hatted hero, sweeping the gorgeous gal off her feet. Then he'd drag himself up out of the chair as reality came crashing back in. He knew poor fat Marvin was never going to be the one who got the girl, yet onstage things were different; he would get double the attention, but in a good way. He still feared the bullies and the shitkickers, but he didn't feel so worthless any more. Didn't feel like roadkill. Onstage he could be anyone he wanted to be, almost. There he could turn that pain inside into something that gave pleasure to the outside.

Speaking to him years later, I wondered if it was this odd mix – of Meat Loaf the scary monster and Marvin the scaredy cat – that drew so many women to his shows? That explained the hot chicks lined up backstage? 'I don't know,' he said, apparently embarrassed by the question. 'I don't think it's me anybody's really interested in. It's the part I play.'

When he was fourteen, he got a part, albeit in the background, in a movie, appearing 'purely by accident' in the 1962 remake of a 1944 Rodgers & Hammerstein musical, *State Fair*, starring Pat Boone and Ann Margaret. 'A friend of mine owned a peanut farm that Pat Boone used to work on. So we went to see this movie being made and they said: "You kids want to be in this movie? Then you go stand up there on the rail and when the hog comes in go: 'Ooh, look at the hog!'"'

As a teenhooder he got a walk-on role in a local production of *Carmen* and saw what the pros got up to when they weren't onstage – smoking pot, having sex with one another . . . So he walked away from the football field and the baseball diamond and hung out with the kids in the musicals. They were the same kids who'd form local bands. Wilma didn't want Meat Loaf getting involved in this rock-music thing that everyone was talking about, but he did it anyway, when he could.

The first song he ever sang live with a band was a cover of 'Satisfaction' by the Stones, which he did with a local band who then asked him to come on the road with them. Wilma put her foot down at that one. 'My mother wouldn't let me travel to Waco, which was ninety miles down the road, to do it. My mother didn't want me in a travelling band.'

But the great cauldron of teenage passion was beginning to bubble. When Meat Loaf stayed out all night for the first time, Wilma grounded him and took away use of the car. Before he could stop himself he'd slapped his mother around the face. Wilma glared back at the boy, making his knees shake. He knew what would happen when she told his father. Knew what hell would descend upon him then. He begged for her forgiveness, vowing to never disrespect her again. Wilma made sure he kept his promise.

When Wilma decided she wanted Meat Loaf to go to a Christian College once he'd left high school, he gladly attended Lubbock Christian University, and there he found himself back in with all the baseball players and other jocks, the same crowd that had publicly shamed him throughout high school, so he transferred to North Texas State, where he began to worry about the draft, like all the other eligible boys. No one wanted to get their asses shot off in Vietnam, so he did whatever he could to avoid it – tried to flunk the physical by getting even fatter, attempted to fail the eye test on account of being colour blind – until he got deferred for four months, and then another two years.

Through all of this, Wilma was becoming sick – she was diagnosed with terminal breast cancer. Meat Loaf didn't really see it at first, but by the spring of 1967 it was bad. He went home from North Texas to visit for the first time in a few weeks, and by then Wilma was so ill she was in an oxygen tent in her bedroom. It scared him so much that he ran straight back to the airport and took the first flight to Los Angeles, where he hung out for a while and tried to forget what he'd seen. In his worst moments – being locked in cupboards at school because he looked like a monster, having other kids' parents tell him he couldn't play with them because he was too fat, all the bull-stabbings and traumas of his terrible teens – he often thought of suicide, mainly as a way of getting back at his tormentors. Really, though, he was terrified of death – the death of his beloved mother, the only one to ever treat him as almost-human, most of all. So he ran away, as he always did when things simply got too heavy – as he always would, even after he'd become a rock star, openly threatening suicide by then as the surest get-out of all. In LA, Meat Loaf let the heads and the freaks transport him from hell to Hollywood in the only way they knew how – weed, wine, beer. But it couldn't last. He finally got the awful call and his newfound friends raised the money for his plane fare home. He was so crazed with grief he tried to lift Wilma from her coffin in the funeral parlour. He blacked it all out, walked around in a daze, but the truth was the truth. And it was not his friend.

'Apparently, at my mother's funeral I was really crazy,' he would tell *Rolling Stone* many years later. 'And my father flipped out as well . . . It was like a movie.' The truth was Meat Loaf had run from Wilma, and so had Orvis. When Meat Loaf got back from California, Orvis was looking for whatever there was to be found in the bottom of a bottle. He was out on four- and five-day drunks. Orvis was a tough guy, a man's man, and drinking and fighting were the only coping methods he knew. That, and taking it out on his son. Wilma had left her boy a small inheritance but as he was a minor still, Orvis tried to take control of it. So Meat Loaf – determined not to allow his father back into his life – went to a judge to have the money given straight to him. Maybe it was because he got it, or maybe it was because Orvis was psychotic with booze and grief, it all came to a head one night when Marvin was at home with his friend Billy, and Orvis crashed in shouting about whores and motherfuckers and who knows what else. Billy got out of the house fast and then Orvis really lost it. He found the butcher's knife in the kitchen and tried to bring it down on his son as he lay on his bed. Meat Loaf got out of the way in a hurry and they got into a fistfight. Meat Loaf was mighty big but Orvis was even bigger and stronger, and he threw his terrified son around like a rag doll – all 250 pounds of him. Then Meat Loaf started to fight back.

'You really wanna know?' he scowled years later. 'My father tried to kill me with a butcher's knife. I was laying in my room and he comes in with a big butcher's knife and I roll off the bed and he plants it right dead in the centre of the bed! I get up, break three of his ribs and decide I'd better leave.'

It was a fight that had been brewing for years. Orvis had never tried to hide his contempt for his son – from the embarrassing and hurtful nickname he'd bestowed on him to the times he'd brutalised him, physically, emotionally, verbally, and left him raw with anger and humiliation. After their fight that night, Meat Loaf got out of the house in just his T-shirt and shorts, jumped into his '65 Chevy and never went back. Orvis wasn't dead but 'ML' had made his feelings clear. Wilma was the force that had somehow held the three of them together, but the void she'd left behind could never be filled. He knew that now, and even though it would haunt him for the rest of his days, Meat Loaf just knew he had to get out. The big little family sprang apart like dark matter in a black hole. Not only did Meat Loaf have the pain of losing Wilma, within a short time he'd lost his father too, having left him behind to wallow as he fled from him.

He took the money that Wilma had left him and rented an apartment in the Turtle Creek Park area of Dallas, where the grand old homes of the original Texas Republic now made way for high-rise blocks on the banks of the creek. Meat closed the door and didn't open it again for three months. He just wanted to shut out the world and everything in it, plus a few things that weren't any more.

Later, he'd sing a lot about Lost Boys.

For now, that's what he was.

CHAPTER THREE

Enlightened Lands

Amherst College wasn't the kind of place Meat Loaf was ever going to see the inside of. Its list of alumni includes one president, three prime ministers, a long line of senators and congressmen, a Supreme Court judge, four Nobel Laureates, twelve winners of the Pulitzer Prize, six winners of a MacArthur Fellowship, engineers, novelists, doctors, actors, scientists, businessmen, diplomats, three astronauts, a director of the FBI and, in the class of 1968, a reluctant, self-absorbed, over-indulged straggler named James Richard Steinman. Plus, another student by the name of David Eisenhower, only grandson of the 34th president of the United States, Dwight Eisenhower. This connection meant the college was permanently guarded by secret service agents, which for some students made it the safest place in the world to indulge in the new 'Mary Jane' culture of the times, as not even the cops were allowed near the place. Not that Jim needed much outside stimulus to fire his already overfed imagination.

'It was probably one of the most exclusive colleges in America, harder to get into than Harvard,' he recalled. 'It was a farce that I got in. The people at my high school were horrified. But the Dean of Admissions had this policy of trying to sculpt a class together. He put in about fifty high-risk people, who could totally fuck up, but we were good for friction. I did fuck up many times, too. But I was good for friction!'

Jim's father was a prosperous businessman who ran a steel distribution warehouse, his mother was a teacher of Latin and Greek. Home life was easy and educated and Jim grew up believing he could be anything he wanted to be, if he worked hard enough. Only snag: Jim didn't want to work, didn't like getting his hands dirty, didn't see the point in breaking his ass, like, why? Unless it was at something he really loved. But what did Jim really love? He'd have to think about it.

His father's steel warehouse was in Brooklyn, on the busy east river shore of Long Island, where Jim grew up. A privileged child of the lovely Five Towns area, where he attended George W Hewlett High School, a rich-kids' campus that produced students who did the stuff that rich kids got to do – TV producers, comedy writers, nightclub owners, poets, fashion designers, comedians . . . liberal arts types who lived lives largely untouched by the thunderous lightning-forked lives of nearby New York.

Jim was smart, everyone could see it, but he didn't seem to try. He wanted the other kids to think he was a slacker, even though the year he graduated Hewlett, 1965 (the same year Meat Loaf was crawling out of Thomas Jefferson High), he was one of four National Merit Scholarship semi-finalists.

What Jim really was already was a fantasist. Not a fantasist in the Billy Liar/conman/sociopath sense, but the truest kind – a dreamer, an imaginer, a creator of rich realms in which his vivid visions of himself and of others could exist. Despite the National Merit Scholarship thing, he would tell people that his high school career was so undistinguished that his counsellor would refuse to sign his application to Amherst College. Instead he said he gave Amherst admission department the full Steinman treatment, a story that he'd spent the summer after he'd graduated from high school hiking in the Kentucky Mountains, where he composed a musical based on Joyce's *A Portrait of the Artist as a Young Man*.

To anyone who knew him, the notion that Jim would go hiking

in Kentucky was ridiculous, and he'd never even read *A Portrait of the Artist as a Young Man*, let alone adapted it for the stage, he just liked the title, just the thought of it, the way it sounded out there in the so-called real world, and how it looked inside his mind, full of caves and streams and moonfall. Whatever the truth, Jim got in. And what a place Amherst was, a storied campus set in lush Massachusetts, in the Connecticut River valley, founded in 1821 and ever since had been one of the leading liberal arts colleges in the country, discreet, moneyed, true to its grand motto: 'Let them enlighten the lands'.

Jim styled a great joke about his freshman year. Having 'achieved' grade point averages of 16 in physics and 33 in calculus (out of a possible 100) he was summoned before his academic committee to explain himself. 'I've always been better at math than science . . .' he said, with an impressively straight face.

He would also claim to have twice used the death of his (very much alive) grandmother to explain away his poor record, and even then he was almost asked to leave Amherst on four occasions. Was *any* of that true?

It was true to Jim.

'In a way, lying was a kind of creativity,' he would tell the *Washington Post*, years later. 'It taught me an important lesson – that I could create myself. I've done a lot of great stuff that started out as pure faking or lying. A lot of the lies I made I had to live up to. I had to stay at Amherst, and I did become the kind of person who would hike through the Blue Mountains and write that opera.'

Well, the bit about the opera was true anyway. But what Jim thought of as true might either be true in the physical world, or his interior one. In his interior world anything was possible, nothing being truly true, yet everything permitted. He had grown up listening to Wagner as well as Little Richard. (A combination that birthed another of his good interview lines: 'Just call me Little Richard Wagner.')

'One of the first things I remember listening to on a record player,' he told his first biographer, Sandy Robertson, 'was Wagner's *Tristan & Isolde*, and I sat through the whole thing. I didn't know what I was hearing but I just thought it was incredible-sounding. And when it was all over I put on a Little Richard album. I think I got the two confused in my mind and I've never been able to untangle them . . . It never occurred to me that they were "different kinds of music" that "shouldn't" go together.'

In another interview from the time, he claimed that the more he played them back to back 'the more I was convinced that Wagner and Little Richard came from the same place. Even though Wagner elevated me to a point that Little Richard couldn't achieve.' Little Richard wasn't so much elevation as revitalisation. 'The thing is,' he went on, 'they were both amplified human beings. The Wagner material was about God, and Little Richard sounded like God. It made me realise that you don't have to remain a human being, that one of the great uses of art . . . is that it was like taking a pill and you were no longer just a human being. That's how I perceived the situation.'

In that interior world of Jim's, where giant eagles swam and talking wolves flew, there simply were no rules. Everything was true, if you wanted it to be. Life could always be made more of. 'All of my heroes were larger than life,' he said. '[The songs] were not personal in terms of my own life, but they were personally obsessive songs. They were all about my obsessions. I mean, none of them takes place in a normal world, for me. They all take place in very extreme worlds, very operatic. The key word is, really, "heightened".'

Jim's sexual awakening happened at a time when sex was becoming weaponised and politicised, when sex began to peak. In the 1950s it had been the preserve of married couples, unmentioned and only hinted at, yearned for but barely acknowledged. By the time he – and his future creation Meat Loaf – graduated high school things were loosening up. Born in the same year, exactly five weeks apart, by the time they hit college age the campuses were full of willing, switched-on girls, peace-sign sisters looking for right-on brothers: full-on summer-of-love stuff, dig, reefer gladness, LSD for tea, freedom for everyone, baby – as long as you knew the right kind of girls and they recognised you (or maybe they were the wrong kind . . . who knew any more? Not Jim. Nor Meat Loaf). The point was, if you were awakened to sex in the mid-sixties you had to encounter this duality: that it was something dark and forbidden and also something free and loving. That it was something so right and yet it felt so wrong. Bad for good, not least for inhibited teenage nerds still living off the fumes of their mamas and papas.

'I was a teenager right when sex was going from being overly repressed in the early sixties to totally free in the seventies, and it was very confusing,' Steinman would tell me years later. 'Shit, I remember shaking like a leaf the first time I was having sex. Terrified I was doing everything wrong, and a little bit horrified.'

But while Meat Loaf absented himself from the scene, even after he'd arrived in LA, the confusion lingered in Jim's psyche, ran so deep he didn't know what to do about it, how to let it out. Eventually it would show itself, unashamedly, in his songs. He may have been a rich kid with a future so bright he'd have to be blind to kill the glare, but in his interior world he was forever that scared, bemused kid full of desire and longing and fear. Everything he would write would be by that kid and for that kid, and somewhere within him a force would seek out others who understood how he felt to help him perform them.

That was the future, though.

First, Jim Steinman of Amherst College had to figure out what he was good at and what he wanted to be. It wasn't maths and it sure wasn't science. Strangely, though, he didn't think it would be music, either. Although he could play piano extremely well, he didn't think he could play it well enough. At the age of nine he'd wanted to be a concert pianist, but when he was thirteen he'd dropped his study for almost five years and barely sat at a piano. Worse, at Amherst he was surrounded by talent – real, unself-conscious talent, wherever he looked. So instead he thought he might write for film and theatre. The more he thought about it, the more it just made sense. Jim had been thinking cinematically in terms of narrative and story all of his life, weighing and judging the facts of his life best in images. Now, he decided, 'I wanted to make music that sounded like a movie . . .' Or, as he put it in 1990, 'I grew up liking extremes in music – big gothic textures. I never have much regard for more subtle stuff. Dire Straits may be good, but it just doesn't do it for me. I was attracted to William Blake, Hieronymus Bosch, I couldn't see the point in writing songs about ordinary, real-life stuff.'

His mother had 'always surrounded me with classical music', he recalled in a 1978 *Rolling Stone* interview. It was as familiar as old furniture. Until one Saturday morning, he said, when he was six or seven. 'I planned to get up early and go ride my bike. I turned on the radio just as this one station was starting a complete broadcast of "The Ring Cycle" by Richard Wagner – which is about 24 hours long. I just lay on the bed listening. I didn't move a muscle for most of the whole thing. I thought if I did, maybe I'd break the spell or something.' When the station humorously followed the broadcast with a parody of the monumental piece, Jim decided 'the juxtaposition made perfect sense to me, all that heroism and majesty followed by humour'.

It was the same with rock and opera – a very new and far-out concept in 1968. On paper, they didn't go together. In Jim's mind, though, they were flip sides of the same invaluable coin. 'They're both about extremes in content and form. Each puts incredible physical demands on a performer. And each of them has that great mix of the sublime and the ridiculous, heroism and humour.

Seems to me that people's barriers to enjoying both have more to do with sociology than the actual music and performances.'

Even though he loved simple pop fare like 'Yakety-Yak' and, one of his 'all-time favourites', 'Woolly Bully', he simply didn't have it in him to be able to write such brilliantly witty – and brief – pop songs. 'I'd give anything if I were. So I'm fascinated by those records.' Instead, he wanted to make music that was big-screen, Technicolor, boom-boom, music that unfolded in your mind like the curtains rising on a grand stage. The way great classics did. The only band that seemed to come close for Jim Steinman was The Doors – the band that brought LA-noir to rock, that combined Bach sinfonias and Coltrane inventions, overlaid with the Gothic acid-spiel of its young lion singer. 'They were like my favourite group from '68 to '72. The only thing is that Morrison wasn't all that funny.'

It was a key observation. When, later, Jim Steinman would preface the album version of Meat Loaf's 'You Took The Words Right Out Of My Mouth' with the famous no-laughing-at-the-back monologue that begins, *'On a hot summer night, would you offer your throat to the wolf with the red roses?'* – and again, to even more dramatic effect on the *Bat Out of Hell II* track 'Wasted Youth' and its deliciously harrowing cry of *'I remember EVERYTHING!'* – it was Jim Morrison's ghost he was summoning up from earnest to the point of suffocation Doors' spoken-word tracks like 'Horse Latitudes' – *'When the still sea conspires an armour and her sullen and aborted currents breed tiny monsters . . .'*

All this said with that queasily parodic, blood-twistingly affectionate humour that the younger Jim revelled in. Meat Loaf – his not-so-tiny monster – there to add his sad clown antics to it.

CHAPTER FOUR

The Chilly Californian Wind

Meat Loaf sat in the rented room in Turtle Park for three months, a quivering wreck, dazed and confused by life and by death, 250 pounds of teenage grief on a strict junk-food diet. He hadn't seen daylight in all of that time. Didn't know whether it was day or night outside, didn't much care. His family and friends didn't have an address for him, couldn't find him. No phone. It was Billy who found him in the end; he stuck his head around the door, saw the fat kid lying on a camp bed surrounded by trash and staring at the ceiling and got him out of there that same day. Meat Loaf said he didn't want to go, wouldn't even get up off the bed, what for? He was still complaining as Billy led him easily towards the door.

He went to stay with cousin Camille and her husband to help out on the little turkey farm they had. He fed the birds and thrashed pecan nuts off the trees. He was living a frontier lifestyle in the summer of love, but it was what he needed while he readjusted to what everyone else had no trouble seeing as the real world. He knew what he should do and one day he did it: he bought a ticket back to LA to find out what the dream factory had to offer a big lost boy from Texas. He knew he would never go back. Not this time. His last months in Dallas had been a nightmare of pain and loss, but, as these things sometimes did, they fed his psyche and his desires. When he got hold of a song now, he knew what he was singing about and who he was singing it for. There was a new meaning building inside him, a new way of standing, his gut swaying around him in rhythm. Anyone who watched him walk into a room, blocking out the light, anyone who heard him sing, thunder rolling down the mountain, could tell right away that he meant it all, every last heavy vibrato syllable.

The anger and grief were still raw by the time Christmas came and Meat Loaf spent it alone in an apartment on Ventura Boulevard observing what he called 'the grotesque glow' of LA's festive season; the happy families and cavorting kids, the fake trees and forced joy, the surprisingly chilly California wind.

It was music that brought him back into the world. He started to hang out at the Balboa Youth Center, in Encino, where he had his ears opened to the new bands that hadn't yet reached Texas. He heard Hendrix for the first time there, tripping out on godhead, and then The Yardbirds, featuring a young and frail-looking Jimmy Page, brandishing his guitar like a wand. The band that really connected, though, that really showed him the way, featured an itty-bitty gal from Port Arthur, Texas, with a voice like a wounded hellcat, named Janis Joplin. Janis was the singer in Big Brother and the Holding Company, and she'd been a star ever since they'd flayed the audience alive at the Monterey International Pop Festival six months before. Janis and the band had also left Texas behind and were now holed-up in San Francisco, but those weren't flowers Janis was tossing into the audience, they were emotional hand grenades.

Like Meat Loaf, Janis wasn't beautiful or anything like that, but man could she sing, and she had a huge voice, a real belter, just like his. It was the voice, so shapely and raw, that made her such a turn-on. It dawned on him that his voice might do the same for him. Turn an ugly duckling into some kind of swan. Maybe . . .

He still couldn't believe it when he started singing 'Piece Of My Heart' himself, stamping his feet as he channelled Janis, and people actually started to pay attention. One of those who took notice was an LA hipster named Gary Spagnola, whose brother, James 'Weasel' Spagnola played guitar in The Electric Prunes, part of LA's garage psychedelia scene. The Prunes worked out of this rickety little studio, not much more than a desk and a sound room, that Gary hooked Meat up with, and it was there that he recorded the sound of his voice for the very first time. He had a bass player called Rick, Gary on guitar and a drummer with no fingers. They recorded two songs that Meat Loaf had written all by himself – well, sort of written, given that he couldn't really play any instruments – one called 'Animal' and another he named 'Deep River Blues'. He sang them as hard as he could and pretended not to notice when the others stood back in awe at the room-quaking sounds he made. He didn't just bring guts, though. For a big guy he had a surprisingly sweet voice, when he wanted to.

Suddenly there was talk of making a tape, of having a band. Why not? This big kid from cowboy country could really sing and, hey, this was 1968, looks didn't kill like they used to. Look at Mama Cass, man, look at the cat from Canned Heat, fat fucks that could really bring it.

He just needed a name – and he already had one of those. He named the band Meat Loaf Soul, which sounded as funky and out there as all of the other names that were beginning to mean something – Iron Butterfly, Jefferson Airplane, Grateful Dead, and the band he really liked, Buffalo Springfield.

The tape got some interest, which felt good. The guy who owned the studio offered to put a record out. A&M Records, a boutique label started six years earlier by easy-listening trumpeter Herb Alpert and record executive Jerry Moss, let it be known that they were into it. The label had made its name on the hits that its co-founder Alpert provided for it, along with other easy listening hits by Burt Bacharach, The Sandpipers and Sergio Mendes. But with the summer of love bringing forth a whole new generation of hipster album artists, the label was now jumping all over any new band they could find. So they approached Meat Loaf Soul with an offer – two singles and maybe an album after that. Meat Loaf, now known by his friends simply as Meat, was ready to leap at the chance. But then came a counter offer from these other guys, Greene and Stone.

Charles Greene and his business partner Brian Stone were managers, were producers, were record company smart guys, were anything they wanted to be when it came to making a deal. They had struck oil when they parlayed their way into becoming the managers of Sonny & Cher. In the mid-sixties they had signed the up-and-coming duo to Greene-Stone Enterprises for management, Ten-East and Five-West for music publishing and York-Pala Records for record production – the latter with a stake in the lucrative Sonny & Cher Atco recordings. They also shared royalties as co-writers of throwaway instrumental B-sides of Sonny-produced singles. They liked to tell the story of how they had hocked their typewriters to finance the recording of 'Baby Don't Go', their second-biggest hit after 'I Got You Babe', but they were hustlers and Cher later claimed she was not sure they even owned the typewriters. Sonny, no stranger to the hustle himself, eventually paid big to get out of their contracts, and Greene and Stone moved on to perform similar tricks for Iron Butterfly and Meat's beloved Buffalo Springfield.

When they got wind of this kid from Dallas who'd blown into town with a voice like thunder and in desperate need of help, they made to swoop. But they were so taken aback when they saw the kid they wondered out loud if they'd been the victims of a practical joke. While Meat saw them immediately for what they were; big cigars and a chequebook with all the cheques made out in their own names. He decided to bail, then realised they'd already slipped out the back door anyway.

'The studio manager wanted to sign me to a contract,' he

recalled. 'Buffalo Springfield's producers wanted to sign me to a production deal and do an album, and A&M gave me a contract.' In the end, though, 'I turned them all down because I didn't know what was going on. I didn't have a clue.'

Instead, Meat Loaf Soul started doing what all of the other cool kids still waiting to be ripped off by the record business did: playing anywhere and everywhere, at all of the little gigs and shows and happenings that sprang up out of nowhere. One thing about this Texan giant – he lived to work. He hid his insecurities well behind the Wizard of Oz façade of crazed facial expressions and sweaty vocal presentation. He stood out, and agents and bookers began seeing his novelty value. Here was a guy who could sing and really throw himself about on the stage, but was too damn ugly to offer any real threat to the big-timers that Meat Loaf Soul now found themselves opening shows for along the west coast. Big deals like Them, Van Morrison's band, Taj Mahal (the cool black hat who'd shared the spotlight in Rising Sons with Ry Cooder) – even Big Brother and The Holding Company. Though Meat was way too shy to try to hang with Janis, who'd never had a shy moment in her life.

Meat was sleeping in the back of his car, up in Highland Hills, but when he made a few bucks, he grabbed a room at the down-at-heel Highland Hotel – 'A wonderful place!' he chuckled darkly. 'I made money doing other little odds 'n' ends. Which I guess some people might say were illegal. But we won't talk about that now.' When pressed, however, he admitted it was 'that stuff coming from Frisco made by Mr Owsley' – aka Owsley acid, the most powerful hallucinogenic of the year, often credited with kick-starting the whole summer of love, beginning with the super-charged batch of 'Monterey Purple' he distributed at Monterey Pop in 1967. But then who wasn't in the market for tabs of acid, loose joints and cheap Thunderbird wine on the streets of LA in 1968?

Meat Loaf's main focus, though, was his band. They would shove their gear into a U-Haul and drive for thirty-six hours straight to Michigan to play on a two-bit bill with unknowns like The Stooges. Musicians came and went, days got left behind by night, and so did band names. For a while they were called The Floating Circus – yeah, baby. Then they tried out Popcorn Blizzard – dig? With no real idea where they were supposed to be heading, just as long as it meant they didn't have to go home early, they kept going on the road for a couple more years. They opened for Ted Nugent and the Amboy Dukes, whose acid-rock hit 'Journey to the Center of the Mind' had been Top 20, then played with MC5.

By now Meat Loaf was already working on his own theatrical presentation. 'I was making homemade bombs and blowing stuff up [onstage]. One night I completely covered this club in smoke and the fire department had to come, it was amazing. Then one night I was playing with Chicago when they were called Chicago Transit Authority and my roadie made a bomb out of this old cannon shell, loaded it with too much powder, and instead of blowing up straight it blew over sideways and covered every horn they were using with black soot. So I went down there with these three roadies and used rags to clean off the horns before the guys [in Chicago] found out.'

Other memorable occasions he wished he could forget included an extraordinary night opening for the Grateful Dead 'at a fucking hog farm. They borrowed all our equipment and played one song for nine hours! And there were all these hogs running around this hall taking craps everywhere. It smelled terrible. I just wanted to get my equipment and leave. I have hated the Grateful Dead from that moment on.'

He paused for breath then sprang back into life. 'You want rock'n'roll roots, man? I'll put you back some, my tree grows deep . . . The Fugs laced me. I asked for a drink of water, they laced me with vodka . . .'

As Popcorn Blizzard, Meat Loaf's band became virtually the house band at the Grande Ballroom, the most happening club in Detroit, opening on bills with The Who, Jimi Hendrix, Sun Ra, Dr John, and often stealing the show and just as often being ignored in the reviews that followed. No one ever remembered the band or the name, but everyone recalled the big, heavy, twenty-one-year-old kid with the full-fat voice. He was gaining in confidence now, too. There were crazy hippy chicks all over America ready to ball with singers in rock'n'roll bands, whatever they looked like, honey. He got so he'd walk up to anyone and say hello. Although he only managed to choke out a few words to Janis, who rewarded him by calling him a 'motherfucker' – which sounded pretty good when it came out of her sweet dirty mouth.

Meat threw his shadow across Roger Daltrey and told him to add a little gravel to his voice. 'Roger came out in a suede, tasseled jacket, which I thought was hilarious. Keith Moon was unbelievable, you couldn't take your eyes off the guy. They used to announce "The Seeker" by saying: "This is a new song that we've never played before." And I thought: "Yeah, right. I bet that's what they say every night." And they did. I also remember that Daltrey stood at the side of the stage when we were on, watching intently. I met him many years later at a music award ceremony. I was in the bathroom taking a piss and he came up behind me and said: "You're Meat Loaf, aren't you? I remember seeing you with a band in Detroit years ago. You were brilliant." I couldn't believe that he remembered me. Years later he sang on one of my albums.'

Introduced to the crazy Jewish kid from The Stooges, Meat listened impatiently as Iggy told him, 'Hey, man . . . we got three chords . . .'

'I saw Iggy play his first show at the Grande Ballroom,' he recalls now. 'His band consisted of the MC5's road crew, none of whom could play an instrument. Iggy came on, immediately took off his T-shirt and then started maiming himself by sticking needles through his fingertips and in his chest. He then somehow got hold of a cream pie, jumped off stage and started making out with this poor guy's girlfriend. So this guy's freaking out, and Iggy just laughs and slams the pie in this poor kid's face and starts rubbing the cream all over himself. And then he jumps back on stage, unzipped his fly, and walks off. That was the whole show. Fucking hilarious! It was over in six minutes.'

Meat also learned how to do things the right way. He still recalls talking with Mark Farner of Grand Funk Railroad, one of the biggest American bands of the era, and the singer telling him about the time his previous band, The Pack, supported a bubblegum act 'who had lucked out with a couple of hits [which was fronted by] a vile egomaniac. When The Pack supported them, the front man wouldn't let the band use his back line and they had to set up on the floor in front of the stage. It was so humiliating, and definitely contributed to the band splitting up. Hearing that story had a huge impact on me and I always made sure our support bands were taken care of and lent out equipment to anyone who needed it.'

Meat's favourite singer was Joe Cocker, whose thunderous blend of raw, wounded-lion vocals and unruly, out-of-control body movements while performing he found inspirational. Cocker proved that 'you didn't have to be a pretty boy to succeed in rock'n'roll'.

Meat's favourite band, though, was Detroit's own MC5. 'I knew the guys really well and they were always great fun to watch. They mixed politics with theatrics. Their manager, John Sinclair, was a member of the White Panthers and was facing a heavy rap for possession of dope. The stage would be covered in American flags and they would have this preacher introduce them, and then it would be straight in: "Kick out the jams, motherfuckers!" It was a cross between the James Brown revue and the Rolling Stones.

LA didn't get it, New York didn't get it; it was a Detroit thing. Wayne Kramer was the best live performer bar none. He'd slide across the stage on his knees. He would have these insane guitar duels with Fred "Sonic" Smith. They dressed up in these silver glitter outfits but they'd be playing this heavy shit. Rob Tyner was a fantastic vocalist, but it was Kramer who stole the show. I would go as far as saying that he was the biggest influence in my life as far as my live performances go.'

His least favourite band was the Grateful Dead. 'Man, they were abysmal. I remember they headlined once at the Grande. The support acts included the MC5, Bob Seger and us – all high energy. Jerry Garcia and his crew came on and started playing this song and it seemed to last for weeks! After about 20 minutes half the audience had gone. The problem was that we couldn't leave. Because of weather problems the Dead's equipment hadn't arrived and we had lent them our back line. I didn't know anything about the band at the time and didn't realise that their sets went on for days [laughs] – well, that's what it felt like. We were stuck there all night.'

All these guys who were getting somewhere while Meat Loaf wasn't, he couldn't figure it out. He could sing as good as anyone, better than most, and he looked more than far out enough for any of the freaks he had ever met, but making a record had never felt further away. He did odd jobs to keep himself solvent and wound up living in Oak Park, with its one road out of town back to LA, and hanging with a pal called Barney, and a gang of guys who were renting Linda Ronstadt's old house in Franklin Canyon.

It was the sixties in California, and this is how it went. Meat Loaf grew his hair, expanded his mind and picked up a few bucks however he could. One night after a show, he found himself in Huntington Beach, at the end of the pier. He was still lost. He felt an urge to jump off the pier and submerge himself in the black velvet ocean. He didn't really know why. He heard a voice that said, 'Don't do that.' An older lady was standing behind him. 'She still loves you . . .' the lady said. 'She still loves you and it's not your fault.' He looked back at the ocean and when he turned around again the old lady was gone and the pier was empty.

He wasn't sure it had even happened, and he told no one about it, and for a while he tried not to even think about it. He walked back to the beach and some guys from the band found him and asked if he'd been dropping acid, he seemed so spaced out.

'No,' he said, 'I . . .'

CHAPTER FIVE

Aquarius

By the end of 1968 Meat Loaf was living in a communal home in Echo Park – a hippy crash pad in Central LA. One of the other guys there, Barney, had a gig parking cars at the parking lot of the Aquarius Theater, a thousand-seater, mural-wrapped psychedelic shack on Sunset Boulevard, and one day someone quit, so Barney told his friend Meat he should try out for the gig. It was a sweet deal; all of these theatregoers in their nice cars, sedans and open-top caddies tipping handsomely for them to park them up and bring them back. Barney was pulling in $50 a night sometimes – fifty bucks a night! It would take Meat a month to make that kind of bread normally. The show that was on was called *Hair*. Even sweeter, he and Barney got called in the next morning because the show was going off on tour and they were holding auditions, so there were stacks more cars to park. In the car park Barney introduced Meat to Greg Carlos, who had the lead role in *Hair*. Greg asked him what else he did and he told Greg how he was trying to put a band together, yadda-yadda, the same story you tell everyone you meet in LA, the same story they tell you right back.

'Then come and audition for *Hair*,' Greg told him, meaning it, not meaning it. 'But I'd seen people standing in line, hundreds deep! I said, "I'm not gonna stand in lines like that! Yer outta yer mind!"' Greg just laughed and before Meat knew what was happening, Meat was cutting past the long line of hopefuls in the car park and through the lobby, Greg behind him all the way. Next thing, he was in the aisle of the theatre and there was this guy in beads and shades and smoke rings and hair lying blissed-out on a pillow. This, Greg told him nonchalantly, was the director of *Hair*, a very cool cat named Armand Coullet.

Armand was so cool he was a director, a producer, a musician – there wasn't anything Armand couldn't do if he put his broad mind to it. He was even sleeping with the lead actress in the production, Rhonda Lee Oglesby, whom he was about to marry. The only thing cooler than Armand was the production itself. *Hair: The American Tribal Love-Rock Musical*, to give it its full title, was the world's first full-blooded rock musical. Musical theatre had flirted with the idea of somehow incorporating rock'n'roll into its more hip productions – in 1957, the *Ziegfeld Follies* controversially featured one number, 'The Juvenile Delinquent', sung by a fifty-year-old washed-up Hollywood ham named Billy De Wolfe; three years later, *Bye Bye Birdie* also flirted with rock'n'roll in the shape of finger-snapping, clean-cut teenagers singing about being on the phone and riding hotrods. But it wasn't until *Hair* that the world got its first authentic hippy counterculture stage show, featuring such new teen staples as nudity, sexual revolution, drugs and the anti-Vietnam War peace movement.

In common with all great late-sixties' phenomenon, *Hair* tore up the rulebook, denigrating the American flag, mocking the old conservative values, using a racially integrated cast and breaking down the fourth wall by inviting the audience onto the stage for its 'Be-In' finale. It also came steeped in commercial approbation and deep, bottom-of-the-well credibility. *Hair* had debuted in October 1967 at Joseph Papp's experimental Public Theater – one of the first significant off-Broadway productions. Six months later it transferred to the real deal – the Biltmore Theater on Broadway's West 47th Street – where it ran for 1,750 performances. By the time Meat wandered in, various productions of *Hair* were being performed in simultaneous places all over the world, including a memorable run in London, which eventually stretched to almost two thousand shows. When the *Original Broadway Cast Recording* of the show was released in the US in 1969, it went straight to Number 1, selling three million copies and notching up four Top Five singles, including a gigantic Number 1 when the Fifth Dimension did a gloriously catchy cover of what became the show's signature tune, 'Aquarius/Let The Sunshine In'.

As he tells the story now, though, when Armand Coullet casually asked Meat Loaf what he wanted to do, Meat shrugged and said he was just trying out for a job in the parking lot. In truth, he knew exactly what was going on but he had learned that self-deprecating humour worked better on strangers when coming from a giant than ambition or, God forbid, actual self-knowledge. Sure enough, everyone laughed at the parking-lot quip. Now they *really* wanted to hear him sing. He sang a blues number, something that sounded almost galactic coming from a voice like that out of a guy like that – and that night he wasn't parking cars, instead he was inside the theatre watching the show.

But something went wrong, the fire sprinklers went off and the show had to be abandoned halfway through. Still, Armand didn't forget and two weeks later when the show was put on again, Meat was invited back – this time to sing 'Aquarius', something his mainsail vocals seemed almost supernaturally suited for, and this time he was offered a cast role in the Detroit production – the role of General Ulysses S Grant: a two-minute spot that he parlayed into a showstopper. 'At one point I got it up to seventeen minutes!' He soon discovered that the other, unspoken reason why Coullet brought him in was because the actor he was replacing – a giant in his own right, Joey Richardson – was 'another big guy . . . It was like equal opportunity for larger-than-life men.'

So what? They paid him $260 a week – he even felt rich

enough to turn down the extra $12.50 that any cast member got who agreed to strip off for the naked scene. That was because he weighed almost 300 pounds now. 'I didn't want to frighten anybody,' he recalled, only half-joking, in his memoir, *To Hell and Back*.

Yet that was partly the reason why they'd jumped him from the car park to the front of the queue at the auditions. He didn't look, or sound, like anyone else. If *Hair* was about anything, it was proving you didn't have to look or sound like anyone else. That everyone could do their own thing, baby. Sure enough, everyone who went to see *Hair* in LA after that first remembered the naked scene, then they remembered the big chubby-cheeked howdy who played the General.

By the time they got to Detroit, Meat was on the front page of the hip local rag, the *Detroit Free Press*. *Hair* did what Meat's ever-changing LA band couldn't – it brought the record companies running. A couple showed up at the production, including a guy from Atlantic, but there was really only one label in Detroit that meant shit and that was Motown. Meat went to see a man called Harry Balk, who offered him a deal, but with a twist. Meat wanted to duet with a girl named Stoney. 'She was one of the best singers I ever heard in my life. I was in awe of this girl.' Harry listened, and began to see the potential of an almost Beauty and the Beast trip – updated for the cosmic generation. He gave it the executive nod. Meat Loaf couldn't wait to tell the rest of the Detroit production of *Hair* of his good fortune. It would mean leaving the show – eventually, after the contracts were signed, which took some months – but he didn't care. He was elated. This was a big step up, he'd decided. For both Meat and Stoney.

'So I went to Stoney and said, "Look, Motown offered me a contract but I said I really wanted you to do it with me." She said, "Hey, that sounds like fun!" . . .' Well her real name wasn't Stoney, but then his real name wasn't Meat Loaf. Her name was Shaun

Murphy, and she was in the cast of *Hair,* too, having taken over from Delores Hall in the lead female role of Sheila.

Meat had known Stoney since her days singing with Wilson Mower Pursuit and had actually recommended her for the gig. The idea of now partnering up with her was almost too good to be true. It was Stoney who was unsure at first. Still in her twenties, she was already a vet of the incendiary late-sixties' Detroit scene. With Wilson Mower she'd become a familiar face at the Grande Ballroom and the first Ann Arbor Blues Festival in 1969.

The contracts went back and forth and the fabled songwriters Holland-Dozier-Holland tried to gazump the deal – ten Number 1 hits with The Supremes, now looking to strike out with their own production company – but in the end Meat and Stoney signed up as a team to Motown, lured by the offer of recording a song they were told The Jackson 5 were desperate to have as their next single: 'What You See Is What You Get' – an obvious ploy. Not only was it a thrusting soul-belter entirely unfitting for the cute vocal stylings of The Jackson 5, but with five straight Number 1 singles already to their name there was no way Motown would have entrusted a sure-fire hit to a couple of newcomers – *white* newcomers at that.

In fact, Motown initially saw Stoney & Meatloaf (singular), as they would be billed, as an ideal addition to their new white rock imprint, Rare Earth – named after the first successful all-white outfit that Motown had signed the year before. None of the previously signed all-white acts – The Rustix, The Dalton Boys or The Underdogs – had even come close. But Rare Earth were self-consciously *heavy* and had helped break the mould by following in the musical footsteps of Vanilla Fudge – who'd had a check-this-out hit with a fully-leaded seven-minute version of an old Supremes hit, 'You Keep Me Hangin' On', in 1968 – by recording an even more audacious/ridiculous 20-minute version of Smokey Robinson's 'Get Ready'. (A drastically edited version of which became an unlikely hit single in 1969.) With Meat's big-balls voice and Stoney's soulful treacle, this was Motown chief Berry Gordy's latest attempt to crash-land the increasingly lucrative white-album-oriented market.

It nearly worked, too. But then 'What You See' began climbing the black R&B charts and suddenly, according to Meat, 'They didn't want anybody to know we were white.' When word inevitably did get out, the single dropped out of sight. Motown reacted the way it always did, blaming the artist and not the song, to the point where they flip-flopped on the track scheduled as the next Stoney & Meatloaf single, 'Who Is The Leader Of The People', giving it to Edwin Starr instead. Starr, who'd just had a worldwide smash with 'War', simply rerecorded the lead vocal. 'You could still hear me and Stoney singing the background vocals,' Meat would tell me years later, 'but of course we were never credited.'

Though it was viewed as little more than a curiosity when it was released in October 1971 (with Meat and Stoney depicted on the cover in late-hippy, Wild Bunch mode; Meat in a tall, medicine-man top hat, Stoney in long, Belle Starr dress and headdress), the album actually laid down the template for the success of *Bat Out of Hell* six years later. Not so much musically, its rock-funk stew was more akin to early seventies groove cats like Little Feat, Humble Pie, Eric Burden and War than the Sturm und Drang of *Bat*, but in the way it very deliberately diffuses the shock of seeing an anguished giant pouring out his overweight emotions alongside the defiantly unbowed feminine grace of his onstage partner.

The swinging, big-shouldered opener '(I'd Love to Be) As Heavy as Jesus' reached, on the surface, for the same gutsy gospel swing of likeminded hits of the day like 'Oh Happy Day' (Number 4 in the US for the Edwin Hawkins Singers in 1969) and 'Put Your Hand in the Hand' (Number 2 in the US for Canadian band Ocean in April in 1971). The heavy irony in the title and overwrought, almost mocking delivery of the two singers also foreshadowed the kind of is-this-for-real, show-tune performances that Meat Loaf tantalised his later audiences with on songs like 'Paradise By The Dashboard Light'. Trading lines with Stoney, both feeding off each other's energy on tracks like 'It Takes All Kind Of People', or the wilfully ecstatic 'Sunshine (Where's Heaven)', it's easy to imagine a parallel universe where Meat and Stoney laid the tracks for the journey into blue-eyed soul that so many white artists in the mid-seventies would embark on.

But Motown wasn't like other record companies. Singers were just singers. The songs were the stars. Meat Loaf would later claim he barged into Motown chief Berry Gordy's office to complain and was so furious that he took off his shoe – Krushchev in New York-style – and banged it on Gordy's desk. It's a good story, redolent of the grandiose imagery he would later learn to bottle and sell, but it's hard to believe. Gordy was one of the richest, most powerful black men in America. Meat Loaf was a no-account white kid from Nowheresville. And all that came of the encounter, such that it was, was that the singer found himself out on the streets again.

He was still bitter about the experience when interviewed in 1978 on his first promo trip to London by early Meat Loaf champion, Sandy Robertson. 'It was junk!' he insisted. 'That was my first record contract and I really didn't know what I was doing, so I just did what they told me to do.'

Maybe things would improve once they took the show on the road, he had hoped. But even there his self-esteem was so low he simply couldn't keep up. Stoney's boyfriend played guitar in a band called Jake Wade and the Soul Searchers, so they became their backing band when they headed out on tour.

Stoney had an 'amazing voice' but onstage 'she never moved, she stood in one place and sang, I had to do all the moving. We had an all-black band, except for one white lead guitar player who could really play! But he sort of went crazy. [They] used to be the house band at a big black Detroit nightclub. Ray Charles would come in and play with them, and Aretha Franklin . . . I used to take them out on the road and make them shave their heads and put earrings in their ears, put on weird suits and sunglasses and stuff, because they always used to wear black suits and nice ties – and I freaked this band out, man!'

After gigs, Meat and the band would shoot craps together – for money. 'They thought they were real good. I'd pay them their money and then I'd say, "Can I play?" "Sure, come on!" And I'd play for about fifteen minutes and win all their money back! And one of them, the bass player, was a pimp, the biggest pimp in Detroit. He used to have the biggest stable of hookers in Detroit and I used to ride with him. He had the greatest car; it had white fur all over everything, white walls and these tyres with all these big rhinestones in them, in the hubcaps. And to ride with him you had to wear a big hat that you had to tilt in a certain way, so when we went riding we had to lean in together.'

The crowd front stage didn't seem to have as much fun, and though the tour staggered on, hitching a riding as support to Rare Earth, Bob Seger and BB King, the moment had passed. Meat Loaf had finally made a record, and even though that hadn't really taken off, it felt good to have something solid in his hand that had his actual voice on. It proved he existed, somehow, even if Motown had wiped some of his vocals and Stoney's backing band didn't really think he could sing. Then the label cancelled his contract – keeping Stoney, who went on to have a big career singing in Bob Seger's band, who became the biggest-selling Detroit act of them all, before Eric Clapton swept her up for his *Behind the Sun* album and a place onstage with him at Live Aid.

Just when he was wondering what the hell he would do next, the phone rang. It was Armand Coullet: *Hair* was going to Broadway. Did Meat want to come too?

CHAPTER SIX

All Revved Up

On paper, Amherst was about as far removed from the countercultural remedy that *Hair* espoused as it was possible to be, but it wasn't completely immune to the changing times, the sudden arrival of vibe and connectedness, of revolution, daddy. Nowhere in America was, though, and twenty-year-old Jim Steinman was determined to push it, or at least try it on to see how it looked – to flaunt it, exploit it. He started small but defiantly weird with a short-lived drama-class offshoot group he named Clitoris That Thought It Was a Puppy. Funny, ha, yeah, don't Bogart that joint my friend . . .

Things got more real when, in March 1968, he wrote the music for an Amherst production of Bertolt Brecht's modernist play *A Man's a Man*, in which the playwright tells the story of a hapless civilian who is transformed into the perfect soldier, exploring human personality as something malleable, interchangeable, that can be picked up and put back together into new shapes like a puzzle, a bigger, more effective machine: a parable that the Pulitzer Prize-winning American critic Walter Kerr described as a 'curious foreshadowing of the art of brainwashing'. Jim, the puppet-master in the making, was enthralled by the idea.

He followed that, in May 1968, as director this time of an Amherst production of Michael McClure's *The Beard*. The McClure production edged Amherst more explicitly towards the counter culture. Thirty-five-year-old McClure was a refugee from the Beat Generation of writers, one of the five poets who read at the famous San Francisco Six Gallery reading in 1955 (where Allen Ginsberg first read 'Howl'), as immortalised in Jack Kerouac's *The Dharma Bums*. Since then the poet who Barry Miles famously once described as 'the Prince of San Francisco' had transmogrified into a hippy, counterculture-vulture, giving a reading at the epochal Human Be-In at Golden Gate Park in January 1967, befriending Jim Morrison of The Doors, whose bad-dream poetry he indulged, and writing *The Beard*. The play was a suitably wiggy piece built around a what-if meeting 'in the blue velvet of eternity' between Billy the Kid and Jean Harlow, with a theme exploring McClure's 'Meat Politics' theory that humans were nothing more than 'bags of meat'.

Kenneth Tynan described *The Beard* as 'a milestone in the history of heterosexual art'. Jim loved its unhinged depiction of the male-female relationship, with its almost cliché obscenities and Grand Guignol set pieces, the gloriously spiralling-out-of-control hurricanes of verboten emotions and final, coming together to be torn apart kiss-off. What *Variety* called 'a reduction of all male-female spats, courtships, fetishes, etc., to simple animal circling, snarling, sniffing, teasing . . .' Exactly the sort of thing Jim liked to write about in his music, to suffuse his own fantasy courtships with – male or female.

Even *The Beard* was nothing, though, compared to Jim's plan for his senior year, a musical that would, in his words, 'make *Hair* look like *Hello, Dolly!*'. The fact that it would count towards his final graduation mark was neither here nor there. Jim's aims were far loftier than that, and they went beyond simple outrage – any fool with a flower in his or her hair and a bare breast could pull that off. The musical would be called *The Dream Engine* and it would be the first visit to the interior hinterland that Jim had been cultivating, a place where his fantasies and obsessions could be fully expressed and visualised. 'I was flunking all over the place,' he explained. 'I had to convince the college governors that I could do this project. So I went to see them, and they were very impressed by my idea.'

The story wasn't up to much, a simple-enough yarn about a character called Baal who falls in with a tribe of kids living a violent and primitive life on the California coast. But the concept and the themes were outrageous and provocative, full of the bullish confidence of privileged, unwasted youth. Jim told the Amherst College newspaper, *The Record*: 'The flower child, sunshine hippie has been replaced with a far more dangerous kind of kid, conditioned by the brutality of assassinations, a war that goes on forever, police riots in Chicago, a political system that refuses to change. American children are being transformed into revolutionaries, willing to fight in the streets if necessary. I think it's more dangerous to live in Greenwich Village today than to fight in Vietnam. The play tries to reflect that physical and moral danger. This is not, I think, the usual kind of musical.'

Cringe-making though the remark about Vietnam was, *The Dream Engine* certainly caught the moment exactly as Jim had wished it. Jim took the role of Baal, a character he described as 'a cross between Che Guevara, Mick Jagger and Billy the Kid', and encouraged the director, his classmate Barry Keating, to push hard, 'using many of the techniques of the avant-garde radical theatre' to produce something purposefully provocative. 'It has been a trying experience, from beginning to end,' Jim explained earnestly in his college newspaper interview. 'But it has been the most exciting thing I've ever done. It may offend some people, but I think it will stand on its own as a work of art.'

That is, he *hoped* it would offend 'some' people. *The Dream Engine* played at Amherst's Kirby Theater for four nights from Friday, 25 April 1971 – but it took just one performance for Jim to know that he was on to something. Speaking in 2003, he gleefully described the musical as 'a three-hour rock epic with tons of nudity, it was everything I dreamed of. It got closed down by the police. Written up in the newspapers. Caused a sensation.'

More important than any of that, though, was the intense reaction the play got from Joseph Papp when he turned up unexpectedly one night – and became so overinvolved he went backstage during the intermission and talked Jim into signing a piece of paper giving the impresario the rights to take the play to his Shakespeare in the Park festival. Fresh from producing *Hair* on Broadway, Papp, the Shakespeare evangelist, the experimental theatre guru, felt *The Dream Engine* offered even more potential for helping define the era: these weren't professional actors dressed up as hippies, these were college students, the real children of the revolution.

'It was like one of those legendary stories,' Steinman recalled in 2003. 'He was in the dressing room and I remember signing the paper, I didn't know what I was signing,' he laughed. 'I just said, what the hell, it's better than going to graduate school studying film. That's what I was going to do. I also remember we were all nude because the second act was almost all nudity.' More laughter.

It was the start of a significant working relationship that would last for almost seven years and would underpin every move Jim would make in his career. 'I identified with [Papp] immediately because he saw no difference between Shakespeare and *Hair*, basically. It was all theatre and I grew up with opera and rock'n'roll and didn't see any difference . . . Papp became sort of my surrogate dad. He loved being a mentor to people and he sort of took me in.'

Within an hour or so of his first original musical hitting the stage, Jim had been recognised as an extraordinary talent, his musical universe already fully acknowledged. Indeed, though *The Dream Engine* would never reach New York, Papp's vision was born out for decades to come as Jim's musical themes and motifs became obsessively recycled and revisited, expanded and refined. 'I still think it's the best thing I'll ever do and it's all been downhill from there,' he would say, not even half-joking.

The story turned on what he later described as 'a really violent pack of kids running amok in some unnamed Californian city, warring against church and state, cops and baron robbers, basically like the Lost Boys. It was all sort of a science-fiction version of *Peter Pan* – that's always been my biggest vision. It's sort of like this huge breast that I suckle on. Everything I take is somewhat related to my Peter Pan vision.'

Every important song he would write would be seeded in this very earliest iteration of his universe. For example, a song called 'Formation Of The Tribe' contained the line and vocal melody *'Turn around Bright Eyes'* – the line that would recur throughout so many of his future songs, most memorably for Bonnie Tyler on her earthshattering hit 'Total Eclipse Of The Heart'. What Papp saw immediately was that Jim's talent was big, but its focus narrow. The return again and again to certain lines and melodies, the constant reworking of those ideas, would characterise the rest of his creative life.

Joseph Papp knew talent when he saw it, though. He was no flyby-night chancer. As well as his lifelong passion for Shakespeare, in particular delivering it free to New Yorkers at Shakespeare in the Park, where he had use of the open-air Delacorte Theater, he'd also worked with almost every major stage actor, and among the new work he delivered to the Public Theater (which would be named after him upon his death in 1991) were early plays by Tony Award winner David Rabe, and the Pulitzer Prize winners Jason Miller and Charles Gordone. His taste in contemporary theatre was also unsurpassed. After *Hair*, Papp would oversee first Broadway productions of *A Chorus Line* and a completely revitalised *Pirates of Penzance*.

Jim understood the value of the patronage of such a theatrical titan – not that he always showed it. Jim Steinman was nothing if not singular, a headstrong young maestro who flounced out on several occasions, once goading Papp into throwing an ashtray at his head, but it was Papp who catapulted Steinman from college weirdo to real-world musical titan in one giant step.

Their first problem was *The Dream Engine* itself. Papp planned to put it on at the Delacorte, but the New York City Council baulked at that. Papp was told that it 'was far too raunchy, sexually explicit and violent to be performed in an open public place owned by the city'. Adding, unintentionally amusingly, that it had 'far more nudity than *Antony and Cleopatra*'. Papp, on Steinman's behalf, would continue battling the ruling for years to come, but *The Dream Engine* remained steadfastly beyond the pale as far as the NYC Council was concerned. Jim had been right. *The Dream Engine* did make *Hair* look like *Hello, Dolly!*. 'It was censured by the city.' He shrugged. 'They kept saying it was too dirty.'

Instead the show had a brief run in Washington DC with Richard Gere in the lead role. 'Gere has one of the great rock'n'roll voices, which he won't use,' recalled Steinman, 'because he feels people won't accept him as an actor if he sings.' In retrospect, however, Jim believed that *The Dream Engine* became 'the seeds of the vision of *Bat Out of Hell* for me, creatively, and Meat Loaf became the physical vessel through which I could get that across'.

Instead Papp told him to go away and write something else, something that he could put on as a new original production. In 1972 he co-wrote a musical called *Rhinegold* with lyricist Barry Keating, based on his hero Richard Wagner's *Das Rheingold*. You can still hear the demos he worked up with Barry on Steinman's website. Some of the songs, like 'Who'd Do The Dirty' – later recorded by another *Hair* alumni, André De Shields – contain future echoes of the kind of overblown epic Jim would compose for Meat Loaf. The play, though, never got beyond the rehearsal room.

Papp suggested that Jim take on a co-writer to help develop his next idea, introducing him to Michael Weller, a young Brooklyn-based playwright and songwriter who had written the screenplay for the film version of *Hair* and who had seen his own original stage play, *Moonchildren*, premiere at London's Royal Court Theatre in 1971, before transferring to Broadway in February 1972. Originally titled *Cancer*, the play centred on a year in the life of eight college students – the moonchildren of the title – living together in an off-campus attic in the mid-sixties, at the very moment when hip butterflied into hippy. Or, as the review in the *New York Times* put it: a play about the generation that came of age during the Vietnam War, written by Weller 'with a discerning eye and a journalist's detachment.'

The play co-starred a raft of upcoming American actors including Kevin Conway, on his way to his first major movie role in *Slaughterhouse Five*, Christopher Guest, who would co-write and star in *This Is Spinal Tap*, Maureen Anderman, who won a Theatre World award for her part, as did a young firebrand named James Woods.

For Jim's part, he couldn't believe his luck when Papp put him together with Weller. Jim was now living back in New York, not out at his parents' luxury pad on Long Island, but in a small apartment in Manhattan, where all the smart kids went to dream. The play that he and Weller began working on was partly based on an idea that Weller had for something called *Souvenirs* – in reference to the severed ears of the killed Viet Cong which US soldiers infamously collected and wore as keepsakes on strings around their necks – and partly a new idea, again based in Vietnam but now centred on something even more dramatic, retitled *More Than You Deserve*. As Jim told me years later: *More Than You Deserve* 'was actually a wonderful, wonderful play, for which I am indebted totally to Michael Weller, who wrote it and co-wrote the lyrics. A brilliant writer.'

The plot concerned an impotent soldier named Michael Dillon, a major stationed at a US army base in Vietnam. When a female reporter joins the base to do a story, she is gang-raped, after which she decides she is a nymphomaniac. Then she gives up her new lusty habits to settle down into a deeper love with the impotent major. In short, it was the sort of play that could only have been taken remotely seriously in that peace-brother anti-Vietnam moment in American cultural history. Maybe . . .

Jim, who was gung-ho for anything far out and grizzly, loved the idea. Weller was appalled, though, when the title was then changed to *More Than You Deserve*. But by then Jim had got his vampire-like teeth into it and the music went from dark and microscopically intense to grandiose and almost comic in places.

Produced by Papp and directed by Kim Friedman, who would go on to become one of American TV's most sought-after directors, *More Than You Deserve* opened at the Public Theater on Wednesday, 21 November 1973, ran for 63 performances and closed on Sunday, 13 January 1974. It was short-burst, mad, ironic, and like a ship on fire went down quickly, leaving behind some very red scenery.

But just as *The Dream Engine* had failed to fulfil its potential, yet brought an even greater gift to Jim Steinman's life in Joseph Papp, so *More Than You Deserve* also burned out quickly, yet brought Jim an even greater gift. As he later recalled for me, 'Meat Loaf turning up when he did was almost like a silent prayer had been answered by some God who's only in charge of singers – even though he wasn't 130-pounds and was in the "extreme" section of the singers' department store.'

CHAPTER SEVEN
Heavy as Two Jesuses

Hair in New York was a fucking disaster. The producers had gone hog crazy and fired half of the existing cast, so everyone who turned up from the Detroit production was stepping into dead men's shoes. Then there was the whole living-for-the-city New York vibe to deal with. When Meat Loaf walked in for the first day of rehearsals the first girl he said hi to curled her pretty lips and called him a straight-up motherfucker. After a few more days of this he had a rash from the stress of it all. He got the hell out of town as soon as he could, joining another production of *Hair*, this one in Pittsburgh. Then he joined another in Buffalo. He wondered if this would go on for the rest of his life – swinging from town to town singing 'Aquarius' every night. There was only so much peace and love that one bad boy from Texas could take.

He did a couple of other shows, including an off-Broadway gospel musical titled *Rainbow in New York* – a project being overseen by the great New York theatrical impresario Joseph Papp. Not that Meat ever clapped eyes on the guy. It didn't hurt, though, when Papp's people offered him a job as part of their Shakespeare in the Park project. Meat knew he was a singer, not a proper thesp, but hey, he needed the dough. 'I remember doing Shakespeare in the Park with Raul Julia,' said Meat Loaf, 'and then immediately heading to Max's Kansas City and singing. It was very schizophrenic.' Or as he later told the British writer Dave Dickson,

'Shakespeare was a rock'n'roller! He wrote for the people on the street. Sure, he wrote the proper things that the kings and queens would have said, but there's so many characters inside those plays that are so funky! Man, they're like pimps on 42nd Street!' He appeared in *As You Like It* alongside future movie stars Meryl Streep and Mary Beth Hurt. 'And Clive Barnes, who's a major reviewer in America, said there were only three real people on the stage out of seventy: Meat Loaf – he called me "Mr Loaf" – Miss Streep and Miss Hurt.'

Years later, he would confide that his Shakespeare in the Park role had drawn the attention of what he referred to as some serious 'patrons of the opera'. They had approached him, he said, and offered 'to pay me $60,000 a year to train for five years and then make my debut at the Met. Oh, I had a voice! Oh, I could have burned 'em! But I'm too rebellious, and I found out that in opera the conductor controls most of it. There's no improv, there's no freedom, there's no, you know, soaring. You can't go off in the clouds and just escape. So . . . I couldn't do that.'

He still wasn't sure if he even wanted to stay in New York. The size and the feel of the place – the shouting, screaming, sirens-wailing, bleeding edge of the place – were still enough to freak him out. Then an old pal from the Buffalo production of *Hair* told him that with his hoodlum looks he might be able to get a part in a new play in New York based on a bunch of fifties greasers called, uh, *Grease*. So he bought a cheap leather jacket and turned up for an audition. He did the *Grease* audition and got offered the part and was on his way to sign his contract when he ran into Jim Rado on the street.

Jim was one of the writers of *Hair*.

Kismet.

Jim Rado had a new play, he said, and he wanted Meat for it. He sent him down to meet his agent, Jeff Hunter, who would soon become Meat Loaf's theatrical agent, too. And before Jim

Rado could do anything about it, Jeff was telling him about *an-other* new play, one that Meat Loaf would be even *more* perfect for, one being produced by the great Joe Papp, something called *More Than You Deserve* – like *Hair*, said Joe, but even more crazy. The auditions were happening right now at the Public Theater. Meat walked down to the East Village and into the auditorium. The only person in the building was this weird-looking, nutty kind of guy named Jim Steinman – a long-haired kid like him but with the air of a much older, more know-it-all kind of a guy. Like some-one who lived in a high tower full of suits of armour and candles.

He sang a song from the album he'd recorded with Stoney: 'I'd Love To Be As Heavy As Jesus'. When he'd finished, Jim looked him up and down and said, 'Well, I think you'd be as heavy as two Jesuses as a matter of fact . . .' Wow, Meat thought. Who the fuck is this guy? 'The first thing I thought when I heard this voice,' Steinman would tell *Rolling Stone* in 1978, 'was, "Get this Negro music away from him. He should be singing Wagnerian rock opera."' As Jim later told me, '[Meat] clenched his hands and his eyes went up into his head. I thought he was great! Everybody else hated him.'

Speaking with me nearly 30 years later, Steinman offered an only slightly less-heightened recollection. 'He auditioned for me, him and a true-genius pianist named Steve Margoshes, whom I still know and I still work with. Steve did every orchestration I ever needed. He's a brilliant orchestrator. He did *Tommy* with The Who. They came and auditioned for me and I was just blown away. It was literally a dream come true. Ironically, I was going through a bad phase with my nose. It came out of nowhere but it was really fairly extreme.'

What Jim meant by 'bad phase' was actually 'this big fight' he claimed to have had, in which he got his nose broken by 'this six-foot-two-inch lady biker with a tattoo'. It sounded too much like a Steinman sexual fantasy to be true, but the part where he insisted the surgeon who operated on it 'messed it up worse' seems to have been true.

'A couple of weeks before I met Meat Loaf, I got into a huge bar-room brawl,' he would recount, years later. 'I'm sort of a pipsqueak, compared to Meat certainly, and I was doing all right, I thought, until I turned around to my left thinking it was almost over and I was jumped on by this enormous lady biker which was a little bit . . . Now, how would I describe this? It was like when she jumped on top of me, it was like being French-kissed by a Buick . . . I mean, it was horrifying! And she bashed me up and broke my nose in about eight spots . . . I went right to this doctor, who I'm convinced was probably living with this lady biker because he did her a great favour by finding the few spots that weren't broken and proceeded to destroy them . . .'

As he told Sandy Robertson in 1981, 'I couldn't even talk for about a year and a half.' Again, the complete accuracy of that statement need not detain us for long. Speaking to me in 2006, he explained more plausibly that in fact the broken nose had left him unable to sing. This was a major inconvenience at a time when Steinman was also being courted as a singer-songwriter in his own right by Eric Clapton's then manager – and future movie mogul – Robert Stigwood. There had even been a country-tinged demo version of 'More Than You Deserve' with Jim on vocals, which Stigwood was planning to release as a single on his own RSO label. 'I had always thought I would sing my own songs,' Jim explained. That dream got squashed along with his nose. In the end, Stigwood, feeling sorry for the kid, took one of his songs, a piece of pop schlock lifted straight out of a Brill building wastebasket called 'Happy Ending', and gave it to Yvonne Elliman, who'd just come out of a four-year stint on *Jesus Christ Superstar* playing Mary Magdalene, for her 1973 album, *Food of Love*. It was not a hit.

So when Jim first met Meat Loaf, 'He was like my dream voice.

I never heard a better voice in my life when I first heard him –
and the pianist [Steve Margoshes], I had never heard a better ac-
companist. So it was like an incredible epiphany, like these guys
are perfect!' Only snag? 'I didn't have any idea for what. I didn't
really know what I was going to do; I just knew Meat was perfect.
I liked his voice so much I had them write a part in [*More Than
You Deserve*] for him. That was my first exposure to Meat as an
actor and when I discovered what a very good actor he was as well
as singer – which was the key to Meat Loaf all along, right from
the beginning – I knew therefore he would be perfect for my own
songs because I knew he would be able to act out what I wanted
to create.'

Jim told Meat to stay put and within a few minutes the room
was full of people, one of them being Joseph Papp. Meat and Margoshes were halfway through their second rendition of 'I'd Love
To Be As Heavy As Jesus' when Papp held up his hand. 'We'd
love you to be in this production,' he told the singer, and handed
him Michael Weller's script for *More Than You Deserve* – the one
about the US army major stationed in Vietnam who fell in love
with a nymphomaniac reporter after she was gang-raped by the
other soldiers. One of who was this maniac called Rabbit, a good-
hearted junkie conscript whose party trick was blowing people
up with grenades. It was weird and dark and queasily funny, and
even before Meat had heard all the songs he knew he wanted to
play Rabbit.

Jim was still callow. Self-obsessed. Deep in a gothic phase, as
he later said, 'wandering around as if I had a bat on my shoulder'.
He'd wear black leathers and a cape to rehearsals. When he played
the piano, he would pound at it dramatically, hitting the notes so
hard his fingers would begin to bleed. He would finish playing
and hold his hands aloft, still dripping blood onto the ivory keys.
'I always wanted to sweep in,' he recalled in 1990, 'speaking in
German, with a bat on my shoulder. You couldn't do that where

I was in New York!' Meat thought the guy might be some kind of genius or possibly insane. A musical Charlie Manson, maybe, with a whole lotta Wagner going on. But they workshopped the play and Weller allowed Jim to rewrite some of it around Meat. Listening now to the 1973 demo that Meat and Jim produced of the song 'More Than You Deserve', one hears instantly what Steinman was talking about when he described having Meat sing his songs as 'a gift from God'. Where Jim's original demo is fine, it's like a gentle spring compared to the torrent of vocal currents that come crashing off the Meat Loaf demo. 'You could literally feel the piano vibrating with his voice.'

Until then, Jim had been thinking of another prospective protégé for his work, a conventionally good-looking blonde kid named Kim Milford. But Meat was 'extreme' and Jim could relate to that far more easily than he could a budding heartthrob like Milford. His high-castle-walls taste was reflected in all the initial casting: the Major was played by Fred Gwynne, whose earlier TV role as Herman Munster belied a commanding stage presence and superb singing voice, while Mary Beth Hurt – from Meat's time in *As You Like It* – played a cross-dressing nurse. Ron Silver was in it, too, and Kathleen Widdoes. These were proper trained actors, born to be famous, nominated for awards. No fooling around. But at the heart of it all were Jim and Meat.

Jimmy – as Meat always called him – unnerved the singer because he seemed to glower a lot and had a razor tongue, which he wasn't afraid to use. As for Jim, he was sort of spellbound by what he called this 'great gothic beast' who quivered and trembled as he sang. 'He was an absolutely mesmerising, wonderful presence,' Jim said. 'His pupils would roll up into his head, and you'd see the whites of his eyes, and his hands would clutch. It was really powerful. He was extraordinary. As a performer, when he's at his best, he ranks among the three or four greatest I've ever seen in my life.'

In the middle of the show, Rabbit gets a letter from his mother telling him that his wife has run away and left him. That's when Meat would stand up and sing 'More Than You Deserve', the title song and an instant showstopper that, even the very first time he sang it in front of an audience at the Public Theater, got an unprompted standing ovation and shouts for more. Much more. It wasn't long coming. 'I'd never seen it before,' Jim admitted. It was the first sign and the first connection, the beginning of everything that happened next.

'More Than You Deserve' is an extraordinary song, in many ways the keystone song for all of Steinman's work, and certainly one of his greatest. It would not be recorded for *Bat Out of Hell*, but instead for *Dead Ringer* (the belated follow-up) where it is given a much more refined orchestrated arrangement. But its true significance lies in that first connection, the meeting of author and subject, the first time that Meat Loaf would come to embody Jim Steinman's interior universe, feeding on planets and shitting stars.

It's a song for and about a loser, and not just any loser but a loser in love, and a loser in love who not only *loses* but is humiliated by the people he loves most. It's a song for the kid in class who could never get a date, the girl who got picked last at the dance, for the outcasts and the beta males and those unfairly left behind. What's extraordinary is the brilliant, mordant humour of the lyric, which is both ridiculous in its excess and somehow still believable, plus the counterpoint that these words make with the unearthly beauty of the melody. Steinman would spend the next forty years constantly exploring and inhabiting this territory in his songs – the yearning of those who don't have and never will, their futures only glimpsed through the raw prism of betrayal and an Olympian desire that finally condemns them to hell. 'More Than You Deserve' is the song that begets 'Two Out Of Three Ain't Bad', 'For Crying Out Loud', 'Surf's Up', 'I'm Gonna

Love Her For Both Of Us', 'I'd Do Anything For Love (But I Won't Do That)' . . . every one of them a fantastical broken-hearted epic with which Meat would sail towards the setting sun.

The lyric begins conventionally, a guy falling instantly in love ('*I knew our joy would last so long*') then discovering he has been betrayed, and not just by anyone but by his best friend. By the final verse he has watched her '*making love to a group of my best friends*' and in his cuckolded, neutered fury utters the killer line, '*won't you take some more boys, it's more than you deserve*'.

For a lyric like that to work it can't be sung by a good-looking, bronzed Robert Plant-type. No girl is going to gangbang his friendship group when she's got the real thing waiting for her back at home. As with so many of Jim's songs, it's only artistically true when someone who's been beaten down by life is singing it, an underdog, someone as far removed from a hero as it's possible to be. It's why Bonnie Tyler would later fit him better than Celine Dion and why Jim could never, ever really do it best without Meat Loaf, even though he would try, try and try again. One of Jim's Amherst classmates had driven at this truth when he said, 'Jim knew what it was to be cool, and he knew that he wasn't.'

As a man, Jim wasn't handsome or heroic, but he was born with certain advantages, like being rich and attending Amherst. Meat Loaf, on the other hand, was just a 350-pound, sweating, semi-orphan from Texas whose mama had died and whose daddy tried to kill him, who looked like a freak, who was a freak, and who was scrabbling to hold on to the edge of the cliff that was his perilous life. Precisely, painfully, the very quality Jim most needed for his songs to work, that and his querulous, desperate, gut-wrenching voice.

Meat and Jimmy: Jimmy and Meat. More than either of them deserved. And still not quite ever enough . . .

CHAPTER EIGHT

Never-Never Land

More serious was the way in which Steinman reacted to the initial success of *More Than You Deserve* – a series of artistic misjudgements that showed what a dizzying learning curve he was on. The show ran for sixty-three performances before it took a summer break.

Joe Papp brought it back in the autumn. The audiences weren't right this time – the blue-rinse set, 'old people and their parents' as Jim put it – and he'd messed around with the book. *More Than You Deserve* had started out as a play with a couple of songs in either half, but then Jim talked Michael Weller into adding more songs. And because 'More Than You Deserve' itself came in the first half of the show, a reprise was thrown in later on, even though it didn't really fit the story.

Jim was still learning how to build the kind of gasp-inducing show he kept imagining, and Meat Loaf was learning how to handle the attention. It took him a while, years in fact. Some say he never quite got used to it – he'd spent so much of his life hiding his bulk, his true voluminous form, in the shadows that he had always felt like he needed a mask when he went out in public. Now the feeling had multiplied into anxiety and paranoia. Not because people recognised him yet, but because he, the supreme actor, no longer recognised himself.

Meat liked to sing in bars, jam with the house band, be one

of the guys, but his agent kept ringing with offers of new auditions and roles. What he really wanted was to take Jim Steinman's songs and make a record, but Jim had other ideas about that and Meat eventually flew down to LA to audition for another hair-sex-guitars-type deal called the *Rocky Horror Show*. He'd see Jimmy later.

They were two lost boys entering the long limbo period before the songs that became *Bat Out of Hell* offered them a route out. Jim was living in a terrifying apartment share on 102nd Street, a place so bad that even Meat Loaf, who had lived in every conceivable shithole, baulked when he saw it. Jim slept on a pull-down bed in the kitchen, his head up against a refrigerator that contained so many horrors people had given up opening it. When he moved to 86th Street, Meat helped him pack his stuff into boxes. Jim dumped them in the new place, where he lived for eight years without ever opening them. Meat would claim that he saw the same boxes thirteen years later at Jim's place in Putnam. Who knew if they were the same boxes? Knowing Jim, though, they almost certainly were.

Meat Loaf got a call to go to LA, where they were casting for the first American production of the breakout hit London musical called the *Rocky Horror Show*. Jim stayed in New York and began talking to Joe Papp about his long-held dream to bring a musical production of *Peter Pan* to the stage. Nothing like the sweet, big-eyed Disney animation, but more specifically like the much darker, original JM Barrie book – itself originally written as a play – which one critic at the time called 'as irresistible and horrific as a nasty daydream'. In Jim Steinman's gloved hands Peter and Wendy would have lost their innocence decades before, but not their deepest desires. Meat would play a heavy-magic fortress character called Tinker. Papp just nodded and told Jim to get on with it. A bisexual from the future named Bowie had recently arrived in the US Top 40, a guy called Alice who chopped his own head off onstage each night was suddenly the hottest ticket in America, even Elton John now sang about rocket men and dressed like a spaced-out Willy Wonka. This was 1973 and nothing was too far-fetched any more.

Meanwhile, out on the west coast Meat Loaf had landed himself the brief but memorable role in *Rocky Horror* of Eddie the crazed biker covered in surgical scars who sings 'Hot Patootie Bless My Soul' and somehow manages to get murdered – *twice* – by the show's star, Dr Frank N Furter, a pansexual, cross-dressing, mad scientist played by Tim Curry, 'a sweet transvestite from Transsexual, Transylvania'.

A pastiche of every sci-fi and B-movie monster flick the show's creator, the English actor and writer Richard O'Brien, had seen growing up in the fifties, *Rocky Horror* had been the surprise hit of London's West End that year. Its first production outside the UK, the 1974 LA show, was modestly staged at the Roxy in Sunset Boulevard, where it became the must-see show for Hollywood hipsters, running for nine months before transferring to the Belasco Theater, on Broadway. It was a relatively minor role – more like a two-scene cameo – but Meat revelled in the play's success. Celebs would come backstage to soak up the anything-goes atmosphere, glad-handing cast members like Meat who they had never heard of before. When Elvis Presley showed up one night Meat thought he'd died and gone to uh-huh-huh heaven.

When word then got out that O'Brien was working on a movie version of the show, to be shot in London, Meat lined up like everyone else with his hand out. He wanted in – bad. It wasn't like there was anything else going on. A few weeks later he was in London, one of the few Broadway cast members, other than Curry and O'Brien, to play their roles on both stage and screen. Now retitled *The Rocky Horror Picture Show*, Meat later recalled how Curry was having difficulties making the adjustment from curtain call to camera – a theatrical bind the singer claimed he helped Curry find his way out of during a fateful taxi ride with his co-star.

'Curry was all upset, so we rode around London for about £45-worth [of travel time] talking about it,' said Meat. 'He'd been doing it so long onstage that he was locked into that role.' He paused a beat. 'I dunno if I helped him or not, but we sure spent a lot of time in a taxi.' In fact, the two men – so very different on the outside, with Curry's suave, boarding-school charm in stark contrast to Meat's grade-school bull-in-a-china-shop sense of fun – had a great deal in common. Born a year apart, they had both survived family trauma – Curry's naval chaplain father died when he was twelve – to grow into strongly independent characters who would use their abilities to act and sing to hide their truer, more brooding natures.

Eventually relinquishing the sanctuary of the taxi, Curry pulled himself together after the first week of shooting. Directed by Jim Sharman, a brilliant young Australian who had previously over-seen productions of both *Hair* and *Jesus Christ Superstar*, and now featuring budding young American stars Barry Bostwick and Susan Sarandon as the two linchpin characters of Brad and Janet, *The Rocky Horror Picture Show*, shot over seven cold wet weeks at the end of 1974, was only a modest success during its initial run. But by the end of the seventies it had gone on to become one of the greatest cult successes of all time, a staple of midnight cinema screenings the world over, with the audience turning up in their favourite characters' costumes and joining in with the deliciously heightened dialogue and deliberately parodic scenes. 'Don't eat the Meat Loaf!' became a familiar cry at screenings as the singer's fame grew. But by then Meat Loaf had already forgot-ten about it. 'I just never thought the movie was put together too well,' he told me. 'But I guess maybe I was wrong.'

Instead he came back to New York, where he took a part in an obscure underground movie he later claimed he couldn't even remember the title of, dismissing it as 'a really stupid movie . . . about the police, and I played a thug and got my face shoved in garbage! It was a real small part. I can remember the plot but not the title. In it I went to this apartment and this stakeout thought I was the guy they were after but I wasn't – I was just some little crook. So these cops chased me down an alley, tackled me and pushed my face in the garbage, which was like vegetable soup! So the only time you saw my face I was covered in these noodles and carrots!'

The real purpose of Meat coming back to New York was to hook up again with Jimmy. Meat was pushing hard on Steinman to make a rock album with him. Being the singer in his own band still ranked higher on his wish list than starring in a Broadway show or a Hollywood movie. He could be himself in a band – no matter what size he was. Being an actor would require going on a diet – for life. Meat Loaf had oversized dreams but he wasn't delusional. He knew where his best chance of success lay.

Jim Steinman had other ideas, though. He wasn't against making records, or the concept of forming a band, but he had even bigger dreams than Meat – ideas for songs and stories that far outweighed the conventions of 40-minute LPs or four-piece backing groups. In an era when the biggest rock artists were having game-changing hits with concept albums of the magnitude of *The Dark Side of the Moon*, *The Rise and Fall of Ziggy Stardust and the Spiders From Mars*, *A Passion Play* and *Quadrophenia*, Jim felt like he was being left behind. Like The Who and David Bowie, Steinman wanted to make big musical statements. He wanted to make rock opera. Still obsessed with writing songs for the Peter Pan-themed musical he'd dubbed *Adventures in Neverland*, Jim talked Meat into helping him out with that, with a view to maybe turning it into a simultaneous concept album – similar to the way *Jesus Christ Superstar* had first drawn breath as a double album.

In the meantime, the pair found work together on the touring version of the *National Lampoon Show*. A spin-off from the satirical American comic of the same name, the original 1973 production effectively launched the performing careers of John Belushi, Christopher Guest and Chevy Chase. The first half of the show was a sketch comedy, the second half was a mock rock festival, 'Woodshuck: Three Days of Peace, Love and Death', a parody of 'Woodstock: Three Days of Peace and Music'. The show was such a cult success that out-of-town dates at mainly college campuses were added and new cast members were brought on board to cover for the loss of key members like Chase and Guest, skyrocketing new talents like Dan Aykroyd, Harold Ramis, Bill Murray, Gilda Radner – and Meat Loaf, who'd managed to get himself hired as understudy to the brilliant but ill-starred Belushi, while Jim became the show's musical director. Jim saw it as an opportunity to keep working on his original material for the *Neverland* project, and Meat went from backroom boy to onstage regular playing dozens of different parts – becoming good pals with the high-living Belushi along the way. 'I owe a lot to John Belushi because he and I were good friends and he taught me a lot,' Meat told me. 'If he'd lived, John would have become one of the best actors in the world, ever. He just had a problem with trusting ... but he was unbelievable, one of the most talented people I've ever known in my entire life.'

It was on tour with the new *National Lampoon* that Meat learned much of the improvisations and spontaneous techniques that would become a feature of his later live performances. Jim Steinman recalls seeing a transformation in Meat Loaf's confidence on that tour. 'They would chant his name at the end and it partly made me realise what a great name it was. To hear 1,500 people who had never seen him before or heard of him, at the end going "Meat Loaf, Meat Loaf!", it was very cool.' He also recalled it as 'a very blasphemous, irreverent show'. It was while they were on tour with *National Lampoon*, Jim said, 'that I started writing the songs for [Meat] that ended up as *Bat Out of Hell*. I never intended to do music. I didn't think I was a good-enough musician. I was gonna do film and theatre, but I figured, "this is fun, let's do this".'

It wasn't all plain sailing. When the tour arrived for a handful of shows 'at these intensely Christian Bible schools' in Pennsylvania, there were near-riots during one sketch that involved a mock crucifixion. The crowd, made up almost entirely of drunken jocks, all as one began chanting the Lord's Prayer and throwing beer bottles at the stage, and one of the bottles hit the lid of Jim's piano, causing it to come crashing down on his fingers. He stormed off the stage. 'When Jim and I did *National Lampoon* together, it was really crazy,' Meat recalled in 1977. 'For the *Lampoon* show, I'd go in a corner and just sit and stare from my chair for maybe four minutes. The lights were down low, and Jim would play piano. I'd just stare at them and Jim would be playing dramatic stuff. They'd get nervous and I'd just sit there; some people would dance, some would giggle and I'd just stare. Then I'd turn to the audience and smile, saying, "I'll bet you'd like to know what the hell is going on, wouldn't you?"'

When, later in 1975, most of the *National Lampoon* gang were hired for a new live comedy-variety TV show called *NBC's Saturday Night* – soon to be retitled *Saturday Night Live* – Meat Loaf was also invited to audition for the show. Meat saw it as a chance to sing on the first show, but the team, led by producer Lorne Michaels, a 28-year-old maverick writer and comedian who'd previously worked on the groundbreaking *Rowan & Martin's Laugh-In* show, had other ideas. As Meat recalled, 'They said to me, "Are you interested in doing a show?" And I said, "No" – a mistake! I should have done it!' (In fact, after he became famous Meat Loaf would appear on the show a further three times and remains the only musician, aside from Mick Jagger, to ever perform anything other than songs. His most notable 'skit' partner was another occasional guest called Eddie Murphy.)

Another talent in the *Lampoon* shows who was destined to become more involved with Meat Loaf's career was composer and musician Paul Jacobs. Speaking in 1985, Meat recalled how he had 'wanted Paul in the band from the very beginning but he didn't want to work with [Steinman] and Jimmy didn't want to work with anybody that was any good, really. That's not to put him down – but he had a fear of musicians at that time (he doesn't now) who knew more about music than he did.'

In truth, when Steinman staged a workshop production of *Neverland*, in 1976, Jacobs served as musical director and co-arranged the show's score. Later, after Steinman left Meat Loaf's touring band, Jacobs, as a pianist and backing vocalist, replaced him.

But that was in the future. Still locked into the idea of making an album of original material with Jimmy, Meat's next paying job came when he grabbed at a stopgap role in *Rockabye Hamlet* – a kind of 'to be or not to be' *Hair* – directed by Gower Champion. 'He'd done a lot of hit stuff.' Meat shrugged. 'And when you have an opportunity to work with people like that, you do it.' Indeed, Champion had enjoyed a successful career in movies as a dancer-choreographer before graduating to musical theatre in the 1960s, directing four hit shows in row, including *Bye Bye Birdie* and *Hello, Dolly!*. This, though, was a step too far for the now-ageing director. Bringing the Bard to the love generation was a laudable aim, but Champion knew as much about the post-hippy audiences of the mid-seventies as Meat Loaf did at the time about vegetarianism. The result was a complete disaster and stumbled along for just seven shows before being unceremoniously dumped.

'It was a terrible show,' the singer conceded, 'it was a dreadful part but I learned from him.' What Meat Loaf learned, he said, was 'how to give and take focus. That's a very important lesson performers need to learn from the viewpoint of how to perform.

You see, if you're me you don't want people looking at you all the time, you want them going somewhere else and then coming back to you. There's very few people who have the kind of strength that I do onstage, so when I give them the focus and then take it back, it rockets. This is not an ego trip, because I don't have anything to do with it, it's just there. I know what I can do and what I can't do. I don't pretend and don't try to fool myself. But in that show, I was onstage with seventy-two other people and I had to take focus. And Gower Champion said, "You're the first person I've ever seen that can take focus from a group of seventy-two people dancing about you at high energy and you're not doing a fucking thing but everyone in the audience is watching you!" And I said, "Well, I figured it out."'

Meat Loaf took another one-off gig adding some vocals to the second album, *Free-For-All*, from his old Detroit pal Ted Nugent. With his flight and hotel paid for, plus a thousand-dollar fee waiting for him, he scooted down for a few days to the Sound Pit studio in Atlanta, Georgia, singing lead on five of the album's nine tracks. As on the Stoney & Meatloaf album, he was credited wrongly as Meatloaf. But he didn't care about that. What stuck in his craw was that $1,000 fee, which seemed like easy money at the time then looked like peanuts after the album sold over a million copies.

There were also one-off, cash-in-hand gigs: recording a song called 'Clap Your Hands And Stand By Me' also featuring Procol Harum drummer BJ Wilson and Deep Purple guitarist Ritchie Blackmore, and destined to become one of the forgotten classics of the era. Meat also took a trip to London to record a song titled 'Tulip Baker', written for a girl who ended up failing to produce the necessary vocal. In stepped Meat Loaf to the rescue. 'You wanna know how high it was?' he laughed. 'Almost blew my brains out!'

Highs and lows, lows and highs, and the story hadn't even got properly started yet.

CHAPTER NINE

Motorcycle Love Songs

Without the same financial imperatives as his workaholic
singer – Jim was still a rich kid even when he was slum-
ming it – Steinman was able to carry on working on what was
now becoming his latest grand obsession, the music to *Neverland*.
It wasn't until Meat was able to fully commit, though, that the
songs really came into sharp relief. The two spent months holed
up together at the Ansonia in New York's Upper West Side. The
Ansonia was one of those boho residential joints in the most expensive part of Manhattan that attracted the kind of artists and
musicianly types whose dreams of grandeur far outstripped their
ability to always come up with the rent on time. As well as the
one-day rock stars and any-day-now actors, Babe Ruth had once
lived there. So had Igor Stravinsky. In the basement lay the Con-
tinental Baths, a gay bathhouse where Bette Midler and Barry
Manilow had provided the cabaret – now being refurbished for
its relaunch as Plato's Retreat, an open-door swingers' club.

Meat and Jim were just glad to have a place they could work
out of – and sleep in.

'We didn't have a demo,' Jim would tell Sandy Robertson.
'It was me pounding away and bleeding, Meat sweating like a
maniac.' None of those that came by to check out what they were
cooking up there, he said, 'could deal with it. They couldn't figure
out what it would sound like when it was finished.'

According to the singer, he personally set to work on altering the Steinman mode of composing. 'I finally convinced Steinman to write some different kinds of stuff,' he reckoned in 1985, 'cos he was writing weird stuff, I mean he was out there.' Even as he spoke the words, though, it was clear a legend was being quietly and painstakingly brewed here. 'The first song that I talked him into writing,' claimed Meat, 'was "You Took The Words Right Out Of My Mouth". Then we sat in a car one night, worked out "Paradise By The Dashboard Light" and I made him extend "Bat Out Of Hell". And I came up with things like "All Revved Up With No Place To Go", which is a lot about me in high school. "Paradise . . .", too, was about my life in high school.' Based on one of his teenage dates in Texas, when he'd driven a girl named Rene Allen down to a make-out spot by the lake, Jim *loved* that one – it was right in his wheelhouse. 'Anyway, Jim is a better writer than I am; I can think of things, of stories, but I don't put it down in words too well.'

Jim had no such hang-ups, and for the first time Jim began to take Meat's suggestions seriously. In *National Lampoon* they had both worked with a beautiful blonde female singer with a lot of spunk named Ellen Foley. Meat thought it would be great if Jim could somehow work a role for her into the project. 'I had him write a duet for me and Ellen Foley on "Paradise",' he explained. 'Cos I thought Foley could sing real well. I just fed him the idea about how I used to hang out by a lake in the car with this girl. Jimmy added to it by making it the life story.'

What wasn't mentioned at the time was that Meat and Ellen had begun an affair. They didn't make a big secret of it but they didn't go out of their way to make a public show of it either. Foley was tiny, blonde, probably weighed about 100 pounds – less than a third of the size of Meat at the time – and Jim recalled people not knowing how to react to that information. 'I'm saying, "It really doesn't involve a crane or anything like that" . . . Meanwhile I'm thinking, maybe a crane *is* involved.'

Foley was the latest to join a growing Steinman/Loaf team of like-minded musicians and thinkers. One such was Rory Dodd (his clear blue-sky voice later heard to stunning effect singing the '*Turn Around, Bright Eyes*' line on 'Total Eclipse Of The Heart', Bonnie Tyler's Steinman-penned 1983 smash hit). Rory and his brother Cal were backing singers with various bands in Canada and, according to Meat, 'Rory invented many of the background parts that were real intricate inside different things like "Paradise" and "Bat".'

The 'Bat' in question was of course 'Bat Out of Hell', a half-finished showstopper Jim had been wrestling with for some time, not quite knowing where exactly to go with it. Meat recalls that the song 'was finished at the second chorus' when Jim first played him the bones of it. 'I made Jim go ahead and write the end of it.' I said, "It's not done, you've gotta finish this story!" And Jimmy had me do stuff, like different ways of singing "For Crying Out Loud". And we had a lot of arguments,' he recalled. 'One time I turned over a piano on him! Then we panicked cos we had to put this piano back together.' They did it, he said, 'with chewing gum and string so no one would know it was broken'.

Speaking with me more than three decades later, Steinman recalls the song 'Bat Out of Hell' as a major turning point for him as a songwriter: the moment he discovered his true nature as a writer of dark, gothic, almost cinematic romances. 'That's the way I write,' he agreed. 'In fact, one of my favourite things that any critic ever said about me was that I was to hard rock what Hitchcock was to movies. Which is, basically, nonsensical but I was really pleased by that because I've always loved Hitchcock and that's kind of exactly how I saw what I did, too.'

Until that moment, he said, 'I never really knew how to write. I had to teach myself how to write when I got out of college. The ten years over that next period, I was busy, intuitively teaching myself how to write. And what I wrote was very influenced by movies and by Hitchcock, who I adore. He's still my favourite of all time, I think, in any field. So it was so refreshing for me to read that because I had no idea that was coming through.

'It wasn't that deliberate but I remember noticing it myself on "Bat Out of Hell" the song. It's written like a Hitchcock movie, in the sense that the opening verses are just like the opening of *Psycho* – to me. Of course, I'm clinically insane and this is all being filtered through my mind, which is an X-rated forbidden zone. But it does function occasionally and the way *Psycho* begins is with a great long shot of Phoenix, Arizona, then it goes to a medium shot of the motel room from the outside, then to a closer shot right outside the motel, and then to a close-up in the motel room of the two lovers in bed. I was so affected by the cinematic language of that as it might pertain to music, without thinking this out, so that the song "Bat Out of Hell" basically starts with that long shot: *"The sirens are screaming and the fires are howling way down in the valley tonight . . ."* So it starts with that overall long picture and then it keeps going closer to the bedroom, which is when the girl and he are together. I realised that I do write that way intuitively, probably having absorbed Hitchcock's language.'

He giggled, bubbles streaming through the air. 'I mean, I'm just guessing. It could be something totally different but you make connections almost after the fact.'

And almost none before, as he and Meat Loaf were about to discover.

Meanwhile, the *Neverland* song cycle that was now transmogrifying into the would-be *Bat Out of Hell* album was being added to and subtracted from, crosscut and rearranged, constantly zig-zagging across its wavy lines, like a musical Rorschach test: you could read anything into these songs, it just depended on how far you allowed your imagination to run free. Months passed during which Jim and Meat would weigh, judge, discard or build on the material. A sprawling 10-minute epic Jim had sweated bullets for, titled 'The Formation Of The Pack', would, at Meat's insistence, eventually be cut by nearly a third, ramped up and retitled 'All Revved Up With No Place To Go'.

The opening piano chords of 'Bat Out of Hell' were amended to sound – to Jim's mind – more like 'Jailhouse Rock'. Instead of '*Bah-baaang . . . Warden threw a party at the county jail . . . bah baaang . . .*' 'Bat' had '*Bah bang . . . the sirens are screaming and the fires are howling down in the valley tonight . . . Bah-bang.*' He tied it to his 'long-standing impulse to write the ultimate motorcycle crash death song' and Meat came at it like centaur gambolling up to the microphone.

The first iterations of 'Two Out Of Three Ain't Bad' Jim had actually heard as a country song, a Hank Williams-type murder ballad ('because country music was so damn dark and so damn desolate'), the lyric coming from a conversation with his friend, the actress Mimi Kennedy: 'I was complaining to my friend Mimi about no one liking my music, and she said, "Well, it's so damn complicated, Jim." Elvis was on the radio in the other room singing "I Want You, I Need You, I Love You" and Mimi said, "Why don't you write something like that?" I thought, well I'll try . . .'

'You Took The Words Right Out Of My Mouth' combined his love of The Who's upstart power chords with a full-on money-shot Phil Spector melody (the spoken-word piece at the start of the song, where Jim asks, '*On a hot summer night, would you offer your throat to the wolf with the red roses?*' and a breathless Ellen Foley replies simply 'yes' was another *Neverland* outtake). 'For Crying Out Loud', another 10-minute cinemascope ultra-ballad, began so tenderly, snowflakes falling like tears, it was easy at first to miss some of Jim's playful wordplay. But then Meat, his voice so soft and yearning until then, comes on strong as the song gets taken over with raw sexual imagery ('the boner line', as he would later describe it), a giant ballad built piece by piece from the simple opening piano motif ('Still one of my favourite progressions,' he would say).

Over a period of two years, the finished songs emerged. The great problem with them was that they were hard to demo. A demo is essentially a simple and cheap early recording of a song that can be played to record companies and A&R scouts. It works perfectly well with most pop songs because most pop songs *are* simple. Jim's songs were anything but, and long before they were recorded they existed in his head as musical visions, dreamscape fantasies, with waves crashing, motorcycles revving, girls swooning and drums pounding. It couldn't be done on a four-track tape machine (indeed, the demos of the early *Bat* songs that do exist and can be found today on YouTube are mostly just Jim noodling the song on piano and working it out vocally on his own).

There was only one thing for it; the songs were bigger than life, and so was the singer. The best thing, they thought, was to call up record companies, find a piano and sit down and play the damn things live, right in front of them. To Meat and Jim, with their shared background in theatre, this sounded logical. To anyone in a record company, the sight of the strangely attired and deliberately mysterious Jim and the 350-pound Meat Loaf wearing a white dress shirt and tuxedo trousers and mopping the endless sweat from his giant moon face with a red handkerchief, sometimes accompanied by the elfin Ellen Foley so that they could duet on 'Paradise By The Dashboard Light', was not the kind of thing you saw every day. Nor was it necessarily a welcome sight to record company talent scouts who were then in thrall to the two big musical trends of the day: skinny-tie new wave and thin-white-lines disco.

Again and again, they crashed and burned. After a few months, as Jim put it, 'We were getting turned down by people that were *thinking* of starting record companies.'

Every time they hit the street after another rejection, they would rage at the unfairness of it all. Every now and again they would catch a break. They opened as a bare-bones voice-piano

outfit for former Ten Wheel Drive singer Genya Ravan at a place
in Greenwich Village called Gino Sweeney's, and realised that
they could get the songs across to an audience, and what's more,
the audience loved them. They got a publishing deal and an advance of $40,000, which seemed like a fortune at the time, but
it didn't last long once they started spending it. They got an ap-
pointment with the greatest pair of ears in the business, Clive
Davis, who'd signed Janis Joplin, Santana, Springsteen and other
big deals when he was head of Columbia Records, and now ran
his own NY label, Arista. Ushered into a small side room with
a piano to run through their set, it felt like this might be it. But
Clive ended up telling Jim he had no idea how to write a pop song
and that he should listen to the radio more. For years, Jim saved
the piece of paper as a bitter little souvenir on which Davis had
scribbled the 'correct' chord sequences he needed to improve his
amateurish songs – the same songs that just a few years later
Meat Loaf would be singing to sold-out arenas all over the world.
'I still have this paper that has A, A, B arrow C, C, C, C, C.' But
as Steinman later put it, he wasn't interested in writing formulaic
pop songs for contemporary radio – whatever the fuck that was
– he was writing 'motorcycle rock songs. Even the ballads were
motorcycle rock ballads.'

But no one was getting that. And the more he tried to persuade
them, the more they pulled away.

And then came Todd.

Todd Rundgren was simply too good, as some musicians are.
He could play stacks of instruments, write an amazing assort-
ment of songs, perform solo or in his band, Utopia, record, arrange, produce – all in a brain-scrambling variety of styles and
genres. Unlike most other long-haired musicians of the day, Todd
wasn't cut out for doing one thing well over and over for the rest
of his career, so despite the occasional big international hit like
'I Saw The Light' and 'Hello, It's Me', he wasn't a big star. The

main group of people that revered Todd Rundgren were other musicians, because they understood how gifted he was. But he'd never been given access into rock's VIP room. It happened some-times – Todd was too good to be a specialist in anything. When he wasn't making his own albums – an eclectic catalogue of pop, psyche, rock, prog, show tunes and soul – he was helping other artists make some of the most singular and influential albums of the seventies. Almost his first gig behind the controls was help-ing record and mix *Stage Fright* for Bob Dylan alumni The Band. Since then he'd produced the first New York Dolls album followed by hit albums for Grand Funk Railroad and Hall & Oates. Todd could tackle anything. The only thing he feared was the mun-dane. The minute he clapped eyes on big, frown-faced Meat and crazy cape-wearing Jim he knew he'd found new friends.

Even Jim, for all of the originality and complexity of his music, did one thing really well. So did Meat. With Todd, you could say to him, as Jim would, 'I want a guitar that sounds like a motor-cycle reproducing in a nocturnal alleyway,' and Todd would fiddle with a few boxes and buttons, strap his guitar on and do it. Jim would soon decide that 'Todd is the only genuine genius I've ever worked with.'

For his part, Todd was simply amused by their songs. 'Oh my God,' he'd said the first time he heard them. 'I've *got* to make that album.' His effortless understanding of music, everything from genre to sound, meant that he heard them as Jim heard them, as songs about heroic, fantastical love, sometimes unrequited, often thwarted, often unfulfilled. Their language was rich and allusive. The music was gothic and dramatic and passionate and outré. It was not for everyone, only the special ones. There was no fey irony. They were not the kind of songs that cool people would necessarily write or listen to. But they were something different, not like anything else, and they rang Todd's bell.

'All you need is a record deal,' Todd said, after listening to Meat and Jim pound through their twenty-five-minute repertoire, 'and we'll go in the studio.'

Yup, that was all they needed. Meat mumbled something about having been signed to RCA – something that hadn't actually happened. But the boys were desperate. In fact, RCA were expected to pass on the deal just as Clive Davis and everyone else had. Some of them liked the songs but left appalled when faced with the odd couple that sang and played them. Jim later called the roll call of companies that passed on them a 'medley of the most brutal rejections you could imagine'.

But they wisely chose not to share that information with their new prospective producer.

'Okay,' said Todd. 'Great. Let's get started.'

CHAPTER TEN

Holding Out For A Hero

They went to Bearsville Studios in Woodstock, upstate New York, where Todd had become a virtual artist in residence, recording five of his own albums there in as many years, and rehearsed for a month. It was 1975 and Christmas was coming and who knew, maybe Santa was real after all? Todd certainly appeared to believe so. He brought in some guys from his band Utopia – Kasim Sulton on bass, Roger Powell on keyboards and Willie Wilcox on drums – and then two members of Bruce Springsteen's E Street Band, the pianist Roy Bittan and drummer Max Weinberg. Todd knew everybody and everybody knew Todd. Now they had the proper tools for the job – musicians who could make *Bat* sound as it should.

In addition to his other gifts, Todd was a wonderful arranger, and he understood structure and dynamics as they pertained to recorded music. The only hitch was the cash. Work on the recording ground to a halt in the New Year when Utopia was booked on a tour of Japan and Todd said that when he got back, they wouldn't be able to carry on until the bill had been paid.

RCA certainly weren't going to cough up – despite one of their smaller offshoot labels, the deliciously titled Tomato Records, showing enough interest to make Meat and Jim a verbal offer of a deal, they thought the idea of having Todd Rundgren produce it completely wrong. The RCA suits felt they needed a proven hit man to make this outlandish project work. Rundgren, who'd recently diversified his own musical direction in favour of progressive rock with his band Utopia, clearly wasn't the right guy, in their eyes. They particularly disliked what Rundgren had done as producer to the Hall & Oates album, *War Babies*, which sharply veered away from their blue-eyed soul pop towards a much more 'out there' sound. Most crucially, it had not been a hit. They suggested Andy Johns and Jimmy Iovine. Andy had worked as an engineer with Zeppelin and the Stones, he knew how to make rock commercial. Jimmy had just come off working with Bruce on *Born To Run*. He also had the magic touch.

But, desperate though the two misfits were, they felt they owed Todd. He had been the only one to really take a chance on them. Plus, he was eccentric enough to make Steinman at least feel at home. With RCA/Tomato now walking away from the deal, things appeared to be in permanent hiatus again. Fortunately, as if by magic, they ran into David Sonenberg, an entertainment industry lawyer who'd worked on *Hair*, now looking to launch his new full-service management company, DAS. They told Sonenberg their sob story and the savvy music biz operator merely smiled. No problem, he told them, he would take them on.

Sonenberg knew what he was doing. Meat could sing, nobody could dispute that, and Jim, for all his idiosyncrasies, could definitely write. If Sonenberg could find someone else to invest some money, he knew he'd have a ballgame. When he found an investor willing to put in $150,000, outside of Todd liking their songs, this was the first decent break they'd had. Meat and Jim wondered what the catch was, but there it was, just as Sonenberg had promised: the cash to pay their studio fees and have enough left to finish the album.

When he got back from Japan, Todd reassembled everyone and recorded the seven tracks that would comprise *Bat Out of Hell* in record time. He knew how it should sound, he kept reassuring them, how big and full and mad, and when he didn't, he had Jim right there to egg him on. The partnership worked because Todd had the chops to turn Jim's aural hallucinations into real-world recordings, and without having to subjugate his own ego, too.

As far as Jim was concerned, Rundgren was the answer to their prayers. Rather than try to manicure the sound for contemporary radio, as every other so-called expert had told them they should do, 'he accepted the music for what it was – and he was just awesome. I can't say enough about Todd.' For Meat, though, the addition of Todd to the team was more of a mixed blessing. With Todd and Jim now joyfully ensconced in the studio in their newfound master and apprentice roles, Meat felt dejected, left outside the loop. Steinman recalls the singer sitting alone in the corner of the studio, the behemoth at bay, the whale aground, as Jim and Todd almost developed a language of their own. Even on those rare occasions when he summoned up the nerve to approach the two with some suggestions of his own, Rundgren would dismiss him like an errant child told to leave the grown-ups alone.

Meat Loaf, whose bulk barely disguised a gossamer-thin skin, took these brush-offs so badly that Jim began to worry he might do something foolish. He'd always been prone to paranoia, since his schooldays of being taunted and bullied mercilessly. Back then he'd kept his thoughts of suicide to himself. Now he began talking of taking his own life the way some guys talked about leaving their wives. He said it so often Jim and everyone else took such remarks as no more than the ill-formed threats of a lonely heart looking for an arm around the shoulder. Now Jim began to seriously wonder. When one night, after another fruitless attempt to get in Todd's face, Meat stormed out of the studio, then failed to show up at the local movie theatre where they had all planned to see the new Clint Eastwood flick *The Outlaw Josey Wales*, Jim began to fret over what he might find when he returned home to the wooden shack they were sharing at the time.

He needn't have worried. The singer had failed to follow the instructions he'd been given on how to get to the theatre, become further enraged when he found himself at the wrong address, decided it was all a deliberate plot, then stomped home to Ellen, hoping she would kiss it better. She did.

Other times, Meat began to act out his suicidal tendencies. Getting everyone's attention by disappearing without warning, or not showing up for a meeting, still getting his own back on the school bullies and their endless hazing. Things went to the next level, though, when one night, according to Steinman, the singer took an overdose of the prescription painkiller Darvon and passed out in the shower. When Jim and Rory Dodd tried to rouse him, the singer just lay there slumped in the corner, moaning, 'I want to die, I want die, I want to die . . .' Jim and Rory somehow managed to drag him out and get him into a car and drove him to the nearest hospital. Jim was furious when he discovered it was *his* supply of Darvon the singer had taken. He yelled: 'Meat, you animal, you stupid animal, I need that stuff!' (Jim had been taking the Darvon for over a year to ease the lingering pain of his badly broken nose.)

After the album was released and became such a hit, Meat would look back on such studio doldrums in an entirely different light. 'Essentially the conception of the record and how it's done are [Jim's] gig,' Meat would tell the writer Ritchie Yorke. 'He doesn't tell me how to do my stage show. When we go into the studio, I interpret his songs because he feels I can do that. We talk about the songs between ourselves and we work back and forth. But in the studio, Jim worked with Todd and I played cards. I made occasional suggestions and several times I got my way because I threatened to kill them. And I'm bigger than both of them.'

Not that Jim had it all his own way with the headstrong producer. 'Todd was very reluctant to do a lot of the things we wanted to try,' Jim revealed in an interview once the record was done. 'He said at the beginning his job was to get our vision onto the record and he really did succeed in doing that. I suspect that he probably disagreed with about sixty per cent of it, but he brilliantly captured it, nonetheless. Anyway, anyone who thinks the album is over-produced should hear what I had to leave out. For instance, in "Bat Out of Hell" I had to delete two of my favourite things. In the soft section, I wanted to have a boys' choir. I argued with Todd about it and he wanted to do it with the existing vocal backup section and then speed up the tape and use other technical tricks to get the boys' choir sound. I said that we needed a real boys' choir, but he insisted. But it didn't work out so we weren't able to use it. You see, I'd heard this symphony by Mahler and I really wanted a boys' choir. There's nothing more beautiful than the sound of twenty boy sopranos singing.'

All this said with the straightest of faces. 'I also wanted a choir in the motorcycle section of "Bat Out of Hell". Just like in the film *2001: A Space Odyssey*, they used a choir sounding like it was singing whole clusters of notes. I wanted to use an entire orchestra, and I wanted to use them viciously.' Talking to him years later, he laughed at the memory: 'All I can say is thank God we knew nothing about making albums because otherwise it couldn't have happened. I wanted to make an album that sounded like a movie.'

Todd would simply nod his head then get back to pushing faders the way he wanted.

'The most important thing is that Meat supports me in my vision of the album,' Jim said. 'There has to be a vision, you know. The real thrill of a voice is how it plays against the instruments. It's almost a battle existing between the instruments and the voice. Wagner used it with spectacular effect – it's extraordinary to see one woman on the stage of an opera house with no amplification rising above a one hundred twenty-piece orchestra. I regard it as one of the heroic feats of humanity.'

Perhaps the most remarkable performance on the record – aside from Meat Loaf's extraordinary vocal pyrotechnics – was Todd's. Along with producing and arranging and finding the other musicians and working out what the hell Jim wanted, he played all of the guitars. According to Meat, he recorded the solo passages for the title song, plus the revving motorcycle guitar that drives a key part of the narrative halfway through, in one take, the whole thing accomplished in under forty-five minutes.

When Meat and Jim needed a hero, Todd Rundgren came through.

Now, finally, they had a record. They just didn't have a deal. They'd gone back and forth on the mixing – Todd had done most of it, but Jimmy Iovine – the in-house producer at New York's Record Plant studios, who'd latterly worked with John Lennon and Bruce Springsteen – smoothed over some wrangles that Jim had with Todd's take on a couple of songs, and John Jansen – a hugely experienced engineer who'd worked with everyone from The Who to Jimi Hendrix – pulled off the only mix of 'Paradise By The Dashboard Light' that Meat Loaf could live with.

'It took us months to mix it,' Meat recalled with exasperation, 'because we were using everybody and their mother; Jimmy Iovine and everybody! We spent four or five months mixing the record over and over again . . . I was ready to kick "Paradise" off until a guy named John Jansen came in and put it together. Nobody knows who John Jansen is but he saved "Paradise" when I was ready to get rid of it because it was dreadful! Rungren's mix was a dog. It was terrible! And it was all done in more studios than you could shake a stick at.' (The only section of the original mix Meat was happy to keep was the baseball commentary by Phil Rizzuto, who took just two takes to get his now famous part down. Rizzuto made his name as a player with the New York Yankees, and Meat Loaf grew up as a Yankees fan.)

Everyone agreed the final results were terrific, godlike even, surely now they had the whole wang-dang-doodle in the can it would be easier for record company deal-makers and their cheque-chewing accountants to grasp the potential, to recognise they had something hot to hold on to here? There were only two problems. The first was that *Bat Out of Hell* didn't sound like anything else – a fact that was guaranteed to make record companies nervous; second was that they'd spent a year visiting every label that they could think of and had been rejected by all of them. The songs were still the same ones, and Meat was still a 350-pound ham, so reapproaching anyone would be doubly tough just trying to get a meeting scheduled.

They needed an entrance via the back door, and they thought they'd got one when Albert Grossman heard the tapes and liked them. Grossman had been Bob Dylan's Svengali manager and as such had the ear of Mo Ostin, who sat on the throne at Warner Bros. Everyone got excited and Jim, Meat, Ellen Foley and Rory Dodd were invited to LA to perform for the label executives. One of those was Lenny Waronker, who had met Jim before. Jim had played 'Who Needs The Young', a song from *The Dream Engine* that Waronker found lyrically revolting, and when Meat Loaf and Ellen started making out during 'Paradise By The Dashboard Light', it sealed their fate. Mo and Larry didn't know where to look. Another wasted trip.

But *Bat* now embarked on a magic carpet ride of its own. David Sonenberg had been courting a start-up label called Cleveland International, which was under the same parent company as Epic Records – who, in turn, were under the Columbia umbrella. Cleveland were prevaricating, so Sonenberg called Steve Van Zandt, aka Little Steven, guitarist in the E Street Band, who went out of his way to talk up *Bat* to Steve Popovitch, the label's garrulous Serbian-American owner known for taking a boom box everywhere he went – a black and silver portable cassette recorder that boomed out a sound as loud as a large in-home stereo. Steve loved making deals almost as much as he actually loved music. Steve was a record man, a dream-maker, of the old school. As the youngest-ever vice president at Columbia in the early seventies, he'd been the head of promotion for dozens of major artists. Moving up to vice president of A&R at Epic, he'd personally signed Boston, Cheap Trick, Ted Nugent, Southside Johnny and several other soon-to-be platinum acts.

Now, in 1977, he'd formed his own label, Cleveland International, and his hot streak was about to get molten when he decided to take a chance with the fat kid with the lion in his throat and the weirdo with the winning way with a mercurial melody – especially so after Van Zandt told Popovitch he thought Meat and Jim were about to sign to Warner's, so Popovitch better make his move right away if he was going to. Van Zandt said he thought *Bat* was going to be a hit. Popovitch took that very seriously because he thought Steve was a genius, plus there was nothing that record companies liked more than beating one another to a hot artist.

Popovitch did the deal.

Bat was almost loose.

They had a killer album cover lined up, too. It was an illustration by a comic book artist called Richard Corben, who had made his name with a popular fantasy series called *Heavy Metal*. From Jim's concept, he drew the heroic biker on his motorcycle, decorated with a horse's skull and bursting upwards from the grave, a large bat perched on a bell tower screeching in unholy joy – or maybe terror and pain – who knew, and who cared? It looked fucking great, a vast blaze of orange madness that caught perfectly the spirit and the aesthetic of the album it enshrined and stood out in the racks like a glowing promise of drama and excess.

Speaking with Sandy Robertson, Jim described Corben's artwork in typically ostentatious, yet in this case entirely appropriate, terms: 'heroic, majestic, multidimensional, tactile, cinematic, erotic, obsessive'. Most of all, he said, Corben's images seemed 'not so much created – as unleashed'.

The illustration also added to the opacity of the concept of Meat Loaf. Who or what was this Meat Loaf exactly? A man? A band? A character? Not even Jim and Meat were sure, and it was this ambiguity that would put the first crack in the artistic relationship, and follow them like a curse over the next four decades.

CHAPTER ELEVEN

The Head of the Match

Ideally, said Jim Steinman years later, the *Bat Out of Hell* album would have come with a front of cover credit as follows: 'written by Jim Steinman, starring Meat Loaf, produced by Todd Rundgren'. But this was the rock market they were launching the album into and that kind of thing would be deemed far too la-de-dah, too filmy, too much like something a chick in a spangled dress would have on her debut album. Jim's idea, not unreasonably, was that the album would be billed as something like 'Meat Loaf and Jim Steinman'. After all, as the writer and conceptual force, his contribution was at least the equivalent of Meat's as the singer, the guy who really inhabited the work. But Cleveland International didn't like that idea either. It was confusing, they said for a first-time artist. No one had heard of Jim or Meat and so having two essentially meaningless names on the cover made the record even harder to market. Meat made the point that people were going to think that Meat Loaf the singer and Meat Loaf the band were interchangeable anyhow. But as he would later say: '[Jim] wanted his name up there. He wanted to be as much a focal point as I was, and I understood that. We had done it together.'

As Steinman would tell me, still writhing with discontent 30 years later, 'It's a little-known fact but originally *Bat Out of Hell* was to have been credited to Meat Loaf *and* Jim Steinman.' That Steinman eventually had his name reduced in size to a quarter of Meat Loaf's is something he said he still got 'extremely upset and angry about' to this day. 'I don't like this idea of forgiving and forgetting,' he fumed. 'You know what they say, move on. Well, no. I like to hold on to my old passions and let them wreak havoc. I don't ever want to forget that. It really hurt me and it still does now. It hurt Meat Loaf, too.'

Jim went on, 'I'm not saying this to try and be self-congratulatory, but part of it was because I left. I had been with him for years, about four years since before the record ever came out and the whole point, in the beginning, was us doing it as a duo. Which I liked, it was an interesting duo, a singer and a songwriter pianist. It wasn't the usual combination of singer-songwriter. It was still Meat Loaf and Jim Steinman and I was into it but the powers that be had the ability to take my name off it and it still bothers me.'

He said it was Meat's then manager – and, ironically, Jim's future manager – David Sonenberg, who did that. 'He wasn't my manager at the time but it's still the same guy. I'm still pissed about it today. I thought it was a heinous thing to do. To his credit Meat Loaf was in tears, literally, about that on the Friday, screaming to the guy – Sonenberg – that he had done that. Now I was listening through a kind of . . . I was eavesdropping, basically. I was in a studio in New Jersey and the way they had it built I was able to just be washing my hands and I could hear this phone conversation in the next room. And without Meat Loaf knowing it I wandered in and heard about eighty per cent of it. And Meat Loaf was literally sobbing. "You can't do this to me! I can't do it without Jimmy! What's gonna happen? Who's gonna write the songs? Who's gonna tell me what to do?" I was very gratified by Meat Loaf's response because to my mind it was a horribly destructive thing. And when I found out that David in the conversation said to Meat, "I'll change it on Monday," meaning he'd change the credit on the sleeve from Meat Loaf and Jim Steinman, simply to Meat Loaf, I didn't believe that. Then Monday came and David came to me [told me]. And to me it was pretty shattering to have that change. But they did change it. I don't think there was any reason to. But what really stays in my memory is David saying, at one point, "It's better to just have it as Meat Loaf. It sounds too Jewish if we add your name." It was a terrible reason and, you know, I'm still offended to this day.

'I never felt the same again afterwards. I remember going to Sonenberg's office about three days later and David being apologetic and saying, "I hope you understand, Jimmy, this way it's just easier to market," and he gave me the line about the name being too Jewish.'

It's worth pointing out at this juncture that Sonenberg has never admitted or denied this claim, nor publicly commented on it.

'I said, "This is getting absurd, David. I think the worst thing you did the other day is you created a monster for Meat Loaf – and he is the monster. And I don't think he's going to be able to function alone out there and that's basically what you're doing. Once I leave that tour, and especially as there's now no compulsory reason for me to be there, as if I had been part of the act, you took that away, you pushed me into the background. And once I leave that tour, I think you're gonna really screw up Meat Loaf's life." I told him I thought Meat Loaf was going to have a crazed, insane time because of this – which is either very absurdly self-promoting of me about me, or, as it turned out, somewhat prophetic.

'I knew that Meat Loaf was an actor and he basically needed someone to write the scripts or he didn't know what to act. And that was what I had done for four years, and I also directed him, bar by bar, about the voice he used. Not to demean what Meat Loaf did, but I thought I was working with a great opera singer, like a Pavarotti. I felt it was a great honour to direct that talent. And I did think that was a really unique relationship within rock'n'roll, and a good one, and I think it was very short-sighted of David to not realise that was a plus.'

It is this, Steinman suggested, that is the key to the way his relationship with the singer has fluctuated so wildly through the years, despite the gazillions of album sales and critical acclaim. Things, he said, could – maybe should – have been so different.

With everyone arguing against him, Jim was forced to settle for third billing with the line 'Songs by Jim Steinman'. It was more than most songwriters got, but then Jim wasn't most songwriters. He also got his picture on the rear sleeve, a semi-ridiculous full-colour image of an ecstatic-looking Meat Loaf, in tuxedo and shades, clutching his red kerchief and groping the backside of a woman with her back to camera, who in turn is embracing Jim, doing his very best to look cool in jeans and a pair of white gloves. It was oddly indicative of the entire argument.

Who had the bigger piece of the pie? Was it Meat or was it Jim?

That dispute was only just getting off the ground.

When the first reviews of the album began to appear, though, both men were able to take their frustrations out on the rock press, then the most powerful gatekeepers in the music world, and its most indefatigably impossible to please faction.

'Meat Loaf has an outstanding voice, but his phrasing is way too stage struck to make the album's pretensions to comic book street life real,' declared Dave Marsh in *Rolling Stone*, missing the point that none of the songs were meant to seem 'real'. They were meant to seem – were, in fact – from another realm. 'Some of the songs here, particularly "You Took the Words Right Out of My Mouth" are swell, but they are entirely mannered and derivative. Steinman is wordy, and his attempts to recapture adolescence are only remembrances.'

Well, duh.

'*Bat Out of Hell* is an album of insurrection and the inces-sant adolescent fight against all odds,' decided Barry Cain, the most authoritative and almost always right critic for *Record Mirror*. 'Meat Loaf hangs out everywhere mainly because of a hamburger-swollen body. He sings all the songs on *Bat Out of Hell* in a hamburger-swollen voice. He's swell.'

And those were the better reviews. The worst passed off the album as some sort of joke. Music by 'Led Zeppelin wannabes', said one. Meat Loaf was no more than 'a bargain-basement Elvis', chimed in another. 'Like Lou Reed met Tom Waits in a very small elevator,' claimed yet another, causing both Meat and Jim to wonder whether that was meant to be a good thing or bad, or whether the reviewer had simply lost their fucking mind.

It was only in retrospect that the music press finally managed to get their heads at least partly around what was going on here. 'As punk seized the UK music world in 1977, *Bat Out of Hell* crash-landed from the States like a monstrous anachronism,' explained Ian Gittens in *Q*, two decades later. 'Packed with eight-minute songs of staggering, grandiloquent verbosity and larynx-straining rock opera, it's impossible to conceive of an album that was more indifferent to the late-seventies' zeitgeist.'

Indeed, but again that only told half the story: *Bat Out of Hell* gave us Grand Guignol superpop at a time when punk was striving to turn rock to ashes. Meat Loaf gave us a vastly overweight thirty-year-old superbeing whose voice could topple mountains, stomping around in a frilly shirt at a time when the coolest rock star in the world was a twenty-year-old with an even sillier name, Sid Vicious, who couldn't sing, couldn't play, and was so junkie-thin he vanished when he turned sideways.

It should have been no contest, with punk rendering such old-wave gothic pretensions to the ground, as it now did to Queen and Led Zeppelin, to name just two. And for the longest time that's how it was, the chances of Meat Loaf replacing the Sex Pistols and The Clash on the covers of *Sounds* and the *NME* were about the same as Jim Morrison being found alive in the jungle. Here and there, though, there were the coming disciples, the Meat Loaf converts and Jim Steinman apostles, who when they finally got what was going on couldn't stay away from it – and couldn't stop talking about it.

First and most prominent of which was the *Sounds* writer Sandy Robertson. The first rock journalist of note to seek out an interview, Robertson proudly planted his flag at the top of the Meat Loaf mountain when others were still trying to get over the fact of his name, his size, the fact that he clearly wasn't anything to do with punk, boo hiss.

'Meat Loaf and Jim Steinman,' Robertson informed his readers in *Sounds* magazine in April 1978, 'are the best visionary/artist team in over-the-top hard rock since the Blue Öyster Cult met [writer/producer] Sandy Pearlman. In the same way that Pearlman used the Cult as a vehicle for the merging of his militaristic/Black Sabbath/Lovecraftian themes and obsessions, Meat Loaf is the perfect interpreter for the Steinman exploration of cliché and young America. The only difference is that it's taken the Cult years to get to the point where they can get in *hooks,* memorable tunes as well as chrome screams from the underground, whereas Meat Loaf's album abounds with them. The Spectorish single with its handclapping middle, "Two Out Of Three Ain't Bad" – ballad mastery; "All Revved Up With No Place To Go"– Springsteen stylisation supreme; the title cut – BÖC meets "Sweet Jane", [live Lou Reed] *Rock And Roll Animal* version, that is.'

'I loved what Sandy wrote,' Steinman told me, 'I've never forgotten it. So cool.' So much so that Steinman's official website is to this day dedicated to Robertson. (Full disclosure: I shared a London flat with Sandy in the early eighties while he was writing his brilliant 1981 Meat Loaf and Jim Steinman encomium, *The Phenomenology of Excess,* and of course couldn't fail to fall under the same carnivalesque musical spell.) As for the majority of his critics, Steinman was dismissive. 'Very few people understood the scope of the project.' He shrugged. 'Even fewer seemed to be able to deal with the narrative. My songs are anthems to those moments when you feel like you're on the head of a match that's burning. They're anthems to the essence of rock'n'roll, to a world that despises inaction and loves passion and rebellion.'

The only thing that *Bat Out of Hell* sounded even vaguely akin to was a record by Bruce Springsteen and the E Street Band called *Born To Run*, released in August 1975, almost two years before *Bat*; specifically epic impressionistic songs like the landmark title track (Roy Bittan's Spectorish sleigh-bell keyboards adding quicksilver to Springsteen's almost Steinman-esque verses about sweating it out *'on the streets of a runaway American dream'* while *'at night we ride . . . in suicide machines'*) and the nine-minute-plus 'Jungleland' with its *'opera out on the turnpike'* and its *'ballet being fought in a back alley'*.

Born To Run had been a huge international hit, and began, finally, to justify the hype that had preceded it. But *Born* was Springsteen's third album, and for years before that he'd fought to overcome first his tag as the 'new Bob Dylan' then, more lastingly, and damagingly, as 'the future of rock'n'roll'. Who was the absurdly named Meat Loaf and what had he done to win the critics over? Surely, it was argued, the *Bat* album was merely a more lightweight, more contrived *Born To Run*? Jimmy Iovine had mixed part of it, as he'd mixed part of *Bat*, and, more significantly, two members of Springsteen's band, Roy Bittan and Max Weinberg, appeared on both albums. Bittan's contributions in particular were extremely distinctive, his style of piano playing immediately recognisable.

Even Todd Rundgren later confessed that on first hearing Steinman's songs he had assumed they were deliberately outré pastiches of some of Springsteen's more self-important and humourless moments. But if they were flip sides of the same coin, Springsteen presented the straight-faced, straight-shooting black-and-white movie version, deeply romantic, but imbued with gritty realism. Meat Loaf's was the face of the sad clown, the crooked jester who saw life as the killing joke. As for Jim's songs, they weren't even set on planet Earth, let alone the backstreets of New Jersey, these were colour TV images, episodic and set in a kind of teenage *Neverland*. Still, the critics latched on and didn't let go, even when it was pointed out that most of the songs on *Bat Out of Hell* were written long before *Born To Run* came out.

As Meat recalled in a 1977 interview with American writer Jim Girard, it was during the recording of *Bat* that one night Jim went down to see Springsteen play in New York. 'He came back and told me that he couldn't believe that Springsteen was doing the same thing we were planning to do. But Jim and I were doing what we were doing before we ever heard of him. We were already working together when we heard of him. We're nothing like he was, though; he's real dramatic, too, but in a different sense.'

Ultimately, talk was cheap. The critics were never more influential on record sales than they were in the late 1970s. But it soon became clear that it wasn't just the kinds of people that bought and read music magazines that would be open to this music. How to bypass the largely unfriendly critics and get to them, though? Well, there was radio – but few of the album-oriented FM stations in America knew what to make of the *Bat* album. Was it deliberately ostentatious rock, like Queen, maybe? Or was it another one of Todd Rungren's weird off-message projects? Or maybe a collection of over-the-top show tunes? A kind of made-in-the-shade, hyperdrive, fatso Barry Manilow? Like, were the guys fucking joking or what?

In the end there was only one way to try to sell an album, certainly a debut album, and that was on the road. The kismet of signing to Cleveland, for whom *Bat* was, for now, essentially the only show in town, probably saved this weird and outrageous record from simple cult status as just another curio of the wild and twisted mid-seventies, the missing link between Broadway and rock'n'roll. The strategy of Steve Popovitch and his partners

Stan Snyder and Sam Lederman was a time-honoured one. Get the band out into every town and city they could, promote the hell out of the gigs and then follow up with every single radio station, send them picture discs, acetates, posters, limited-run cassettes, coke, weed, wine, pussy, ass, whatever-whatever, anything that would get *Bat* to stick in their mind and out on the airwaves. The only difference, as Stan Snyder would tell *Rolling Stone* in 1978, the year the record finally broke: 'Most new records get six weeks' promotion if they're lucky. We decided to push *Bat Out of Hell* for a least a year, or for however long it took CBS [Cleveland's parent company and bank-roller] to sink extra bucks into the project . . .'

They began with some support shows, again a traditional route for an unknown group. They went to Chicago to play with Cheap Trick, a hometown Illinois band just hitting their commercial sweet spot with some heavily Beatles-influenced rawk an' roll. They were hot straight out of the box, as those hazy record company cats would say, and the kids were lapping them up. They had an out-there guitarist in a baseball cap who made nerdy faces when he played, named Rick Nielsen, and a blonde dreamboat singer in Robin Zander. Best of all, they had a huge radio hit called 'I Want You To Want Me'. This was good because it guaranteed a packed hall. This was also bad because nobody had even heard of Meat Loaf yet. Maybe if he came out with his band and just socked 'em dead from the get-go he might have stood a chance, but that wasn't how Jim Steinman saw things. Jim wasn't interested in competing with obvious crowd-pleasers like Cheap Trick. Jim wasn't into the communality of rock'n'roll, he wanted his show to be ritualistic, staged, a fully loaded presentation, not a ragbag of feel-all-right boogie. Meat Loaf was a stand-alone act as far as Jim was concerned. Unique, one-off, a purely take it or leave it proposition.

Chicago decided to take it – then throw it right back at them.

Jim had decided to play piano on the tour, and was deep into his theatrical fantasy of what a *Bat Out of Hell* stage show should be. He had put together a wardrobe that made him look like a cross between Boris Karloff and Liberace, a ludicrous confection of capes, boots and hats that Meat Loaf would describe as 'the most bizarre things in the world'. He would start the show by peeling off his large black biker gloves – only to reveal a pair of silk white gloves beneath. With Ellen Foley in demand for better-paid stage work, they'd found a new female foil for Meat in twenty-four-year-old Karla DeVito, a hot homecoming Queen (she actually *had* been homecoming queen at her school in the Midwest) who'd left college and gone straight into *Godspell*, before appearing in – you guessed it – *Hair*.

Karla was a brunette bombshell from Chicago who wasn't afraid to be upfront and sensuous, and to wear some costumes Meat Loaf claimed were 'so extreme I've blotted some of them from my brain'. With Meat in full tuxedo, frilled dress shirt and loose red kerchief dangling inelegantly around his neck, they were an extraordinary sight.

The show then started with Steinman reading from a 400-word spoken-word lyric he titled 'Great Boleros Of Fire', a partly tongue-in-cheek piece he'd first written for the *National Lampoon* show, full of breathless images of cold winds and cruel suns and tears that turn to dust, pivoting around the phrase, 'It's all coming back to me now', which would form the basis of a future Steinman song that for years he would refuse to allow Meat to record, insisting it was 'a woman's song'. (Céline Dion would have a huge worldwide hit with it in 1996.) The booing started almost immediately, people yelling, 'Fat boy!' and 'Fucking pig!' Stunned, Meat wheeled back towards the piano where Jim was sitting, and asked him what he should do. Not knowing what to do, Jim made a joke and told Meat he should tell the audience their mother wears army boots. Desperate, Meat did exactly that. Only to be told to shut up and go back to the zoo.

CHAPTER TWELVE

Crying Out Loud

The drummer in the first Meat Loaf touring band, which Steinman dubbed the Neverland Express, was twenty-year-old Joe Stefko. Joe was still young but he thought he'd seen it all. His last gig had been with former Velvet Underground star John Cale, a series of UK dates that Joe bailed out of after the night Cale killed a chicken on stage. But at least Cale had the crowd on his side. As Stefko recalls of that first night with Meat Loaf in Chicago, 'The main thing I remember is they started the show off with speeches, not music, and that was wrong.' The band also featured hotshot guitarist brothers Bob and Bruce Kulick. 'Bob Kulick and myself were trying to tell them: "We really don't think this is how we should start the show. They're not gonna get it." And we kinda got, you know: "Shut up. We're from Broadway, we know how to put on a show." Yeah, I thought, but this is rock'n'roll.'

The band would then pick up the pace, extemporising around Ravel's original triumphal 'Bolero' motif, before finally – finally – crunching into the intro of 'Bat Out of Hell'. It meant that for the first six or seven minutes Meat Loaf didn't utter a word, just stomped around the stage, bug-eyed and blowing like a buffalo. All of this rehearsed like a Broadway show, according to Steinman, minus the cavalcade of abuse from the unimpressed crowd. 'It was one of the greatest things I've ever seen,' Jim was still insisting nearly thirty years later. But Cheap Trick's crowd had no idea how to react to it. All they saw was this fat guy prancing around like a bull, snorting and puffing out his cheeks while making a grab for this hometown doll he didn't deserve. All they heard was the angry thunder of their own baffled voices as they hurled first abuse then fruit, vegetables, and then anything else they could get their hands on. Meat Loaf would not perform in Chicago again for six years.

Afterwards, according to Stefko, 'Meat was so upset he destroyed the dressing room. Chairs were going – Meat just throwing shit all over the place. So we all had a meeting afterwards, and I remember saying: "Look, you've gotta punch them in the face right away. You've gotta get the first punch in and just shut 'em up. Show them how great you are, and then you can do your speeches and your balloon acts or whatever the fuck you want to do." So we retooled the show. We never opened for anyone again, either.'

Meat Loaf would recall that at their next show in New Jersey, in a small 300-capacity club called Creations, when the album had been out for a couple of weeks, that they turned up for sound-check to find actual real-life fans waiting for them. This was the moment he felt that *Bat* may actually start to happen (the evening would feature another small but significant moment – the photograph of Meat Loaf that appears on the back cover of the *Dead Ringer* album was taken at the show, a tight head shot of his drenched hair, light haloing him angelically . . .).

The singer had been so scarred by the experience in Chicago, however, that he was shaking in his boots when he ran out on stage. Convinced that he was in for another barrage of fat jokes, he forgot most of what Jimmy had told him to say and just tore into the set as he had in the old Meat Loaf Soul days. He couldn't believe it – and neither could Jim or anyone else – when the whole audience sang along, almost word perfect, to every song. Unbeknown to Meat and Jimmy, a local New York radio station,

WNEW-FM, had begun playing tracks from *Bat* on its afternoon show, hosted by legendary DJ Scott Muni. The only other station in America that would touch the album at that point was WMMS in Cleveland – and that was mainly because it had been released on Cleveland Records and was seen as a 'hometown' record. Muni was one of the pioneers of what was then known in the US as progressive rock – that is, album-oriented rock. Scott knew gold when he heard it. He also, as he later confessed to Steinman, loved the longer tracks on *Bat* because they allowed him to take a lengthy toilet break while they were playing. 'They were so fucking long, I could put one on, go take a dump, read the paper, still have two or three minutes to come back, wipe myself and I was ready to go again.'

In reality the breakthrough was still a long way off. *Bat Out of Hell* was a classic sleeper hit, seeping slowly into the public consciousness and spread as much by word of mouth as by any sort of heavy-rotation airplay. The first genuine turning point came in the January of 1978, when Cleveland International put Meat Loaf up as their act at the annual CBS conference in New Orleans. It was the smartest hustle that Steve Popovitch could have pulled off. The cream of the label's executives gathered there to shoot the shit, talk the talk and watch some of their signings in the flesh. On the bill were Cheap Trick, Billy Joel, Elvis Costello, Ted Nugent – an eclectic mix.

Meat Loaf was last on, and finished with 'For Crying Out Loud', the song that closes *Bat Out of Hell*, a long, moody ballad that has some odd tempo changes (and Jim's famous 'boner line' about the *'faded Levi's bursting apart'* . . .) but that, perhaps more than any other song on *Bat*, highlighted Meat's voice, laid bare at the start and end with just Jim's piano for accompaniment. By his own estimation, it was the best he'd sung it, before or since, and at the end there were several seconds of silence before the room almost exploded with applause. He had taken them deep inside the song, showed them how, once you allowed yourself to travel there, the music of *Bat Out of Hell* could be an experience like no other.

The band ploughed through 'Johnny B. Good', then as an encore, a towering and supremely apt version of 'River Deep, Mountain High', the lost Phil Spector classic that Steinman would give his vampire teeth to have written. The ballroom began to vibrate as people stood on tables to get a view. CBS's doubts over Meat Loaf, Jim and *Bat* had vanished during those nine minutes of 'For Crying Out Loud'. The rest was gravy. 'We blew away everybody down in New Orleans,' Bruce Kulick recalled. 'After that the label "got it", and they committed a lot of money, and it was a much, much better tour after that.'

'There must have been two hundred people on stage while the band was still playing,' Meat recalls in his autobiography. 'We were that stunned. People were jumping and dancing and carrying on. They went crazy, completely berserk. They did something like $40,000 worth of damage to the room . . . That night set the wheels in motion. Whether they hated *Bat Out of Hell* with a passion or not, they finally got behind it.'

Immediately after the conference, they sanctioned the making of three promotional films (this being the very cusp of the video age, and long before MTV would make such things central to any marketing campaign), for 'Paradise By The Dashboard Light', 'You Took The Words Right Out Of My Mouth' and 'Bat' itself.

The 'Bat' clip would offer the way into Great Britain, a country that would prove one of *Bat*'s great and enduring heartlands, and where the album would spend 485 consecutive weeks in the chart, a record surpassed only by Fleetwood Mac's *Rumours*. It was something of a fluke, too. The BBC2 TV late-night music show *The Old Grey Whistle Test* usually featured live bands only, but closed their weekly slot by showing the 'Bat' promo clip. The response was immediate, and so overwhelming that they agreed to show it again the following week, 'back by public demand'.

The clips also broke down walls in Australia and Canada, where the sight of Meat and Karla, the latter miming to Ellen Foley's vocals, was enough make many wonder if their TV sets needed adjusting. In the US, Meat's connection with his old pal from the *National Lampoon* show, John Belushi, got them a priceless slot on *Saturday Night Live*. Introduced by guest host Christopher Lee with the line: 'And now, ladies and gentlemen, I would like you to meet . . . Loaf!' they boomed through 'All Revved Up . . .' and soon that song and others were all over American Top 40 radio.

Jim later recalled how nervous Meat was before doing the show. 'They didn't let us do the long songs. I wish we could have done "Paradise By The Dashboard Light", but we did "All Revved Up With No Place To Go" and "Two Out Of Three Ain't Bad". When the show was over we went backstage and Meat was always just as intense after the show – you had to be really careful, cos it didn't go away . . . it was still there, all that volcanic energy. We were in the green room, and he said, "How'd I do, Jimmy? I did okay, didn't I?" I said, "You did really good, Meat."'

The singer was so relieved he thrust his fist into the air – and smashed it into an overhanging chandelier. Cue: mayhem. Jim was so freaked out he ran back to his apartment to take a shower and try to get all the tiny pieces of broken glass out of his hair – in time to rush back to the after-show party. Meat just shrugged it off. 'He probably had swallowed the glass and ate it,' said Jim. 'But I remember that was kind of metaphoric, like perfect. His moment of triumph also involved catastrophe and danger.'

The same month, Meat and Jim were profiled in *People* magazine. The album began to sell so quickly the figures were giddying, impossible even. In Toronto, they went from 2,000 sales to 26,000 in a single week. As the first anniversary of the release approached and Jim and Meat were interviewed by *Rolling Stone*, Steve Popovitch, in his inimitable style, was predicting that 'The record will top out at over five million and "Two Out Of Three Ain't Bad" is destined to become a standard sung in every Vegas nightclub by Jerry Vale and Steve Lawrence, and on *The Tonight Show* three times a week.' [In terms of *Bat's* final 'topping out', Popovitch was only wide by around 38 million copies.] The record was a juggernaut, and once it started rolling, no one was going to stop it. Plans were made to present Meat and Jim with platinum albums in Cleveland – in the time it took to have the platinum presentation albums made and framed, it had sold another million . . .

Fashionable, unfashionable, who gave a shit?

Some radio stations wanted to ban 'Paradise . . .' because of its 'sexually graphic' nature. It didn't matter. No radio station in Los Angeles would play songs from *Bat*, because they didn't think it was 'cool'? It didn't matter. The people were speaking, and the people *fucking loved it*. And CBS loved them, too . . . Now.

Bat was not only successful, more importantly it was profitable, because it had cost comparatively little to record (not that CBS had put up any of that money anyway). When sales were still at 200,000 they had begun pushing Popovitch to get Jim and Meat back in the studio to make album number two. Popovitch resisted for as long as he could because he knew that *Bat* would keep selling if they kept playing and promoting it.

Everyone was getting greedy, and the only people without any money were the band. Meat was struggling to pay a couple of hundred dollars a month in rent, because the royalties from the sales of the album were still in the pipeline, and the accountants at CBS were already beginning to wrangle about who would get what. He started getting angry and temperamental, his state not helped when they pulled Jimmy off the road so that he could start writing the follow-up album. He was drinking too much, and beginning to partake in the devil's dandruff – cocaine, the drug that killed all of that road weariness with a couple of uplifting snorts.

The show's centrepiece was 'Paradise By The Dashboard Light'. Meat worked himself into a 350-pound blob of sweat, hormones and hair, often falling to his knees at particularly fraught moments, at others stalking the edge of the stage like a rampaging line-backer. In 'Paradise', as the teen couple parked up at the lake and began to get fresh to the song's mid-section radio baseball commentary, he would envelop the tiny Karla DeVito into the folds of his sopping shirt, groping at her while trying to ram his tongue down her throat until she finally fought him off and screamed, 'STOP RIGHT THERE . . .' The cue for the song to rampage towards a climax brought on by the declarations of undying love, Meat bawling like a harpooned whale, Karla all big eyes and barely restrained passion.

It was extraordinary, deeply weird and not just a little disturbing, a mix of adolescent rock'n'roll fantasy and the more outrageous moments of *Hair* or *The Dream Engine*. The first time Meat grabbed Karla, in fact, was the first she knew about it. None of it had been rehearsed or even discussed. But Karla already knew enough about the singer to simply go with it. She felt it wasn't sexual or opportunistic, more something Meat did to misdirect the audience, confound expectation about just how far a deeply insecure and overweight giant could take things. 'He's a tortured guy,' Karla DeVito laughingly recalled in 2007. 'I said to Steinman: "Exactly what happens in 'Paradise'?" And he goes: "You'll figure it out when you get there." So, swear to God, literally, we had not rehearsed the make-out scene until we performed it live. It was just improvisational theatre out there.'

Eventually the skit became the highlight of the show, and it got wilder as the tour wore on. Steinman said: 'Karla had one of the most difficult jobs in the world. I remember her saying: "I can't believe how far down my throat he gets his tongue. It doesn't seem possible. It's like he's doing a stomach X-ray with his tongue!"' Karla was constantly surprised. 'There was one time

I came up earlier in the song than I normally would, and this giant heavy steel mic stand bottom whizzed by my head within an inch! I didn't realise that every night at that point in the show he threw that at me!' Another time, Meat wrestled Karla so hard in their extended embrace he ended up pushing her off the stage. For Meat Loaf, though, the performances were so immersive he simply knew no limits. Jim would stare bug-eyed at the steam he saw coming off Meat's body as he prowled the stage, like the hissing of a New York subway. Halfway through the show he rushed to the wings to receive oxygen while lying on a gurney in a tent. Sometimes he didn't make it and would simply sag to the floor. When pictures of him lying face down on the stage in Atlanta receiving help from local paramedics were published, the news spread that he had died. 'I know the pain that will come when I walk on that stage, from what I am about to give of myself to that audience,' he told *Classic Rock* magazine in 2007. 'In the words of Sally Fields: "When you give everything you have to give in a performance, it is like cutting yourself with razor blades."'

As the tour wore on, Meat was constantly losing his voice. He had also taken to fainting each night as he left the stage. At first, Jim and the crew would become alarmed, wondering if he really was dying. But then it became as regular a feature of the show as the rest of his theatrics. As Steinman recalled for me, 'Meat lost his voice about a month into the tour. I remember one show in Nebraska, a really cold winter's night. After the show, he was on the floor of the dressing room, sort of passed out, and pulling me towards him. Which was a horrifying thing, by the way – like being slightly raped by Moby Dick. And he says, "Jimmy, I did it! I did it! I got 'em to cheer, even though I couldn't fucking sing! They loved it!" And I thought that was a scary observation.'

On the *Bat Out of Hell* tour, everything was theatre, with Meat and Jimmy constantly clashing. When the singer deviated from the script Jim had written for him, inviting audiences to stand up and get their rocks off, making them scream and shout, Jim was horrified. 'This was never meant to be just another regular rock show,' he told me. 'This was meant to be something much bigger, more powerful.'

The two would have furious rows about it. Finally, Jim ordered Meat Loaf not to speak at all onstage because, 'When he speaks, the audience suddenly sees he's just the fat kid who works at the gas station.' Meat went out the next night and never shut up. The audience lapped it up. Finally, after a show in Pittsburgh, after Jim tried explaining that it was like he was Francis Ford Coppola directing *The Godfather* and Meat was Marlon Brando, the singer just stopped listening and went berserk, picking up the nearest chair and hurling it through the window of his hotel room, followed by various lamps, smashing the wall mirror with his fist. Then storming out of the room, threatening to end it all.

Jim had heard it all before, but this time was different. He'd never seen Meat so thunderously out of control. He and the tour manager went looking for him, finally finding him crouching behind some cars in a nearby parking lot. As Steinman later recalled in an interview for his website, 'Meat was a football player and boy he was powerful and he was set position down like a rhino or an elephant, something about to charge.' Jim and the tour manager approached Meat gingerly, almost on tiptoe, Jim whispering, asking if Meat was all right. 'He says, "I'm not a Frankenstein monster. I'm me! I'm Meat Loaf. I'm not your Frankenstein monster."' Then he ran charging towards a huge truck parked opposite, his head detonating against its heavy steel fender, blood fountaining into the sky.

Jim left the tour soon after, ostensibly to return to New York and start writing material for the next album. In reality it was because he couldn't take the night after night grind any more – things were getting more out of control with each new city they landed in. In Toronto, someone had broken into their dressing room and stolen guitars, cash and – holiest of holies – Jimmy's lyrics book. Every song he had written for the next album, already titled *Renegade Angel*, at least in Jim's mind, was in the book. Now gone. 'After that,' Meat recalls in his memoirs, 'he sank down in the deep end.' Some of them – 'Surf's Up', 'Renegade Angel', 'Left Behind', he would recall enough of to recreate again. 'But he could never, ever get them all back in his head – the second album got lost there.'

Things had come to a head when the tour landed in Australia, where 'You Took The Words Right Out Of My Mouth' was Number 1 at the same time as *Bat* was top of the album chart. Jim had been festering for months over the lack of recognition he was getting for writing the songs on the album – the media much more focused, as always, on the singer, not least when it's *his* name in lights, and even more so when he looks like the giant at the top of the beanstalk. During a press conference at the airport, as the waiting press hordes began firing questions at Meat Loaf and Karla DeVito, leaving Jimmy sitting to one side, the ghost at the feast, then asking him to step aside while they got pictures of Meat and Karla posing together, he flipped out.

'I hate you,' the creator finally confessed to his creation. 'Nobody knows who I am and we started this together.' By the time the tour returned to the States, Jim was back home, back to sitting up all night devising plans for his revenge on the world in a series of songs that would, he was determined, prove once and for all who the real genius in this Meat Loaf story was. 'You see, Jim always wanted to be famous,' said Meat Loaf. 'Jim likes the circus. I don't like the circus.'

But the circus was all that was left for Meat Loaf now.

BAT TWO

I'll Kill You If You Don't Come Back

CHAPTER THIRTEEN

I Am God

'Hell hath no limits, nor is circumscribed in one self place,
for where we are is hell, and where hell is must we ever be.'
—*Doctor Faustus*, Christopher Marlowe

When a TV reporter in Australia asked the singer, 'When are you going to lose some weight and give us a real show?' he tried to jump over the table and punch him. The truth was that as he piled show upon show, the character of Meat Loaf, the giant, fraught, lovelorn sucker who transformed himself into a leading man through the songs, had begun to bleed out into his offstage life. He could feel the intensity – sometimes he saw photographs of himself and saw the Meat Loaf character there, just under the skin, showing through in his mad expressions. He liked to decompress after a show, spend some time alone and let the character fall away, but as he got more famous, people wouldn't leave him alone, and so he allowed himself to be dragged to clubs and bars, everyone wanting a piece of him, and the way he dealt with that was to stay in character. And to take cocaine, which smoothed the process, fed the monster – and to have what he'd later describe as 'orgies'. It was the seventies, *Bat Out of Hell* had knocked the soundtrack to *Saturday Night Fever* off the Number 1 position. What the hell else was he supposed to damn well do with his time?

Ten days after the Australian tour closed, Meat Loaf finally arrived in London, for a one-off show at the Hammersmith Odeon. The show was far from sold out, those that were there were just the first wave of devotees that would eventually buy more than two million copies of *Bat* in Britain alone. Meat's mood was not helped afterwards when a notoriously 'nutty' music journalist from *Record Mirror*, asked gaily, 'So what's up with you then, Meat? Is it glandular or what?' He was ejected from the dressing room and warned as to the safety of his own glands should he try to return.

The big and much more lasting highlight of that first UK trip was Meat and the band performing 'Paradise By The Dashboard Light' live in the studios of *The Old Grey Whistle Test* – then the gatekeeper for all things good albums-wise in the UK. They played the whole eleven-minute version of the song. The singer's voice was rough as a cat's tongue but that wasn't the talking point. It was the cameras catching every graphic inch of Meat's killer-clown seduction of Karla.

He plants his behemoth's mouth on her unspoiled flower lips for two seconds, she throws him off, he retreats, turns his back on her as she scolds him, then, bold as love itself, comes back to land again – and this time hangs on like a bee to its honey, the two clinging to each other and dry humping for a full nine seconds. This time, though, when they break the clinch, the flower finally yields fully, drawing the sting back, and they begin kissing and groping each other for *over a minute* – a universe-traversing snog that was as shocking and unfathomable to the uninitiated as the gargantuan success that *Bat Out of Hell* was now becoming. Nearly forty years later, it's difficult to appreciate what a transgressive moment this was, not just for rock music, but also for television in general; a moment symbolic of everything that made Meat Loaf special. The moment where Frankenstein finally gets the girl, where rock starts to really roll in ways previously thought

. . . disgusting. If Sid Vicious singing 'My Way', also released that year, was meant to be funny, irreverent, Meat Loaf bellowing 'Paradise By The Dashboard Light' while mauling at Karla DeVito's breasts was laughter as hysteria, mocking and vengeful. Eyes glued to the screen. Ears pinned back.

It became renowned as one of the most-requested, all-time highlights from the longstanding series. It also gave most of Britain its first real idea of what Meat Loaf was all about: loud, ostentatious, sexy, lewd, unapologetic, gothic rock with a strangely self-lacerating twist. Like nothing you'd ever seen before. Singing songs so ribald and camp, so excessively hooky and deliberately outrageous they would have made Freddie Mercury blush.

Back on the road for the rest of the summer, with Jim having retreated into the shadows, Meat Loaf now came under increasing pressure to make decisions on the fly. When one major radio station offered to play their next single, 'Paradise By The Dashboard Light' but only in exchange for Meat Loaf performing at their annual Christmas show, he told them to fuck off. Big mistake. 'Paradise' still became a hit but he had made enemies of people who might have helped him further down the road when the excitement over *Bat* had died down and Meat really needed new friends.

Another turning point came in Ottawa when Meat Loaf fell off the stage and ended up with his leg in a cast. Some said he deliberately jumped into the orchestra pit in another petrifying attempt to do himself serious harm. It was getting harder and harder to tell dream from reality.

But a simple leg break was not enough to interrupt the tour, this once-in-a-lifetime moment. He carried on, singing from a wheelchair until he could hobble to his feet again. It was the sort of thing that used to happen back in the murky fifties, when Gene Vincent and his shattered left leg would be tied to the mic stand to stop him toppling over. But Gene was a one-hit wonder who worked for beans. By now *Bat Out of Hell* was a monster hit the world over, outselling Zeppelin and the Stones. If Mick Jagger or Jimmy Page had broken their legs, the tours would have been called off, the best doctors available summoned. But Meat Loaf was not sexy like Jagger, or ravishing like Page. Meat Loaf was a monster, still the freak despite his growing fame, and nobody could quite believe this was anything but a one-off deal. There wasn't any time to waste. They had to sell and sell hard while the monster was still breathing and the novelty had not yet worn off, the spell broken. Anything to do with his personal life was now completely subsumed by his success. 'There's a lot of my childhood that I've just blocked out,' he confessed years later. 'My mother died and that's something – maybe a psychologist would help me deal with that but I'm perfectly okay and I don't want to deal with that. If I could go back to my teenage self I'd tell him not to yell at his mother. Her last words were "Where were you?" because I had run away to California because I couldn't deal with it. It took me ten years to deal with her death.'

As for his father, though he would later claim that 'I don't hold a grudge and I love my father,' the trauma of the many childhood beatings, the alcoholism and rage was something he could never truly get past. 'I don't remember him hitting my mother, though that could be blocked out, but he would hit me and throw me around. But alcohol is a disease. And I take responsibility for my own actions as an adult. As far as I'm concerned, my dad has no part in my personality. When I get mad it's not my dad's fault, it's mine.'

As the *Bat Out of Hell* world tour wound on, Meat Loaf became crazed and unmanageable, his anger and confusion compounded by the booze and drugs and the rapid way in which his whole life had changed; the sheer effort and emotional energy he needed to get into character each night drained him of his humanity. Every night there would be another tantrum, chairs, tables and equipment being thrown across the room, the beast roaring and snarling at the bars of his cage. Now he was just a rock pig like all of the others, a walking nightmare of ego and road madness, snorting, drinking and fucking, his head deep in a trough that was being topped up nightly. With more experience he might have seen what was happening, but as it was he careened on until, in the spring of 1978 and after 170 shows, he hit the barriers in spectacular fashion, metaphorically talked down off the ledge of several, what he later described as 'imaginative', suicide attempts, though he would never elucidate, claiming the anger and paranoia had simply become 'too much', and into a deep well of depression from which he would take months, years, to return. If he managed to at all . . .

'Fame makes me depressed,' said Meat Loaf, more than thirty years after first becoming famous. 'I hate fame. I wasn't born for this. It frightens me, it crushes me, I still can't handle it after all these years.' It was true. Having spent the best years of his life desperately seeking validation through singing, through acting different parts – it all in the end boiled down to the same bedevilled masque: the (Fat) Bat from Hell – Meat Loaf would spend the next forty years hiding from his gigantic, overweening fame, playing it down, mocking it, jaundiced with the incurable sickness of it.

In middle age he would find new ways of dealing with it, of keeping the worst of the symptoms at bay. 'When depression hits I find spending at least one and a half hours in the gym on the cross-trainer and doing weights helps. I also talk to a psychologist every day. I don't know how else to deal with it.'

In 1978, however, in a pre-AIDS, post-permissive, mind-expanded world where cocaine was regarded as champagne – a rich man's delight and salve, certainly not addictive or troublesome – and whisky and wine were the mineral water and organic juice of the age, an everyday pleasure and stress-reducer – Meat

Loaf's way of dealing with being the Most Famous And Least Likely Rock Star In The World was only to be expected.

The *Bat Out of Hell* tour had finally come to an end with a long worn-out sigh of a show at the sold-out 12,500-seater Congress Centre Hamburg, in West Germany, in October 1978. He flew home the next morning and arrived back in a terrible state. Physically, emotionally, spiritually, he was gone. The cage may have stopped moving and shaking momentarily, but he was still locked inside it in his mind. He just carried on as he had been doing for the past year on the road, only without the interruption of having to do a show every night. He had been talking about and threatening suicide for years. Without realising it, he had now embarked on the slowest and surest way of killing himself yet: death by overindulgence – the fat man in the bathtub, born to bloat, Humpty Dumpty having his great fall.

For three months in the summer of 1978, *Bat Out of Hell* was selling, globally, half a million copies a week. Jim's songwriting royalties had started to come in, but Meat still wasn't seeing any of the money, even though he was the one who'd been out there on the road for a year. There were several reasons for this, all of them familiar to musical stars throughout the ages: paying back advances, which covered everything from the cost of making the album to the cost of touring, including mountainous expenses. Plus the long list of 'extras' the record company always found a way of adding to the list of outgoings. The root of it for Metal Loaf was the fact that he hadn't written any of the songs and therefore – unlike Jim – had no publishing money coming his way; he hadn't been involved in the production of the record and therefore – unlike Todd – he had no percentage of that to look forward to either.

Meat Loaf could only expect royalty money from 'mechanicals', that is, his share of record sales, which his label claimed might take years to fully calculate – not unusual in that pre-internet era – and the small percentage of monies derived from radio and TV play. He didn't even make much money from touring, the seventies being a time when ticket prices were deliberately kept low, touring being seen, at best, as a loss leader, a way of promoting record sales. And then there were the people who simply stole from him, though he never came anywhere near grasping that until many years later.

It was all very rock'n'roll, beyond the wildest dreams of young Marvin from Texas who couldn't get his fat legs into Levi jeans, let alone face down record company bigwigs who kept promising jam tomorrow. It was also, after so long away from home, and for a man like him, dehumanising.

He lost himself in the persona of big bad biker-boy Meat Loaf. He had childish temper tantrums and convinced himself that he was doing it so that he could 'maintain the tension' of the shows. Maybe that was half-true, too. When he got back to New York, he couldn't walk around unrecognised. When he left his apartment there were always twenty or thirty people outside waiting for him. He checked into the Mayflower Hotel and didn't come out for a month.

Rock stardom, like most other types of fame, impacts on the psyche. And the psyche of rock stars is generally fragile to begin with. Success in other fields of achievement can restrain the worst excesses of the ego (they don't have dwarves with bowls of cocaine on their heads at the Nobel Prize-giving ceremony), but the rock star has an open field. Meat Loaf knew this, as did every other *Rolling Stone* reader of the 1970s. Rock stars could do whatever they want, until whatever they want is fetishised and approved of. Sex? On tap and practically compulsory. Drugs? No problem, how many do you want? Money? Don't worry about it, just spend it . . . Indulgence? Sure – throw as many tantrums as you want over the brown M&Ms not being taken out of the bowl – it's what we *want* you to do . . .

Meat Loaf, the rock star who appeared so different from the

others, singing not two-minute razor-slashed punk ditties but nine-minute overblown rock operas, thought fame would allow him to look down at last upon everyone else from the top of the mountain, allow him his moment in the sun, freed from the opinions of others. But what if the emptiness isn't filled by excess? What if finally getting your own back on your father who beat you, your mother who left you and all the others over the years who had bullied and taunted you, driven you into the shadows with their flaming pitchforks, didn't ease the pain at all? What if all the success had left you feeling lonelier, more isolated and cut off from normality than ever?

It was the life that Jim wrote about in his dream world, but that he didn't live.

It was the life Meat Loaf lived now but didn't want. He would lock himself inside his hotel room with the curtains drawn for days at a time, the phone unplugged, the ceaseless knocking on the door going unanswered, just the booze and the mirror for company. On those days when he wasn't down he was so far up he turned into Elvis, buying cars for himself and the newfound 'friends' his success had suddenly brought him. Then yelling down the phone at hapless record company executives, chewing the heads off his own band, sneering at those who thought they knew better than he how the next chapter was meant to go. 'I am God!' he recalls ranting. 'You are fools!'

By then, according to Steinman, 'he was really like the character in *Bat Out of Hell*. He was always that close to annihilation.' Onstage, people saw the wonderfully flamboyant ham, singing what on the surface could be cheesy songs but that in his hands had great depth and weight and meaning, and that demanded everything he had to sing them, until the show began to run on fumes, his voice blown to pieces. 'I was nuts,' Meat Loaf recalled in a 1993 *Rolling Stone* interview. 'I mostly turned it inward . . . I didn't want people to call me a star.'

Jim Steinman, who very much did want people to call him a star, was now meant to be back in control, nesting in the comfort zone of the same Woodstock studio, just him and his moonlit piano, finessing the songs that would become the follow-up to *Bat*. That had been the plan anyway, but with his book of lyrics gone, he now had to write new songs to add to the few he was able to reconstruct from memory. It would have helped if Meat had gone shoulder to shoulder with him on this, as he had through-out so much of the writing process on *Bat*. But the Meat Loaf that workshopped so hard in 1975 was now missing, too, stolen somewhere out there on the road, never to be seen again. The Meat Loaf that Jim tried so hard to work with in 1979 now lived on another planet, somewhere cold and hostile and paranoid and unreachable.

Renegade Angel. That's what Jim was going to call it, the second *Bat*, the follow-up. *Renegade Angel*. He loved the way the words sounded together, loved the world that they evoked in his mind. *Renegade Angel*. Jim had it all worked out. It would be darker, more romantic, more dangerous and more sensual than anything he or anyone else had done before. He had a big new notebook in which he began writing all of the lyrics. The way he composed he didn't particularly commit them to memory, instead he would work on the music and the melodies and then begin to shape the lyrics over the top, finding the perfect line for each moment. He was getting it, too. The songs as they had existed until someone stole his lyric book had been coming to him as if in a feverish dream: 'Left In The Dark', 'Surf's Up', 'Everything Is Permitted', 'Renegade Angel' . . . all of them further adventures in his noc-turnal world, songs about lust and longing and betrayal, songs about sex and love and death. He knew how much Meat would love them, especially 'Renegade Angel' itself. After all, that's what Meat was, wasn't it? What they both were, in fact . . . Renegade Angels . . .

But it was endlessly tormenting trying to recreate what he'd originally had in his lost book, in his mind. He knew – *knew* – that what he'd had in the book was the first and most perfect iteration of his vision, that he could never get *Renegade Angel* back into full-spectrum view the way that it had been, and it almost destroyed him. He felt himself sinking deeper and deeper into make-do, into approximation. This wasn't building up something new, it was raking through the ashes and trying to reassemble. He managed to pull out of it and start writing again, but when – in years to come – he and Meat looked back, they both knew that this was the moment that their second record was lost. Whatever happened next would be something different, something less pure. *Renegade Angel.* The album they lost, and could never find again. A sliding doors moment that would come back to haunt them for the rest of their often bitterly entwined lives.

CHAPTER FOURTEEN

You Are Fools

So began Meat Loaf's true season in hell. Its most defining aspect: the seemingly now permanent loss of his voice. To everyone else around him this was clearly a psychosomatic problem. With Meat back in Woodstock with Jimmy, trying to piece together new material for the sequel to *Bat*, the pressure was on as never before, for both of them. But while Jimmy could take his frustrations, his bafflement and personal agonies out on his piano, Meat only had his voice – and it simply would not obey. Doctors were called in but none of them could find anything 'physically' wrong with him. There were even sessions where his voice appeared to be coming back, not strong but at least breaking the fall. But Meat wouldn't have it. There was something *wrong* with him, he declaimed. This wasn't just in his head. This was an open wound. You could hear it every time he tried to hit the high notes. Instead of the sweet summer winds of before, all that came out of his strangled vocal chords now were terrifying shrieks and yowls, clefts and fissures.

'It was the weirdest thing,' Steinman recalled. 'One day he was fine, and the next it was literally like hearing a dog barking.' Jim later said that when Meat Loaf 'started singing like Linda Blair in *The Exorcist*, I left'. But what really set him back was Meat's refusal to recognise that the songs Jimmy was putting before him were just as good as anything on *Bat*. After the ignominy of 'losing' his original drafts of the key songs, followed by the sheer brute strength needed to try to piece them back together again, Frankenstein-like, against a lightning-shocked sky, Jim wasn't in any mood to hear Meat tell him he didn't think they were, you know, *good enough*.

Against what would have been insurmountable obstacles for most songwriters, Jim was now entering a period in which he'd produce many of his greatest songs, and much of his catalogue. His life had its strange avenues, but he had never really known failure. His music, right from the off, had attracted interest and praise as well as bafflement at its baroque appeal. Now, his very first full offering to be set before the public was selling in its millions. And whatever it said on the album sleeve, it *was* his creation; surely no one could argue with that? It had begun with him. It certainly couldn't happen without him. This was his itch that wouldn't quite be scratched, as first Meat belittled the songs then claimed he couldn't even find the voice to sing them. This was the feeling that just wouldn't quit. That Jim had faced down the demons that threatened to relegate his success to a one-off novelty act. But that Meat Loaf still had not.

The new vision was no longer called *Renegade Angel*. *Renegade Angel* had vanished with that notebook. In its place came *Bad For Good*. Jim loved wordplay almost as much as he loved music. He loved to invert their meanings, to take a cliché and spin it back on itself, turn it inside out. *'You think that I'll be bad for just a little while / But I know that I'll be bad for good . . .'* A typical little twist of meaning that Jim would return to later in the song with an epic list of exactly what he'd be good for.

Or from the reconstituted 'Left In The Dark', an exquisitely painful song of betrayal: *'But don't tell me now, I don't need any answers tonight / I just need some love so turn out the light, and I'll be left in the dark again . . .'*

And 'Surf's Up', a lusty paean to beach culture with a killer boner line:

'Surf's up
Surf's up
Surf's up . . .
And so am I . . .'

Not Meat Loaf, though, Jim. And not for a long time yet.

There had been a meeting in New York in November 1978, just a few weeks after Meat had come off the road. Jim had tried to sell him on the *Bad For Good* concept but Meat was still hiding out at the Mayfair, his head in bits. Nothing sounded good right then, everything was bad. They parted agreeing to at least get back into the studio in Woodstock in the New Year. Then just before Christmas Jim signed his own separate management contract with David Sonenberg, an acknowledgement that his career would develop along more lines than just the one that connected him to Meat Loaf. After all, if he had created one monster, how many more might be out there, just waiting to be juddered into life with his electricity? Then he flew up to Woodstock, where he spent December staying at Roy Bittan's house and readying the material for *Bad For Good* at Bearsville Studios. The fact that Meat Loaf had had an almost allergic reaction to most of it counted for nothing in Jim's mind. He knew what he had and wasn't going to lose it a second time.

Anyway, Meat had been wasted. Maybe after Christmas, a break, he'd feel differently once they started working together in the studio again. Through all of the rough times when they were schlepping the songs from *Bat* around any record company that would entertain them, it had been Meat and Jim, Jim and Meat. If they'd had a third wheel, it was Ellen Foley, who had played her role immaculately. In the studio, Todd Rundgren had, with great good humour, acted as their wingman, bringing their aural hallucinations into shimmering reality. On the road, Karla had brought a new focus and a different sexual charge to the live shows and the promo tours. Surely Meat could see that? Why throw the baby out with the bathwater now?

When Meat finally travelled up to Bearsville he discovered that the dynamic had shifted once again. Jim and Todd were already in the studio, and some of the backing tracks were now down on tape. Todd and Jim were yukking it up together, the best of friends, picking straight up from where they'd left it on *Bat*, and just as three years before when Meat made suggestions about the music, he felt that he was essentially being told to 'shut up and sing'.

And when he tried to remind them that it wasn't about singing, it was about inhabiting the songs, developing a character that could tune them into the same perfect emotional pitch that they'd hit on *Bat*, 'They'd look at one another and roll their eyes.' It seemed as though they couldn't agree on anything, from who should play on the album to how the songs should sound. Meat felt that Jim had gone too far down the road in writing a *Bat Out of Hell* sequel. If you thought about *Bad For Good* in those terms, both of the title songs were long and phantasmagorical epics, 'Dance In My Pants', one of the new numbers, was a rerun of 'Paradise By The Dashboard Light'; 'Stark Raving Love' could be another 'All Revved Up'; 'Lost Boys And Golden Girls' another 'Two Out Of Three Ain't Bad'. While 'Left In The Dark' was an album track closer in the style of 'For Crying Out Loud' . . . There was another of Jim's monologues, too, 'Love, Death And An American Guitar', this one longer and even more self-consciously theatrical than the '*Wolf with the red roses*' lines that cued up 'You Took The Words Right Out Of My Mouth'.

Meat Loaf found all of that troubling, and he thought that the title song 'Bad For Good' sounded too much like a Springsteen song, which was all he needed given what so many people had said about *Bat Out of Hell* being a *Born To Run* knock-off. Behind it all was the record company, hungry like the wolf and urging Jim to produce a new record that would in every respect – artistic and commercial – simply duplicate *Bat*. Meat tried in vain to tell them, to point out what seemed so obvious to him, but Jim and Todd weren't having any of it. They were locked together in their vision for *Bad For Good*, and he was on the outside. Again.

Third wheel, baby. Only this time the third wheel was him . . .

Still raging about the indignity of it all in 1985, he said: 'The next record came along and I was being left out of it – everybody knew what to do for me at that point and I said, "Fuck you" and left! I quit and said, "Everyone can go to hell. I don't wanna do another *Bat Out of Hell*. I don't like 'Stark Raving Love'; I love 'Left In The Dark', 'Out Of The Frying Pan (And Into The Fire)', 'Surf's Up'" . . . I loved the stuff that was different from what was on *Bat*. There was a song called "Rock'n'roll Dreams Come Through" that I really liked but I didn't like the other stuff. "Bad For Good" was all right but it wasn't great. "Stark Raving Love" I hated. Steinman turned it into "Holding Out For A Hero" which they [later used] for the Channel 4 American Football programme every week! And I really hated "Dance In My Pants", where everyone was trying to get Jim to write another "Paradise". [But] you can't write another one! And it was making me crazy; no one was talking to me about anything. And then Rundgren said to me, "If you can't talk to me in musical terms don't speak to me at all!" I said, "Fine, I'll never talk to you again . . ."'

Twenty years after that conversation, Meat still bristled at the memory when talking to me. 'I disagreed with doing *Bad For Good* in 1979. I just thought [those songs] were way, way . . . I think that if we would have done *Bad For Good* [as the follow-up to *Bat Out Of Hell*] I don't think I'd still be sitting here talking to you. I still believe that. I felt that then, I feel that now.'

But why: because it was too obvious a follow-up?

'Too obvious, right. Way too obvious. "Stark Raving Love" was nothing but "All Revved Up" again, and "Dance In My Pants" was trying *so* hard to be "Paradise By The Dashboard Light". And I am not blaming Jimmy at all because Jimmy was . . . they were feeding him this, these record company people were feeding him this stuff. All I could say was, "No, no, don't do this. This is the wrong thing to do. We should wait. We shouldn't have a record come out in two years. This has been too much." I said, "If anything we should have a record come out in six years!"'

A pretty radical idea back then, I said. 'Well, just what I was thinking,' he replied. But most major artists were putting out at least one new album a year in the late seventies, sometimes two or even three. 'Yeah,' he chided, 'but not when you have *Bat Out of Hell*. That was something completely different. That wasn't, "Let's get together with an acoustic guitar and sit on the bus and write a song." That's not what that is. Or, you know, a song about my cat got run over by my truck when I was backing out of the driveway stuff. I mean, there's an awful lot of that – not necessarily cat-got-run-over-stuff, but to me that's the same emotional content. There's too much of that stuff, playing into that same game over and over again.'

Yet speaking to Steinman around the same time, he still saw *Bad For Good* as the legitimate, rightful follow-up to *Bat*. 'Meat rejected all the songs and now claims he thought they were too close to *Bat Out of Hell*, but that wasn't the case. He was going through all kinds of hell of his own . . . a lot of physical, psychic disturbances. He'd lost his voice and we weren't really working together the way we had. The success had changed things. It wasn't that simple but that's the quick way to say it. It was just a mess.'

Speaking to me nearly three decades later, Jim Steinman was still adamant. *Bad For Good* was, he repeated, 'absolutely the follow-up to *Bat*. It was recorded as a Meat Loaf album.'

Meat Loaf, he said, was going through hell.

CHAPTER FIFTEEN

Chrome Hearts

Woodstock had always been an interesting hangout. Most people knew its name because of the festival, but that had taken place more than sixty miles away on Max Yasgur's 600-acre dairy farm in Bethel. The town itself, home in the late sixties and early seventies to a few thousand full-time residents, was a genuine artists' enclave, a trippy, hippy, arty country retreat for the New York rock'n'roll nouveau-riche kids. Utopianism had come to Woodstock in 1903 with the foundation of the Byrdcliffe Art Colony, a community of studios and workshops set up to 'nurture creativity in all forms'. In 1905, one of the Byrdcliffe founders, the novelist and poet Hervey White, bought a farm and allowed it to transform into a more radical version of Byrdcliffe, with artists, writers and musicians coming to live in wooden shacks on the property. By 1915, White, who wore his hair long (for the time at least), grew his beard and dressed in flowing linen get-ups, had begun the first festival in Woodstock. He called it the Maverick. A future echo of the 1969 version – revellers wore flowers in their hair and the vibe was both bohemian and utopian. White constructed a 'music chapel' in the woods, a hand-built auditorium with almost-perfect acoustics that would in coming years debut work by John Cage and other avant-garde composers.

The town had always had a vibe and a force of its own, it seemed. Bob Dylan moved to Woodstock in 1965, had his famous motorcycle accident in Bearsville the following year and remained a resident until 1972. In 1969, Dylan's manager, Albert Grossman, at whose house in Woodstock Dylan had lived when he first arrived, founded Bearsville recording studio and began a record label to which Todd Rundgren would soon sign. The band shared a Woodstock house they named the Big Pink, and recorded their debut album there – named *Big Pink* – and a bunch of other songs with the still recovering Dylan, that formed the basis of the first really well-known bootleg, *Great White Wonder*. Soon afterwards Todd moved to Woodstock full-time and joined the long list of musos who had turned up, tuned in and dropped out – everyone from Hendrix to Van Morrison, Bonnie Raitt, Johnny Cash, Ravi Shankar, Paul Butterfield . . .

Woodstock wasn't quite the utopia it seemed, though, certainly not by 1979. Leslie Edmonds lived in the town with her daughter Pearl, who was three. She had to make ends meet as a gofer for rock stars and their managers, driving them around, running errands, cleaning houses, babysitting, cooking, doing laundry, whatever they needed – all, more often than not, for bed and board and not much more. Rock stars wanted the good ol' hippy vibe but, you know, didn't ever want to actually have to *do* anything or *look after themselves*, so people like Leslie filled the breach, the town's second-class citizens, there to fetch and carry for their rich employers.

Finally, she landed the job that would, indirectly, change her life, as an assistant studio manager at Bearsville, where the princely wage of $120 a week enabled her to move into a house share with Paul Butterfield – she and Pearl were downstairs, Paul had the top floor. The job wasn't vastly different to the ones she'd been doing: rock stars that showed up to record at Bearsville needed somewhere to stay, so Leslie would drive them around showing them the various places the studio had an arrangement with. There was the Cummings House, which had apartments for a couple of people; there were rooms above Bearsville's accounting office; there was the Turtle Creek House that had been divided into three apartments.

She had Pearl in nursery every day until 3pm and then had to bring her to the studio office until she finished work at six. The Woodstock scene involved a lot of drinking and partying. There were always drugs floating around, and it was a tough place for a young mother with a child to raise. Although Leslie was young and aspired to the lifestyle, after a long day at the studio she wasn't into listening to the radio or going to gigs, so when Jim Steinman showed up, she wasn't sure who he was or what kind of record he was in Bearsville to make.

All of that changed when Meat Loaf arrived to work with him and the studio assistant was asked to find him a place to stay. The singer's affair with Ellen Foley had not survived the release of *Bat Out of Hell*. Since then, though, there had been no significant others in Meat's life, just the usual backstage 'well-wishers' that always inhabited the road. Now all that changed, almost overnight. 'We fell in love in a matter of days,' Meat would recall in his autobiography. 'It was kind of scary and crazy at the same time . . . It was like looking in the mirror. I looked at her and I saw something in her face – it was like, where have you been? I've been looking for you for three hundred years.'

It sounded like something from one of Jim's more fanciful songs. There was snow on the ground in Woodstock as Leslie drove Meat around to look at the accommodation. He chose the Cummings House. He wanted her to know what he did, so they went to the record store and bought a copy of *Bat*, which he played for her back at Paul Butterfield's house. He found a VHS player and they watched his turn as Eddie, the lobotomised delivery boy in *The Rocky Horror Picture Show*.

He wasn't trying to make her think he was a big star – the

opposite, in fact. Just like Meat Loaf the onstage schlub, the fat guy that never got the girl, he was worried that she wouldn't like his singing and his acting. But she did, and what's more she was charmed by his insecurity. Here was this giant guy, this force of nature blowing into town like a storm, a guy with a hit album that was selling in its millions, and all he wanted to do was to hang out with her, the studio assistant that all of the rock stars regarded as another of the little people put on Earth to make their life run smoothly.

Very quickly Meat Loaf became Leslie Edmonds's white knight, her salvation, her rock'n'roll dream that had, against all odds, finally come through. He would have screaming rows with Albert Grossman and Paul Butterfield about the way they treated her. He took her on dates to New York and promised her that he would rescue her from her drudgery. After they'd known each other for a week, he proposed to her. They were at the Cummings House and the snow was still falling outside. With the same flare for melodrama that had fuelled *Bat*, he told her that he would take a knife and cut his heart out if she refused.

She didn't.

Twenty-one days after they laid eyes on one another for the first time, Meat and Leslie married at Todd Rundgren's place at the top of Mink Hollow Road. The snow and ice were thick on the ground. Two hundred people braved the drive up the mountainside. Jim was best man. The minister was ninety-five years old, and during the service a candle set light to his vestment. 'I said, if you don't marry me I'm going to rip my heart out and throw it in the snow and lie here bleeding,' he recalled years later. 'It was supposed to be on video. Todd Rundgren was shooting it, because he's supposed to be Mr Tech. And all we got was the audio because he'd left it on pause.'

Just like one of Jim's songs, the romance had its filmic ending; the lost boy finally had his golden girl. All that remained was the happy ever after. That's when things got complicated – and Meat's life began to fall apart.

It began with a noise, an unholy noise, a noise that no one had heard before. It came out whenever he tried to sing. It began with the high notes, the ones he used to hit with the accuracy of an army sniper.

'HHGGGGGUUUUURRRRGGGGHHHH!'

The sound of air being forced from a kettle, of strangulation. The sound of a bat trying to find its way out of a deep, dark cave. 'I asked Meat Loaf to come up and start just rehearsing, just so I could hear what shape his voice was in,' Steinman recalled in a BBC Radio interview. 'And he opened his mouth and we both like just looked at each other in shock – because the sound that came out of his mouth didn't even resemble a human voice . . . It was like this low, guttural sound – like a dragon trying to sing. It was a horrifying sound, and there was no way we'd be able to do a record like that and he didn't know what to do. He just stared at me, sort of helplessly, and said, "What do I do now?" I said, "I think you better go get help."'

'HHGGGGGUUUUURRRRGGGGHHHH!'

Jim and Todd just fucking *stared* at him.

'I can tell you very specifically,' Steinman told me, 'his voice was great for about month but he didn't do anything to train it, or keep it going right, it just got abused or something happened psychologically, which was part of my [original] point to David Sonenberg. About a month into the tour his voice basically had gone, and he didn't take time to rest it. And it just was a very kind of horrifying, fascinating situation for me to see crowds of up to twenty thousand screaming along with this record and per-former of my music. And I'm on stage at that point . . . where he didn't sing one good note the whole night. The perverse thing for Meat Loaf was not being even a bit self-aware of the situation.' He got away with it, 'because sometimes people bring enough of the record with them that the last thing they're paying attention to is the performance. There are performances that are very well known, such as the *Old Grey Whistle Test* thing, where he didn't sound great. It's like only if you listen to the record can you [detect] an appreciable depreciation, so to speak.'

A year on, Meat's voice sounded inhuman, animalistic. He knew that he *could* sing. It was still there at the lower end. At least it was at first. The damage wasn't physical, it was psychological. As he later wriote in his autobiography, 'The doctors all said, "Meat is fine physically. It's all mental." But psychosomatic or not I still couldn't sing.' From somewhere deep down inside, his body was in rebellion, refusing to do the thing he loved to do.

It was weird.

'HHGGGGGUUUUURRRRGGGGHHHH!'

It was fucked.

He thought about Jim working on the album with Roy Bittan and not him. He thought about Todd dismissing his ideas. He thought about the songs he couldn't fully embrace and hadn't had the chance to shape. He thought about the great effort it took him to get into character to sing them. He wondered if his subconscious was stopping him, trying to save him from the madness that he'd lived through during the end of the *Bat* tour, the hideous physical and moral decline he'd fallen into.

'HHGGGGGUUUUURRRRGGGGHHHH!'

They sent him to doctors, one after the other, progressively more senior and eminent, New York thousand-dollars-an-hour specialists, and they all told him the same thing: 'There's nothing wrong with you.' And then the whispers began. He wasn't sure if they were real or not at first, but it soon became clear they were. He'd lost his voice and now he was losing Jim. Jim was the guy who wrote the songs. Jim was the dark and brilliant presence behind *Bat*. He was just the singer and if he couldn't sing, then what use was he, to Jim or to Cleveland International, who were getting increasingly freaked out and impatient? Everyone around him was wired up, crazed by excess, fuelled by booze and cocaine. Everyone wanted something, and for a while what they wanted had been him.

Now it wasn't, not any more.

'HHGGGGGUUUUURRRRGGGGHHHH!'

He stopped going to doctors and started going to faith healers and oddballs – guys that hit him with kitchen implements while he hung upside down like a fucking *bat*. Steinman later told an incredulous Sandy Robertson about 'the witchdoctor' in California that Springsteen's manager had recommended. Claiming the guy had fixed things for Jackson Browne and Bonnie Raitt. A guy named Warren Berrigan who told Meat that he'd been traumatised when he fell off stage and injured his leg all those months back in Ottawa. Said Steinman: 'The guy's treatment is he injects you with your own urine and then he beats the shit out of you! He has Black & Decker power tools, huge saws, axes . . . He puts rubber pads on your body and he pounds for three hours and you scream.' He added, nonchalantly, 'I can't imagine Jackson Browne going through this.'

Jim went on to tell Sandy that the doctor had made Meat put his head in a 'glass box full of cat hairs . . .' All based on the doctor's own esoteric theory about the urine containing some magic property, some kind of essential oil, and how the pounding of the body helped unclog certain restrictions that built up physically and psychologically. 'God knows why it works,' concluded Steinman, 'but after three months his voice had improved one thousand per cent because of it.' I remember Sandy telling me this improbable story at the time and both of us just sitting there grinning at the absurdity of it. Not entirely sure if Jim wasn't putting Sandy on. What was certain was that, as Steinman would later put it, 'He started out on a procession of doctors, vocal coaches, vocal teachers, throat specialists, hypnotists . . . he would see anybody!

And all this time I just kept writing because I had nothing else to do.'

By the time Meat began to regain some control over his singing voice, though, it was too late. It was Jim that delivered the bullet to his head. Towards the end of the year, he told Meat Loaf that he was going to record *Bad For Good* himself. He didn't need Meat for the project; Jim would sing the songs himself. As Jim told me, it was no longer just about the singer's lost voice. It never had been, not for him. It was his flat-out rejection of the songs, the ideas – of Jim. 'Meat Loaf didn't want to do it, so I did it myself . . .' Cue the sound of two goliath egos butting heads.

Jim assured Meat that when his voice came back – *if* Meat's voice came back – he would write him another album, an even better one. But Meat was no dummy. He could see where this was headed. If Jim's solo career took off, the next album he wrote wouldn't be for Meat Loaf. Suddenly, he was an ex-singer; a man with a past but no future. Once again, the old feelings of betrayal and paranoia overtook him. All the success had been a charade, a stupid game devised to strip him of what was left of his dignity. Well, fuck them! He would take his revenge on all of them – especially Jim – one day. Wait and see.

Almost simultaneously, he was offered a part in a movie, a thing called *Roadie*, directed by Alan Rudolph, who'd started out in TV working on *The Brady Bunch*, and then had got into film with an arty, auteur flick called *Welcome to LA*. The person behind the whole enterprise, though, was Shep Gordon, manager at the time of both Alice Cooper and Blondie, and something of a legend in Sunset Strip circles. It was Shep who saw Meat Loaf as perfect for the lead role in the movie. He instructed Rudolph to offer it to him – and keep offering until he caved. *Roadie* was about a beer-drinking, hell-raising truck driver named Travis Redfish who somehow or other becomes the world's greatest roadie. Lots of rock stars were going to be in it playing themselves – Alice

Cooper, Blondie, Hank Williams. Meat Loaf, who wasn't sure who he was any more anyway, would be the only one actually acting. 'I did *Roadie* because I liked the script,' Meat would later say. 'I thought it was funny. And I liked the film we shot – I just didn't like the film they edited.'

Around the same time, he also appeared in *Americathon*, a zany comedy film starring John Ritter and his wife Nancy Morgan, with narration by comedian George Carlin. Set twenty years in the future, the movie was remarkably prophetic in its predictions for what the late nineties would look like, anticipating both the collapse of the USSR and the advent of reality television. Meat Loaf played a minor but memorable character named Roy Budnitz.

The sort of *Animal House*-style drive-in movie beloved of gawky teenage boys, *Americathon* was hardly of the same calibre as *Rocky Horror*, but Meat Loaf loved it. Speaking to me some years later, he recalled being affronted when he learned that his theatrical agent had originally turned down the part for him.

'I went in to the office and was rummaging through scripts and happened to open that one up right to the character! Bam!! I said: "Hey, this is great!" But they said, "Oh, you don't want to do that! We already turned it down."'

But Meat did want to do it. 'Now the character only had two scenes and one of them was with Dorothy Stratten,' the *Playboy* bunny and Playmate of the Year, who was infamously shot to death by her insanely jealous husband in 1980, 'which was really weird. That was about a year and a half before her death and I asked her about being a *Playboy* bunny and I got the whole rap about: "My boyfriend wanted me to do it because he thought it would be great!" I went through the whole thing with her; it was wild, really weird. There I was on the set with Dorothy Stratton sitting on my lap, telling me, "You're comfortable." I'm glad that guy didn't hear or he'd be shooting me!'

He guffawed. 'The other scene I was dressed up as Captain America in tights and shorts, a big shirt with an "A" on my chest, a helmet with red and white stripes – it was great fun. You ever see that? You gotta see that, that's unbelievable! I kill this car! It's the car from the movie *The Car* that's supposed to be alive. Possessed by the devil, it's the same car! And I had to fight it so I stabbed it in the crank case with this big spear and it spurted oil like blood and then I took a flare and blew it up! It was great, unbelievable!'

He went on. 'I got to do all my own stunts on that, too. And one time I got hit by the car but I didn't tell anybody. I got hit and went spinning away on the ground and they went: "Great! Great!" I went, "You like that?" "Yeah, yeah, wow, you're good!" I didn't tell them but it almost crushed my leg . . .'

Movies like *Americathon* and *Roadie* brought some money in and kept Meat Loaf busy while he was still unable to sing. But they did little to enhance his public profile. Having spent a year performing and touring, working hard to convince the world that the vision of a grossly obese monster singing fantastical songs of love from the underworld was not somehow just too silly for words, whatever rock-cool mystique he had built up in that time was now rapidly eroded as he went back to playing the clown.

Jim Steinman was both appalled and forgiving. From a distance he could see what was really happening to his old friend. 'So he went to do this film,' said Jim. 'He only did it to get his mind off the music business. I actually think he knew that it wasn't much of a movie, but he wanted to forget about the record. He thought maybe . . . because this whole problem with his voice, everyone realised, was about 50 per cent physical and 50 per cent psychological. He really was in terror of trying to follow up *Bat Out of Hell* because you have to remember that he had thought at most it would sell 700,000. I was the insane one who thought it would sell five million, but when it ended up selling eight million

. . . I think he was just paralysed with fear about how to top it.'

'HHGGGGGUUUUURRRRGGGGHHHH!'

The fates were calling, doing their thing . . .

Meat Loaf knew what was really happening, too. Filming movies like *Roadie* became 'the perfect escape' from the convoluted mess that his life as a real rock star had become. 'I became Travis Redfish! I'm a mechanical failure but when I got the part of Travis, I could fix anything. I was going around fixing vacuum cleaners, radios, TVs . . . I was doing stuff I can't even do.' Whether acting in film or singing on stage, he explained, 'I *become* these people. I'm not an actor, I become possessed, another human being. It drives my wife Leslie crazy! She didn't know who she was living with . . .' He laughed but he really wasn't joking any more.

CHAPTER SIXTEEN

East Side Story

Jim Steinman was nearly sixty years old. I was nearly fifty. In the decades that had passed since we'd first spoken for a magazine article, my life had settled into a middle-aged fug of school runs and work deadlines. His life was what it always had been – waking like a vampire as the sun went down, up all night, his great works to perform. For me, it was the start of another bright cold day when I phoned. For him, thousands of miles and several lifetimes away, it was the middle of another hot, dark night. It was true what he wrote, all those years before, what he sang when Meat Loaf either couldn't or wouldn't sing the words himself: Jim wasn't bad for just a little while, Jim was bad for good.

We were going over old ground. It was decades later but Jim was still talking about his musical vision, where it came from, how he alchemised it. 'From rock'n'roll, from opera . . . Not from Broadway show tunes, as has been suggested. It really was my own rock opera, quite literally. All my life, those were the two musical forms I was most attracted to. In fact, I don't even see a separation. I would listen to Wagner followed by Phil Spector, followed by The Beatles and The Beach Boys. The common denominator was that they were at the same time thrilling and spectacular and ridiculous and absurd, and I like that combination. That's why the concept of having a 350-pound guy called Meat Loaf singing my songs wasn't weird to me.'

But then, just as the world was also coming round to that idea, Jim had changed the picture again and replaced the 350-pound freak with – himself. Then later still with Bonnie Tyler, with Barbra Streisand, with Céline Dion and so many others. Why? Was the meltdown that followed the *Bat* tour really so insurmountable?

'Absolutely,' he told me. But why? 'How much time do you have? There's no way to put it simply, I'm sorry . . .' Clearly, this was about more than just singing, though. This was also about Jim finally getting the star billing he felt was his due on *Bat*. Jim had always liked to think he could sing.

Jim's voice is good but not great. Up until that lady biker had danced a tattoo on his nose, Jim had always considered himself a singer, too. Meat Loaf had a great voice. But Jim could hit the notes. His natural pitch was high, his tone slightly querulous, his power somewhat lacking. But although he was a remarkable character in his own strange way, he didn't have the kind of star quality that held a big stage in the way that Meat Loaf did. He lacked the physical charge, the electric jolt that real rock stars had. Jim may have forgotten more about music and writing songs than someone like Jim Morrison or Janis Joplin ever knew, but they had a quality that he didn't possess.

He wasn't the man to sing *Bat Out of Hell*, and he wasn't really the man to sing *Bad For Good*, either, but that was what he did. 'I always liked singing more than writing,' he said, wishfully, at the time. 'I taught the songs to Meat Loaf. He became my voice. I used to sing Doors and Stones rockers in 1972. My voice is edgier and there's a different texture to it. Drummer Max Weinberg describes it as sounding like "I have to go to the bathroom".' This wasn't quite the endorsement Jim seemed to think it was. It was perhaps fair to say that the person who liked Jim's voice best of all was Jim. Was it confidence, arrogance, hubris? Did he have a point to prove?

Yes to all of those. More important, though, Jim still had his dream of turning *Neverland* into an album, a show, a vehicle that would establish the universe in which many of his best songs took place: 'Really every song I write, my idea is that the whole album should sound like a soundtrack to a movie that hasn't been made yet,' he said, 'so that you could listen to the movie and basically create the film yourself. But I try to write them so visually and cinematically, as much as possible, because to me they are films. Every song is one, and the entire album fits together. It's just a very powerful film to me, and this one in particular.'

But where Steinman had talked in the past of *Bat Out of Hell* being his more realised version of the Peter Pan story, he now chose to reconfigure history, drawing the same comparison to the material on *Bad For Good*, claiming the songs on the album had been written 'with a very specific movie in mind, which has sort of been my dream project for almost two years now, and that's a film called *Neverland* which is a rock'n'roll, science-fiction version of *Peter Pan*. *Peter Pan*'s always been about my favourite story and I've always looked at it from the perspective that it's a great rock'n'roll myth because it's about – when you get right down to it – it's about a gang of lost boys who never grow up, who are going to be young for ever and that's about as perfect an image for rock'n'roll as I can think of. I mean, the way I see this movie, it's like a mixture of *West Side Story*, *A Clockwork Orange* and *Star Wars* . . . I mean, it's a real dance, real musical, singing and dancing like a *West Side Story*, and the dancing is like *West Side Story* twenty-five years later. I mean, it's very athletic, virtuosic, real tough dancing – much tougher than *West Side Story*, but it's that style – real showy, and it's got a lot of special effects, science-fiction *Star Wars* kind of tradition . . .' He went on to breathlessly explain how the title track of his album, 'Bad For Good', was from *Neverland*, as evinced in the lines, *'You know I'm gonna be like this forever: I'm never gonna be what I should.'* As was the second track, 'Lost Boys And Golden Girls'. 'It's one of the songs that Peter sings to Wendy. It's like a love song he sings to her.'

It was as though he was saying that *Bat* had been merely a run-through for the songs on the album he had now produced under his own name. That we should ignore the fact that *Bat* had been a Meat Loaf album. It was the Jim Steinman album that really contained the gold. But the more Jim tried to sell it to the press, the more *Bad For Good* sounded exactly like the album Meat Loaf did not want to make: *Bat Out of Hell II*. Right down to using the nucleus of the ensemble that had created the now emblematic sound of *Bat*: Todd Rundgren at the controls, Roy Bittan and Max Weinberg moonlighting from the E Street Band, Rory Dodd on those cathedral-like backing vocals, and one track, 'Dance In My Pants', featuring a duet with Karla DeVito. Even the cover harked back to the original template: another Richard Corben winged hero embracing another scantily clad Tinker-babe.

Released in April 1981, there was no mistaking the scope of Steinman's ambition. This was no humble side project, issued in the shadows for completists only. This really was, to all intents, the (un)official follow-up to *Bat Out of Hell*. It even came with the added value of a separate EP, with two tracks either side – 'The Storm' and 'Rock And Roll Dreams Come Through' – that were meant to be taken as the prelude and epilogue to the story behind the album. The latter, replete with wonderfully lush, uncredited lead vocals by the magnificent Rory Dodd, would grace the US Top 30 when it was released in edited form as a single – Jim's lone Top 40 hit as a solo artist. (In fact, fans examining the credits on *Bad For Good* would also find the words 'Lead vocal by Rory Dodd' in smaller type next to 'Lost Boys And Golden Girls' and 'Surf's Up'. Rory's voice sounded very similar in tone to Jim's but he was a much better singer, an accomplished session man who contributed many of the mountain-stream backing vocals to Jim and Meat's songs. Begging the question: if Jim was as good a singer as he said he was, why did he have Rory Dodd singing three of the biggest songs on the album? The answer was obvious.)

'The Storm' was something else again: a grandiose neo-classical instrumental recorded at huge expense with the New York Philharmonic Orchestra, in homage to Bernard Herrmann – the legendary movie soundtrack composer whose scores for Hollywood classics like *Citizen Kane*, *The Birds* and *Taxi Driver* placed him among the immortals, as far as Jim was concerned. 'I also wrote it because I was really into the idea of what Stravinsky would do if he put out singles,' Jim told Sandy.

But while *Bad For Good* went Top 10 in Britain, it barely bruised the US charts, tiptoeing into the Top 75 then tiptoeing out again.

Jim promoted it hard, and gave his interviewers his full Little Richard-Wagner shtick, camping it up and slightly rewriting history where he felt it necessary. He had a bullish confidence in everything he said and everything he did.

Then came the reviews . . .

'*Bad For Good* establishes that Steinman was *Bat* in all departments except that of vocal melodrama,' explained Mark Cooper earnestly in *Record Mirror*. 'Trouble is, that's a fairly central bureau both there and here, and though Steinman has a fine voice it lacks Meat Loaf's weight or drama.' Parke Puterbaugh, in *Rolling Stone*, complained that 'Steinman's thin reedy voice simply can't carry the absurd precocity of the lyrics. Throughout, *Bad For Good* is marred by Wagnerian excess, feral "rock" playing and vile choristering.' *People Magazine* cut straight to the chase: 'On the title cut Steinman wails, "*I wasn't built for comfort/I was built for speed*". He may not have been built for a lead role in rock either . . .'

In the end, it was left to the ever-prophetic Sandy Robertson to really nail it. 'Rock'n'roll genius is never obvious,' he wrote in *Sounds*. 'Jim Steinman is one of my two or three favourites, and if you haven't noticed him it's because he's been hiding in plain sight. His concept of a two-ton man singing eight-minute operatic heavy rock may now be considered vulgar populism, but that's the luxury of retrospective snobbery. Steinman has now conducted the niftiest salvage job since Francis Ford Coppola brought *Apocalypse Now* back alive from the jungle. His voice may lack the dynamic range of Meat Loaf's, but when you couple the fact that there's nothing like the real, old-fashioned songwriter singing his own material, with production and playing (again) by Todd Rundgren and some E Street mafia, you get a *Bad For Good* that's a lot more than the pale shadow of what might have been.'

Without a world tour to help spread his message either, Jim had to spend all of his interviews explaining why *he'd* made the album and not Meat, and however he framed it, the underlying message was always: THIS IS NOT THE GUY YOU'VE BEEN WAITING FOR. In big block caps. And it played into his fears, the seam of insecurity and ego that had so wanted equal billing with Meat Loaf on *Bat Out of Hell*. Instead, he had been cast in the role of Dr Frankenstein, the éminence-grise tugging at the puppet's strings, a new Phil Spector with an even bigger wall of sound.

Yet the arguments that audiences may not 'get' Jim as a performer proved prescient. He'd told *Rolling Stone*: 'Everyone thinks this guy Steinman must sing like a wimp because he's got Meat Loaf singing everything. But really, Meat sings a lot like me. I would do a lot of the phrasing, and he would not so much imitate as use it as a base, a foundation. A lot of people say I sing like Meat Loaf. I say Meat Loaf sings like me – when he's doing my songs.'

Unwittingly, he was clouding the waters further, adding to the confusion. Inevitably, when an album sells in the numbers that *Bat* had, a large percentage of those purchasers are not rabid fans, just people who have heard the songs on the radio and liked them. To sell to them again, a message had to be clear, the connection easy to make. Jim's message was far from clear. Not even Meat Loaf was sure what he was talking about any more.

As a musical statement, *Bad For Good* would remain one of the most complete and compelling works Jim Steinman would ever make. A body of work so overfilled with highlights it would be plundered again and again as the years sped by and Meat Loaf, though he still won't admit it to this day, privately realised his mistake and returned to it in search of the hits that his career without Jim would sorely miss. As a commercial proposition, though, *Bad For Good* was a dud. For Jim, and for many others, it may have been as good as the best of *Bat Out of Hell*, but it didn't sell even a tenth of what the latter did. It didn't become a byword for rock'n'roll excess and mock-opera glory, the way *Bat* did. It was a flop.

Jim had an explanation for that, too, though. There was a conspiracy among US radio stations to avoid playing his songs. 'They've even done surveys that have proved that after listening to one of my songs, people don't take note of the adverts immediately afterwards because they're too involved in the song. The radio programmers are very blatant about stuff like that. They'd rather have Madonna.' Ultimately, he insisted, 'What all that proved to me was that I was right. There was a world out there waiting to hear operatic, gothic stuff! At the time, I was real disillusioned, though.'

As a barstool story it was terrific, as inventively told as all of Jim's yarns, but in terms of moving both his and Meat's careers forward at a time when they were among the most successful artists in the world, it simply mixed the message further, diluted the appeal. Could Meat sing or couldn't he? Was *Bad For Good* the follow-up to *Bat* or would it the next Meat Loaf album? (Whose title, *Dead Ringer*, had already been leaked just as *Bad For Good* came out.) Had Jim put his favourite songs on *Bad For Good*, or would we have to wait for *Dead Ringer* for the real juicy stuff? And why were the records coming out so close together when Meat Loaf was supposed to have lost his voice?

Bad For Good was stalled before it got out of the traps. For all of its triumphs and all of its mad ambition, it was fatally compromised by the name of the guy on the cover. Perhaps Jim would have realised, had he not been overworked, distracted and caught up in his fantasies about singing and making movies and all the rest of it. The record limped to a high of 63 on the Billboard Top 200. It went Top 10 in the UK, but not for long, soon slipping below *Bat* again. It made Number 14 in Sweden. All of this would have been okay for the average debut artist, but it wasn't for a record that was following *Bat Out of Hell*.

History would come to see *Bad For Good* as carrion there to be picked off when other artists needed its songs, not least Meat Loaf himself. It was a flawed masterpiece, an act of hubris, ultimately destined to be an all-but-forgotten rock'n'roll curio. The wreck of a great idea, the shadow of its grand, lost inspiration *Renegade Angel*.

And it was over almost before it had begun.

As a solo artist and as a singer, Jim was already finished. Now it was Meat's turn . . .

CHAPTER SEVENTEEN

Constipated with Gold

Both Meat Loaf and Jim Steinman learned an important lesson from *Bad For Good*, though of course each would be loath to admit it. The music, the act of creation, may have all belonged in the leather-gloved hands of Steinman, but the franchise – the magic, the moneymaking code – belonged simply to Meat Loaf. Outside the business, few would ever know who Jim Steinman was. Inside and out, though, by the early 1980s, everyone knew who Meat Loaf was. Or thought they did.

But the magic only happened when the two worked together in symbiosis. Day and night, yin and yang, fire and water. Meat Loaf couldn't even fall back on his career as an actor any more – despite some goodwill reviews, *Roadie* had bombed at the box office. A review by revered American movie critic Tom Wiener summed up the mood: 'It won't win any awards for subtlety, but *Roadie* is a hoot of a comedy that is also a good excuse for its producers to pack a soundtrack album with as diverse a group of pop music artists as ever assembled for a feature film. One of the film's jokes is that its star, pop singer Meat Loaf, doesn't warble a note; his character, Travis W. Redfish, has showbiz ambitions, but they extend only to the backstage area. Travis comes off as something of a redneck idiot savant, a beer delivery truck driver who is a dynamo when it comes to making sure that the microphone wires don't get mixed up with the ones for the amplifiers.'

It might have been a joke that Meat Loaf didn't sing, but what the not-so-many filmgoers who showed up when *Roadie* was released on 13 June 1980 didn't know was that he *couldn't* sing. The voice had gone completely by now. *Roadie* wasn't a bad movie, but it wasn't a hit, in part because another knockabout musical comedy called *The Blues Brothers* was released the following week, starring his old pal John Belushi. Seems there was only room for one fat guy musical comedy from Hollywood that summer.

Meat and Leslie went back to New York. They found an apartment and nested down, barely going out and living a regular – well, sort of regular – life as a new family. Meat got to know Pearl better. He played softball in Central Park with his old friends from the theatre – all of them people he'd known before *Bat Out of Hell* came out. He decompressed. Slowly, the mad *Bat* persona left him – he still had outbursts of temper, but gradually, as Leslie refused to engage with them, he learned to control it.

Slowly his voice came back. It was subtly different, never again the wild, unforced instrument it had been in his younger years, but it was still his voice – expressive and formidable. By the end of 1980, just as Jim Steinman was getting ready to launch his solo career, Meat Loaf was ready to work again. He made Jimmy promise him he would write him an album when he'd finished promoting *Bad For Good* – and Jimmy, hedging his bets perhaps, kept his word.

By the time *Bad For Good* was released in April 1981, *Dead Ringer* was already on the schedules and was due that September. Jim would even find himself talking about it, instead of his own album, reassuring interviewers how good the songs on *Dead Ringer* were. Indeed, the recording of *Bad* had barely been completed in March before work on *Dead Ringer* began in earnest. It made the whole thing doubly confusing and even harder to market when both albums came out so close to each other. Jim had tried so hard to put *Bad* across as the real follow-up to *Bat*, yet here we were just weeks later, hearing all about *Dead Ringer*, the *real* real follow-up to *Bat*. But Meat's voice had returned, and Jim had been as good as his word. He had written another album for him – well, he wrote another five songs: 'Peel Out' (with wife Leslie on the call-back vocal, 'What is it, boy?'), 'I'm Gonna Love Her For Both Of Us' (with a Karla-like babe in the video for the single version), 'I'll Kill You If You Don't Come Back', 'Read 'Em And Weep', 'Dead Ringer For Love', featuring a chart-bait duet with Cher, which along with 'Everything Is Permitted' (which sprang out of an extended instrumental section on 'For Crying Out Loud' the band worked out during the *Bat* tour), 'More Than You Deserve' (barely reworked from its mid-seventies original stage show production) and a reworked Jim monologue titled 'Nocturnal Pleasure'. All these tracks would make up the second album by Meat Loaf – and the third written by Jim Steinman.

Jim had actually completed the new *Dead Ringer* songs while he was still working feverishly on *Bad For Good*, as he tried to explain as simply as possible to the BBC's Richard Skinner: 'Since I kind of thrive on pressure a lot more than I think Meat Loaf does and I kind of enjoy it, I said fine [I'd write another record]. I was dying to get these [*Bad For Good*] songs recorded. So I went in a sort of a blaze and wrote the other seventy-five per cent of the album really fast and started recording it in the summer of 1980 and really worked straight through until I finished it. And right before I did that, though, Meat did ask me to have another record ready for him – totally different. And so just on the assumption that he would get his voice back, I . . . wrote an entire album for him. Did all the tracks, co-produced it, arranged it, and had it all sitting there – sort of sitting waiting in the cans ready for him for when he did get his voice back. And then I went and did my record.'

While it sounds quicker than it was the way Jim breathlessly described it, it was, by his nit-picking standards, a period of peak creativity, that time in an artist's life understood only in retro-spect, when their energy is at its height and the craftsmanship has become second nature, and everything combines into a sweet spot that produces the work for which they will always be remembered.

It was certainly that way with Jim. 'I was creatively constipated; not to imply this is the stuff you'd be constipated with,' he said. 'Constipated with gold . . .'

By now, with every move each man made in their career freighted with meaning, it was hard not to read into Jim's title for the album – *Dead Ringer* – as a somehow ironic comment on the fact that the real follow-up to *Bat* had been scorned by Meat Loaf for being too much of a musical replicant, while this, ostensibly just the next Meat Loaf album, bore more than just a trace of the original *Bat Out of Hell* DNA. Where what had been seen three years before as something mould-breaking, even genre-defying, had now been fairly well boiled down into a formula. A winning formula, yes, but a built-in-the-lab, if you liked that you're gonna love this formula nonetheless.

Or maybe it had a deeper significance for Jim. A tacit declar-ation that Meat was actually Jim's *Dead Ringer*, a doppelganger; his representative in the world. The rollercoaster title song itself, although it would become the album's most enduring hit, was almost a throwaway, a boy-girl duet not in the epic fashion of 'Paradise By The Dashboard Light' but a straight-up, tuneful rock'n'roller, a good earworm if not much else. The star power of Cher would lift the finished recording, but it stood in the shad-ows of *Dead Ringer*'s other songs. Alongside 'More Than You De-serve', 'I'm Gonna Love Her For Both Of Us' was a citadel of misplaced longing that built to a shattering and slyly humorous finale; 'Read 'Em And Weep' a crystalline ballad with a melody more luxuriant and covert than the hushed interior of a five-star hotel; 'Everything Is Permitted' was one of Steinman's darkest songs, subdued but full of menace; and perhaps best of all was 'I'll Kill You If You Don't Come Back', a bellicose rock song that suddenly descended to the most unexpected and tender two-minute coda, filled with an impossible yearning.

'This album is a little more intimate, the lyrics are more personal,' Jim said as he completed the writing. 'It's had like three different titles in the last week. One of the songs is called "Dead Ringer", and that might be the title. The title I wanted to use was considered too strong, which was "I'll Kill You If You Don't Come Back", one of the best love songs I ever wrote, great chorus line: *"In every way I want you out of my life/ But I'll kill you if you don't come back."'* A love song, to whom, though – Meat Loaf? 'Then there's a nice song there called "Everything Is Permitted" . . . *"Everything is permitted/ Nothing ever is taboo/ And there is always something shattered/ When there is something breaking through."* Meat wanted to use this title for a while, but I asked him not to because it's a Dostoevsky line.

'I think what I figured is that in *Bat Out of Hell* those qualities that I've been mentioning – the operatic, the real heroic, the epic style – was really a lot more my own personality than it was Meat Loaf's, really. But I think when I sat down to do this new Meat Loaf album I tried to think of a different style, even though it's still got a lot of my qualities in the writing. I mean, it's a very passionate record. It's much more intimate in that it's more personal. It's not so much mythic and epic as it is about people. You know, it's the difference between a movie that's about four people and a movie that's like *Star Wars*. You know it's not so much a big spectacular as it is every song is really a love song of some sort, so it's scaled down a bit in a sense and that's what his album is and the songs in a way are more traditional in terms of rock'n'roll musical styles.'

Was he saying it was actually a simpler record than either *Bat* or *Bad*? Or that he hadn't had to try as hard?

Either way, it was the work of a master, no doubt. Yet they were now split into separate camps. Work on *Bad For Good* had gone on for so long it meant that Todd Rundgren was unavailable to Meat even if he had wanted him, which he sorely didn't. Instead, *Dead Ringer* was produced by Stephan Galfas, a journeyman engineer and orchestral arranger who Meat had met in 1976 while guesting on 'Keeper Keep Us', a track from the album, *Intergalactic Touring Band*, a fictitious space-rock ensemble comprising guest performances from a number of well- and lesser-known singers and musicians (including Ben E King, Rod Argent and various members of Genesis, Status Quo, Strawbs, Sharks and others), released at a time when similar multi-artist concept albums like Jeff Wayne's *The War of the Worlds* were briefly popular around the world.

Jim had created the backing tracks, with help from both Rundgren and Jimmy Iovine, then the songs had been handed on to Meat Loaf and Galfas, who had some high-quality musicians with them: former Bowie guitarist Mick Ronson, bassist Steve Buslowe, synthesiser king Larry Fast and on guitar, in Todd's stead, Davey Johnstone, whose day job was with Elton John.

Jim had almost a year's start on Meat Loaf, but it became obvious that the two albums were going to be finished at around the same time. That meant that they would be released around the same time, too, which seemed to be madness. But then, madness was all around them and it was only growing. *Bat* was still selling hundreds of thousands of copies a week when *Dead Ringer* was released in September 1981, and although the latter would go to Number 1 in Britain, it didn't even make the US Top 40, only 'I'm Gonna Love Her For Both Of Us' making any headway at all on American radio. Meanwhile, whatever credibility Meat and Steinman still had was being eroded. The pop mags still loved the bizarre novelty of the fat man singing the big hits. As *Smash Hits*, then the UK's biggest-selling music weekly, put it in its review of *Dead Ringer*: 'Meat Loaf is about glorious immersion in fantasy. Look at the pudgy face in the photo on the back of *Dead Ringer* and then the Mr Universe ideal in the painting on the front: they're both Meat Loaf, the flesh and the dream, the bulk and the incredible hulk. Irresistible.' But the serious critics now looked on with bafflement, even, in the case of *Creem*, with outright contempt: 'The opening song of this musical gridlock,' its review of the album went, 'goes, "My body is the car and my soul is the ignition." Could be. The composer's mind, however, is the empty gas tank.' Meat took such criticism as he always did: as personal insults, made by people who didn't know what they were talking about, didn't realise the pain he had been through just to get this far. People who liked to point fingers and make fat jokes.

More gallingly, the single 'Dead Ringer For Love' may have hit Number 5 in the UK but it didn't even get released in the US. Internal political squabbling at Epic Records resulted in 350 people being axed from their posts a week after *Dead Ringer* reached US record-store racks. Among the victims in the Epic purge were all the people who had supported the *Bat Out of Hell* project. As the singer later put it to me, he and his album 'went down with the regime' – and looked unlikely to get back up again quickly. With ticket sales 'soft' through lack of an accompanying hit, an autumn-winter tour of the US was quietly 'postponed' after just four shows. Meat Loaf was devastated. Couldn't figure out what was happening to him. Then he began looking around for someone to blame. It was a pattern that would begin to repeat itself more and more as the eighties began to crumble beneath his feet. Suicide was no longer something he flirted with or spoke openly about, he now had a young family to support. But he felt the tides turning as surely as he saw his career slipping into the margins.

Instead, a comedy/documentary movie was hurriedly filmed to fill the gap, co-written and produced by Meat Loaf's manager David Sonenberg and his new right-hand man, Al Dellentash, in conjunction with the film's director, Allan Nicholls, after talking the record label into advancing the money for that in lieu of a tour.

Nicholls was a Canadian actor, director, producer, screenwriter, composer and musician. In recent times he'd played minor roles in cool-de-jour movies like *Nashville*, *Popeye* and *A Wedding*. More pertinently, he was another old-school *Hair* cast member, playing Claude before returning to Montreal. He seemed just the guy to make the Meat Loaf thing work. Whatever it was meant to be, nobody seemed entirely sure.

Early in December, Meat Loaf and his band were the musical guests on *Saturday Night Live*, where they performed 'Bat Out of Hell' and Chuck Berry's 'The Promised Land'. Meat was also reunited with fellow *Rocky Horror Picture Show* star Tim Curry, in a skit depicting a One-Stop Rocky Horror Shop. It was funny enough on the night but it didn't stop the slide out of focus in America. By the start of 1982, the Meat Loaf flame was only being kept alive by the support coming out of Europe, where a seven-week tour in the spring found him headlining arenas across Germany, Scandinavia, France and Britain, including four nights at the 12,500-capacity Wembley Arena in London. His duet with Cher on 'Dead Ringer For Love' had become his biggest hit single up to that point – aided by the now-famous video featuring a barroom confrontation with the leather-clad Cher. 'Working with Cher,' the singer declared breathlessly, 'I can never say enough good things about her – she's a pro, she's great, I love working with pros.' Onstage at the Brighton Centre in April, he looked like what he was. The same guy we'd met on the *Bat Out of Hell* videos, same kitsch tux and mind-expanded waistline, only this time going through the motions – until suddenly he wasn't. Towards the end of the show, he attacked the stage equipment, not like Pete Townshend smashing his guitar, but like a sun-maddened rhino attacking anything that caught his gimlet eye. Even the contrived smooch with Karla DeVito's replacement, the similarly dark and svelte Pam Moore, took on a more frenzied aspect when he turned accusingly to her and screamed: 'I want you to read my lips very carefully . . . *Fuck you!*' To which, Moore screamed back at him, in an apparently unscripted moment, 'Fuck you!' Followed by the pair of them exiting the stage. Show over after barely an hour. There was a twenty-five-minute encore, but both the audience and I were still in shock. Nobody was aware during those years that the man mountain who could sing so sweetly one moment, then seemingly smash all our preconceptions by running around the stage like a man unhinged while belting out operatic masterpieces, could be so personally undone by insecurity and rage. But then none of us in that concert hall knew of any of his other troubles. We just saw the guy who had one of the biggest and best albums of all time. What was his problem?

He still harboured plans to tour America but the financial sluice gates were now opening up at both ends just as he was spending his last promotional dime on videos that would not even be seen in America.

And then the bills came in, each one like a bullet to the gut.

It was as if Jim and Meat had cancelled each other out, releasing two versions of the same follow-up album within months of each other. The story too overlapping, the waters smudged with bad blood. For years afterwards, cherry-picking your favourite tracks from each album to come up with the parallel dimension *real* follow-up to *Bat* became an enduring parlour game among Meat Loaf – and Jim Steinman – fans.

Maybe a manager could have worked out a more coherent strategy, but then again maybe not, if the manager is tied up running drugs for Pablo Escobar . . .

CHAPTER EIGHTEEN

Helicopter Al

Al Dellentash had balls of steel. He needed them to be. In the seventies, he had begun heading multimillion-dollar operations flying Pablo Escobar's primo-manufactured cocaine from Columbia to Carlo Gambino's crime family in New York. Neither Escobar – then busy massacring police officers, judges, locals and prominent politicians with impunity – nor the Gambino organisation – responsible, though never convicted, for nearly two hundred contract killings during the late seventies and mid-eighties – had reputations as soft and fuzzy new-age employers, so you did your best not to fuck up. Al found out what the drug-smuggling business was about when he flew his first mission, somewhere around 1974 he reckoned. Born in 1948, he'd had a pilot's licence since he was sixteen years old. It just seemed magical to him, a chance of freedom and escape from his humdrum life in New Rochelle, Westchester County, one of the plusher environs in New York State.

Al's dad – Alfred Senior – was in construction – the chief 'legitimate business' owned by the Gambino family – and his mom was a local Republican and fine, upstanding American. Growing up, Al had just two passions: music and flying – well, three if you counted women, and four if you counted drinking and having a good time. He followed his father into construction, married young and had two kids, but he found suburban life stultifying.

He bought a wrecked plane from a dead guy called 'Flamin' Eddie' and discovered in the process that the bank would give him a substantial loan against the title of the aircraft. He set up a sales and charter operation at an airfield in New Jersey, where he ran into a guy called Lenny, who wanted to buy as many of these Swedish light planes with trapdoors in the bottom as Al could get his hands on. It turned out that flying drugs into America under the radar was a fast-growing business in the mid-seventies, and planes with trapdoors were perfect for the job. The *New York Times* had even written about it. Al read that some guys were making $50,000 per flight! That sounded good to Al, who seemed to be permanently on the breadline and struggling to keep his business going.

His first job for Lenny involved a trip to Belize. He used a Cessna Skymaster 337, which had its propellers on the front and rear, an unusual design. One of the Belize guys walked into the rear propeller almost as soon as Al had taxied to a halt. As he lay on the runway bleeding to death, a man pulled out a revolver and put the poor guy out of his misery right in front of Al. No fucking around.

Welcome to the jungle, baby . . .

Al got into the music business when he was chartered to pick up Mick Jagger and fly him from Woodstock to New York. He got talking to Mick and discovered that all of the rock bands that were making millions of dollars on the road in America were chartering their own planes, so Al forged a bank loan agreement to buy a Falcon jet and soon he was flying ELP and the Grateful Dead, Kiss and the Doobie Brothers, his plane full of rock stars, groupies, booze and everything else on the menu in the star-crossed 1970s. Al loved the action, absolutely fucking *adored* it, and soon he was rocking the skies with his own fleet, each chartered out to a different band. *People* magazine wrote an article about Al and his floating palaces of excess, kitted out with 'thick

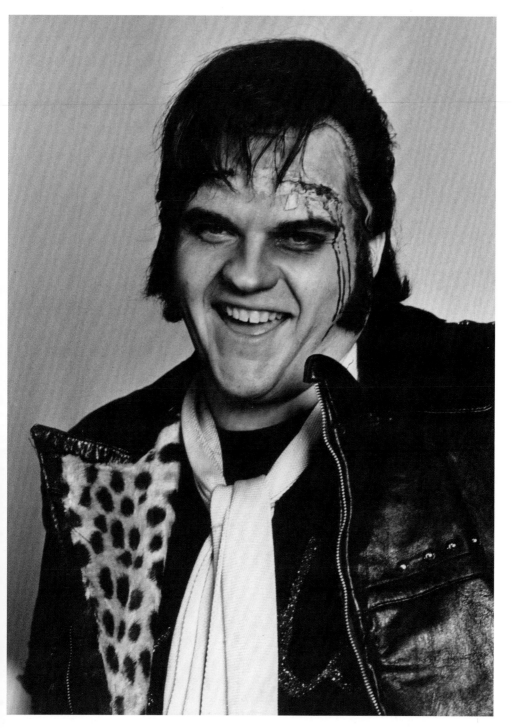

28-year-old Meat Loaf in *The Rocky Horror Picture Show* movie, playing Eddie, the crazed biker covered in surgical scars, who sings 'Hot Patootie – Bless My Soul' and somehow manages to get murdered. Twice. A harbinger of the characters he was to play later singing Jim Steinman's songs. (Getty Images)

Meat on the phone during a press call in London, 1978. He would always be a bigger star in the UK than in America. (Getty Images)

The monster and his creator. Meat Loaf and Jim Steinman, Woodstock, 1981. Jim had just finished *Bad For Good*, his 'real' follow-up to *Bat Out Of Hell*; Meat was in process of finishing *Dead Ringer*, his 'real' follow-up to *Bat*. (Getty Images)

Pam Moore – as Beauty – readies herself for Meat Loaf's – as Beast – now nightly onstage lunge, 1982. The Monster and his Bride had become a running theme of all Meat Loaf's shows. (Getty Images)

According to Jim Steinman, in order to write 'Total Eclipse Of The Heart' for Bonnie Tyler, 'I had to envision a situation where Joan Sutherland is on a stage backed up by The Who and Phil Spector's group – and then I could go ahead.' (Rex Shutterstock)

Meat Loaf and Ellen Foley, New York City, April 1985. Ellen and Meat had begun a love affair during the recording of *Bat Out Of Hell*, on which Foley sang all the lead female parts. Eight years later, her part in the story was all but forgotten. But not by Meat, who would unsuccessfully try to involve her in *Bat II*. (Getty Images)

Sharing a moment on stage in the 90s with Patti Russo, the longest lasting of Meat Loaf's duettists. Like Karla De Vito before her, Patti had been brought in for the *Bat II* tour, singing the vocal parts that on the album were sung by unknown British singer Lorraine Crosby. (Getty Images)

Nearly 20 years after playing scarred and monstrous Eddie in *Rocky Horror*, Meat gets into even more garish character for his *Beauty and The Beast* performance in the 1992 video for 'I'd Do Anything For Love (But I Won't Do That)'. (Getty Images)

Let Bitch Tits kiss it better: Edward Norton and Meat Loaf in *Fight Club*, 1999. The movie that made Meat Loaf a star in Hollywood at last. (Rex Shutterstock)

Meat Loaf leaving the set of the ITV show, Loose Women, where he had been taken ill shortly before transmission. The breakdowns and ailments piled up as he grew older. (Rex Shutterstock)

Meat Loaf now. After his latest health scare, collapsing on stage in 2016, Meat Loaf insists he will be back on stage soon. But in truth it now seems unlikely. (Rex Shutterstock)

Jim Steinman and Meat Loaf today. Both men turned 70 in 2017. Both now suffer the effects of long-term illnesses. Jim ended up in a wheelchair after the first of his strokes in 2006; Meat now walks with a cane. (Getty Images)

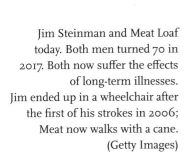

Billed as Jim Steinman's *Bat Out Of Hell: The Musical*, the name Meat Loaf is nowhere to be seen on the posters or tickets. Forty years later, the two men are still tussling over who deserves the most recognition. Riding the motorcycle, co-star Christina Bennington as Raven, and aloft, Andrew Polec as Strat. (Rex Shutterstock)

carpeting, plants, phones, telex printer, electric typewriter, bedroom and bar' – everything a self-respecting rock star might need at 30,000 feet.

Al boasted to his friends about his money and his lifestyle, about all of the contacts he'd made in the entertainment industry. Then he began to think that maybe *he* could become a mogul, too, like Albert Grossman and all of those fat cats. He signed up a few bands and tried to manage them, but that didn't really work out, until one day in 1980, when a couple of guys he'd chartered flights for introduced him to David Sonenberg, music business lawyer and manager of the writer and singer of the biggest album of 1978, *Bat Out of Hell*.

The only problem was, Al was still in the drug-smuggling business via the Gambino family's main drug trafficker 'Steve Teri', a ruthless mobster named Salvatore Ruggiero – aka 'Sal the Sphinx', aka 'Sal Quack Quack', aka 'Sally'. Steve Teri introduced Al to his 'Columbian connection', aka Carlos Lehder, a big-time cocaine supplier with a direct line to Pablo Escobar. Al pondered, it was strange how the drug business was a lot like the music business – you knew a guy who knew a guy, and you sort of hooked it all together and you were away, up into the clear blue skies, where no one on Earth could touch you . . . At least, that's what Al thought, anyway. The perfect guy, then, to manage an overweight, oversensitive singer in a mid-career crisis – yet that's what happened in 1981.

Around the time that Meat was finishing up *Dead Ringer* and making plans to go on the road: 'David Sonenberg had come to me and asked if he might transfer half of my management contract to Al Dellentash,' the singer later wrote. 'I gave him my permission. Dellentash leased planes to celebrities. They called him "Helicopter Al".'

Meat knew that Sonenberg was super smart, and that in many ways Dellentash seemed to complement him, to fit Sonenberg in the same way that he fit Jim. Sonenberg was a Harvard lawyer who dressed in expensive linen suits. Al was a more classic Noo Yawk Italian-American street guy ... shirt unbuttoned to the navel, shades, chunky jewellery, moustache, respectable wife, lots of sexy girlfriends. Al was now the frontman in Meat Loaf's management company, the negotiator, the guy who walked in and demanded the money. After all, once you'd negotiated with the Mob and Pablo Escobar's guys, how hard was it to walk into CBS Records and get them to write a cheque? As the British writer Jeff Maysh put it: 'Dellentash brought street charm and muscle to the bargaining table; Sonenberg crunched the numbers.'

It was Helicopter Al who'd tough-talked CBS into paying $1.5 million for the *Dead Ringer* movie. By the start of the eighties and his increasing involvement in Meat Loaf's career, Al had money pouring in from all sides: from CBS (he'd got another $250,000 out of them for a Bay City Rollers' album, which he had *Dead Ringer* producer Stephan Galfas oversee); from the aircraft leasing business, where he now owned three Convairs, two helicopters, a Boeing 707 and a Lear Jet; from the other business he conducted in the skies between central and North America ... With all of that cash burning a hole in his pocket he decided he needed an HQ fit for a mogul like him. He found a grand place on Riverside Drive on the West Side of Manhattan and set about filling it with expensive crap. He had Louis XV furniture in reception, a pink 'party room' with a pale pink grand piano, a gold lobby, an in-house chef, all real rock-star shit. In his office, Al's desk was twenty-five feet long and his chair was from the first-class section of a decommissioned airliner. He had a bodyguard called the Brick, and as he told Jeff Maysh, he had: 'a full-time guy just to keep the fireplaces roaring at all times and a theatre room with a twenty-foot screen. We'd host sex parties with all the best girls.'

Sex parties were of no interest to Meat Loaf, with Leslie now expecting their first child together; a girl, Amanda, born in January 1981. In fact, Al's excesses were starting to seriously freak Meat Loaf out. Al was full of stories – the Pakistan gun-running trip that ended in a shoot-out, the box-loads of US currency he was moving to an offshore tax haven using his own planes . . . He'd get up in the middle of meetings and disappear, too, sometimes for days on end. As Meat Loaf recalled in his memoir, 'The music biz was just a sideline for Al . . . He would tell these stories of flying to Libya with a load of automatic weapons.'

The idea was that the movie would not only be great (obviously, how could it not be with Big Al behind it . . .?) but that the videos for the singles would be recut from the footage. The castings for *Dead Ringer* were held on Riverside Drive. While Al was calling in girls to jiggle about in front of his twenty-five-foot desk, he met Bonnie, a *Playboy* bunny for whom he would eventually leave his wife.

A combination of real concert footage mixed with a fantasy storyline, *Dead Ringer* called for Meat Loaf to take the two leading roles, that of himself and Meat Loaf's biggest fan. The plot was pretty basic: there's a contest to go to a Meat Loaf show that is won by Meat Loaf's biggest fan, a shy, hulking character who is socially awkward and almost mute. When it comes to the time for the show, Meat Loaf falls ill and the fan takes his place, emerging from chrysalis to butterfly in the process. Allan Nicholls, as director, managed to bring out some deeper themes of identity, of the separation of the star and the real person in his original version, which was shown just once, at the Toronto Film Festival. But then, as Meat Loaf wrote in his autobiography: 'Dellentash and Sonenberg took over and started editing it themselves.' The finished product was a car crash, never generally released and only useful for the videos that spun off it.

The movie picked up some lukewarm reviews – 'Lively, but simple-minded fun' said the *Hollywood Reporter*; 'Should play well in midnight screenings,' chimed *Variety* – but it never achieved a theatrical release until the early nineties. Clips of it now reside in the bowels of YouTube, if you should care to find it. But there really is no need. It was abysmal – erratic concert footage, hammy performances; a *Hard Day's Night* done wrong.

Maybe Jim had been onto something with this *Dead Ringer* idea. Not only did it have all of its subtle little meanings in the relationship between him and Meat, it worked pretty well as a description of Al Dellentash, too. Al was a real dead ringer for himself; there was the flamboyant, fast-talking, high-living music-biz big shot Al.

That was his day job, his first life. Then by night he became Al Dellentash the drug runner, flying his plane from the tip of Florida down to Columbia, stopping off in the Bahamas to refuel. This was his extraordinary second life.

Al and his old pal Lenny even devised a route back to America that took them over the infamous 'Cape Fear' coast of North Carolina, a graveyard for ships and planes and the place where a few years later another flamboyant music-biz figure, the manager of Mötley Crüe and Bon Jovi, Doc McGhee, would become embroiled in a record-breaking marijuana bust. Al and Lenny flew in low, hundreds rather than thousands of feet above the sea. It was physically risky but there was far less chance of being caught. Once they were safely back over the mainland, they'd fly to a little airfield in New Jersey, unload the plane and run the drugs up the turnpike to the city by truck.

Al did what all good conmen do; he hid in plain sight. The music business connections and the house on Riverside Drive were the perfect cover for his other life. As his clients Jim Steinman and Meat Loaf prepared to release albums in 1981, Al had seven million dollars of drug money hidden behind a fake wall in his house.

Not even that was offering enough excitement for him. When he wasn't trying to create an entertainment empire or drug-running for Pablo Escobar, he was living it up in New York's nightclubs, where champagne and cocaine flowed like rivers, and juggling his wife and kids with his affair with Bonnie, his new girlfriend from the *Dead Ringer* movie.

As Al would later admit, with an admirably straight face: 'keeping all the plates spinning was becoming impossible'.

But for Meat Loaf, the perennial bull in a china shop, it was already too late. Every last piece of crockery he owned was now at his feet in pieces. A new father, a new husband, his life was very different now. The voice was back but it was different too. No longer the rampaging *Bat* monster, he had both feet on the ground. *Dead Ringer* was a bad film but a fine record. It felt more like it was *his* record, too. At least, to his mind. He'd been scarred by those early attempts to start *Bad For Good*, before his voice had gone, scarred by the way he felt Jim and Todd had treated him as a third wheel. *Dead Ringer* had put that right. He'd barely seen Jim, and working with Stephan Galfas he'd been able to put his own ideas onto the tape. He still needed to get into character to inhabit the songs, but they didn't require the same possessive mania that *Bat* had sucked out of him. He still needed to take oxygen during the shows on the European tour in 1982, but he didn't need the booze and the drugs. Didn't even need Jim, his place at the keyboard now permanently taken by Paul Jacobs.

In the US it was tough. *Dead Ringer* had done better than *Bad For Good* (Meat had heard that copies were now being stickered 'By the creator of Meat Loaf', which raised his hackles) but it was hardly the billion-dollar hit that everyone had been sure it would be when they commissioned the film and sat around telling one another how great it all was. Then just as it seemed things could not get more complicated, something decisive happened. In his autobiography, Meat Loaf recounted verbatim what Dellentash had said when the singer told him that he wanted to end their management agreement: 'Well you can do what you want but I can tell you right now, if you leave, your career is over. And Meat? I really *love* your kids and I really *love* your wife and I think you are one of the hardest-working guys I have ever seen and I have a lot of respect for you, but there are people who have a lot invested in this situation and if you don't come back to us right now you are going down. Your career is over. You will never work again. Everything you have will be taken away from you, including your name.'

It was the sort of thing you'd expect a guy like Al to say, but this time it started a war, the kind of war in which everyone was a casualty. The first of what would eventually total more than forty-five lawsuits, totalling $85 million in claims, landed within days, and the nightmare began. Every bank account Meat Loaf had was frozen. He and Leslie survived only because he had kept $10,000 in cash from the European tour tucked away at home.

Then Jim Steinman announced he would be suing Meat Loaf, too, for money he reckoned he was due. Years later he would say this was because his manager forced him to. That through an endless maze of legal technicalities that he never fully understood, he was left with no choice. The relationship between Meat and Jim had been slowly going downhill for years, but this now felt like the night of the long knives.

'Jimmy was talked into that,' Meat insisted years later. 'He figures there was a $200,000 payment due to him and the money was in a bank and I declared bankruptcy. And when that happened it was in a trust set up through lawyers, and these lawyers, who were owed money, went for it, and there was nothing I could do about it. The bankruptcy people took the rest.' At the time, though, a furious Meat Loaf couldn't understand it. 'I felt like a leper,' he said. 'I felt like I was on an island with my wife and my two daughters.'

The fall-out would last for ten years.

CHAPTER NINETEEN

Shark Bait

Karma was a bitch, man. By the time he threatened Meat Loaf and his wife Leslie in November 1981, Al Dellentash's spinning plates were one by one starting to fall. Salvatore Ruggiero wanted to get into the heroin trade, something Al realised might be too rich for his blood, not least because it would bring him into the orbit of Salvatore's even more fearsome older brother, Angelo – an out-of-control mob enforcer who the FBI regarded as 'an unpredictable psychopath'. Nonetheless, Salvatore ordered Al to stop fucking around in the music business. He wanted to come up to New York from Florida to see Al face to face and reinforce the message. Al sent his Lear Jet to pick up Salvatore and his wife, and on the return flight it crashed into the sea off the Georgia coast, killing both passengers and the pilot. The bodies were eaten by sharks. Al had to call Angelo to tell him what had happened. Unbeknown to him, the FBI was listening in when he did.

The events of that day spread outwards in a baroque pattern, reaching as far as John Gotti, then head of the Gambino family, for whom big brother Angelo worked directly. Al Dellentash was caught between a rock and a hard place and ended up testifying against members of the Gotti family in return for immunity on certain charges and a lighter sentence. In 1983 he received twenty-five years, served five and disappeared, some said into the witness protection programme. He didn't surface again until

2014, when Jeff Maysh found him working as a car salesman in Los Angeles, married to Bonnie and adamant that the death of Salvatore Ruggiero was nothing more than a terrible coincidence. 'Whatever the truth is,' Maysh wrote, 'he still prefers to sit where he can see the door.'

It was during this crazed period after the death of Salvatore Ruggiero that Meat Loaf's life fell completely to pieces. He now declared personal bankruptcy in order to allay the gathering lawsuits. He also vowed never to work with Steinman again. 'The problem was with a million different forces – his manager, his lawyers, his vocal chords, his brain,' Jim Steinman tried to explain to *Rolling Stone* in 1993. 'He had lost his voice, he had lost his house, and he was pretty much losing his mind.' Not helped by the fact that Jimmy was now suing him, too. 'It was padded-cell time,' Meat recalled in the same interview. 'When I declared bankruptcy, they said, "It's not like this big scourge." But it was a big scourge. It was horrible. The kids took a beating. My wife would try to write a cheque at the grocery store, and they wouldn't take it, even though it was fine. So I just worked. I always have. No big deal.'

He certainly worked, but to ever-diminishing returns. If you could call an entire decade a write-off, that was the rest of the 1980s for Meat Loaf. 'There was a period of time when it was ridiculous. I couldn't work; I couldn't do anything for nine months. I had injunctions on me.' These were his wilderness years and he roamed them like a sore and wounded beast, doing what he had to do to pull through. 'It wasn't that I didn't pay my electric bill, my phone bill or my credit card bill or my tax. It upset my wife no end because people look at you funny.'

One thing the world learned about him now, though: he was no quitter. But he was apart from Jim, and whatever Meat Loaf the entity was, a large part of it would always be Jim Steinman.

America was a bust, but *Dead Ringer* had done well enough in

Europe and Australia to keep the ball rolling. He owed Epic Records an album that both parties knew would be the last of their contract, so he made one called *Midnight at the Lost and Found*, the first of what would become the dark half of his catalogue, the half that didn't involve Jim. The common theme on each of these records would be a striving to recreate Steinman's style and sound. It was more complicated than just being a kind of pseudo-Jim. It was the parts of Meat Loaf that existed *without* Jim, which were mostly the attitude and the psyche and the voice.

Even though the lawsuits were still flying, Jim had offered him a couple of songs but Meat turned them down – officially because the label refused to pay Jim's high price, but more likely because the legalities had become insurmountable. Jim would write songs that would help Meat Loaf sell records, so that Meat could then settle Jim's lawsuit? Wait a minute . . .

The songs in question, though, were destined to become two of the biggest hits of the eighties – though not for Meat. The first, a grandiose piece of pop genius titled 'Total Eclipse Of The Heart', ended up being recorded by British singer Bonnie Tyler. Until then Tyler had been a modestly successful singer for whom one of her last two hits had been 'It's A Heartache' in 1977. Granted, the song had given her a Top Five smash in both Britain and America, but by 1983 she was largely remembered as 'the female Rod Stewart', due to her unnaturally gravelly voice. (Her voice on her debut hit, 'Lost In France' had been markedly gravel-free.)

The second was 'Making Love Out Of Nothing At All', an exquisite Steinman ballad that he instead gave to Air Supply to record – thereby bequeathing the soft-rock duo from Australia the biggest record of their career. (Their best-known hit to that point was the obsequiously polite ballad 'All Out Of Love'.) When both 'Total Eclipse' and 'Making Love' reached the top of the US charts in the summer of 1983 – the Bonnie Tyler track sitting at Number 1 with the Air Supply single sitting right behind it at

Number 2 for three weeks, making Jim Steinman suddenly the most sought-after songwriter and producer in the world – it felt to Meat Loaf like one more turn of the screw, and a particularly vicious one at that.

'I was being sued for $85 million by Jim's manager – Jim had no idea what was going on. I spent $1 million on lawyers and was seeking protection from being sued again. The record company said I shouldn't have anything to do with Jim, that nobody wanted to hear his songs. These morons – and I'm gonna sit here and call them morons – passed on "Total Eclipse Of The Heart" and "Making Love Out Of Nothing At All" which reached Number 1 and 2 in America in the same week. They couldn't care less about me.'

The irony was that there was no way that Epic were going to invest serious money in the project without any gold-standard Steinman epics to rely on, and so while veteran producer Tom Dowd agreed to take the producer's chair, the writers of *Midnight* were for the most part Meat Loaf and his touring band. Bassist Steve Buslowe, keyboardist Paul Jacobs, guitarist Mark Doyle, keyboardist George Meyer and backing vocalist Ted Neeley (the latter two co-writing the soporific single and non-hit, 'If You Really Want To') in various combinations to seven of the album's ten tracks, while Meat Loaf was also listed for the first time as co-writer on four of the tracks. The rest of the material came from a hodgepodge of different sources, including Jacobs's wife, Sarah 'Sandy' Durkee, who wrote songs for cool kids' show *Sesame Street*; Paul Christie, a former *Crawdaddy* writer then doing stand-up comedy in New York; Danny Peyronel, former keyboardist with British rock band UFO. Even Leslie Aday, who wrote the lyrics to 'Wolf At Your Door', a clearly autobiographical song about what it was like to be a broke and lonely Meat Loaf during that time: *'There's a wolf at your door/He wants your money, wants your soul/A wolf at your door, you give it all, he wants more . . .'*

The three tracks that weren't covered by the gang were all covers: Chuck Berry's 'The Promised Land', Meat's vocals so far down in the mix it sounds like it's being sung exclusively by the backing vocalists; 'Don't You Look At Me Like That', written by fellow Texan Marshall James Styler for his band Duke Jupiter's album the previous year, and featuring a duet with Dale Krantz Rossington, wife of former Lynyrd Skynyrd guitarist Gary Ross-ington. Considering Meat's previous objections to a Steinman track like 'Stark Raving Love', for being too formulaic in the *Bat* mould, it's disappointing how dreary and formulaic 'Don't You Look At Me' was. Much better, in that department, was the final track 'Fallen Angel', written specifically for Meat Loaf by former Lou Reed and Alice Cooper hotshot guitarist Dick Wagner.

'I'm really happy with this album,' Meat insisted when inter-viewed at the time by *Melody Maker*. 'The only way that it's dif-ferent to me is that the songs are shorter and everything's more concise. All the dramatics are there – that's the one thing no one can take away from me – and I think this one's better produced than the other two. But I'm dealing with Tom Dowd, who's like . . . phew!'

Years later, however, when it no longer mattered, Meat would tell me: 'I *hated* that album. *Midnight at the Lost and Found* was a joke album! We couldn't do a record properly; I knew it was the last album for Epic and they were really trying to control my life! It's like the old saying: "Kick him while he's down." I was down and they were trying to throw in as many kicks as they could.'

He was right. *Midnight* was a dud. Even the cover was sub-dued and downbeat: in place of the heart-leaping fantasy images of *Bat* and *Dead Ringer* came a straight-up black-and-white photo of Meat Loaf's face. Released in May 1983, *Midnight* limped into the shops, making only the slightest of impacts, mostly in the UK where the *Bat* fan base remained loyal enough to get it, briefly, into the Top 10. It barely got into the Australian Top 100 and didn't figure at all at home in America. It did mean the opportunity to tour again and he grabbed hold of that, trekking back through Britain and Europe with an arena show that had some sparkle and buzz. The Meat character onstage still inhabited him, his popularity as a live act, his saving grave during this washout era. He played just sixteen US dates, mostly theatres and auditoriums, and began his European shows at the Monster of Rock festival in Donington, which offered reinforcement of his credentials to the tribal UK rock fans. But for the next seven years it was a case of wash, rinse, repeat.

Despite the nearly twenty million albums of his that Epic had sold over the past six years, the label execs appeared quite happy to see the back of him. Everyone in the industry was interested in taking a meeting with the man who'd recorded one of the biggest-selling albums of all time. But what the singer needed was someone to help guide his career now that Steinman wasn't there to do it for him. Signed by new Arista Records chief Clive Davis – the very man who had poured so much cold water on them when Meat and Jim played him the bare bones of *Bat Out of Hell* in his office back in the seventies – Meat felt he'd found the answer. He knew he'd have to put his best work into whatever he did next, but that was okay. Davis had privately regretted not signing Meat and Jim when he'd had the golden opportunity. Now he saw the chance for redemption in being the man to put Meat Loaf's career back on track.

In May 1984 he began recording *Bad Attitude*. Like its predecessor, it tried to pull off the impossible trick of making a Jim Steinman-like Meat Loaf album – without Steinman. This time, though, it did include two Steinman tracks: Meat's wooden version of 'Surf's Up' – a shorter version of the *Bad For Good* original with the extended fade finale of mandolins, strings, synths, etc. replaced by a much punchier, more generic rock sound, anthemic drums pounding, the guitar offering a back-arching solo.

It sounded blustery and busy enough to be a cracking Meat Loaf tune. But if you knew the original, it made you realise how far away Meat's voice was from that of his former understudy, Rory Dodd. Like comparing a water pistol to a clear running stream.

Then there was 'Nowhere Fast', written by Steinman for the soundtrack to the movie *Streets of Fire*, released the same year. The original featured Meat Loaf refugees Dave Johnstone, Steve Buslowe, Larry Fast, Max Weinberg and Jim on keyboards. It also had Holly Sherwood, a new recruit to the Steinman stable of stars-for-hire, on lead vocals and Rory Dodd adding his usual superb backing vocal beds. The new Meat Loaf version was again ramped up and streamlined to make it single size, but again it failed to please anyone outside the studio.

The return of Steinman's name to the credits on a Meat Loaf album had a greater significance. It signalled the end of legal hostilities between the two. 'We settled that over the phone ourselves because it was stupid for me and Jimmy, who are friends, to do that,' he explained at the time. 'I settled with him, giving him all kinds of publishing and money and things. I did the best I could with Jimmy.'

Five of the remaining seven tracks were penned by Sarah Durkee and Paul Jacobs, now her fiancé, and were, ironically, more in the classic Meat Loaf mould than either of the Steinman add-ons. An obvious highlight was the predictably rabble-rousing title track, which also featured a duet with Roger Daltrey. It's easy to see why commercially it was thought that the addition of The Who singer might add value. Musically, however, it seemed kitchen-sink unnecessary, the two singers sounding so alike with their gruff rocktastic voices, if anything it only underlined again how much Meat's voice had lost over the years. The best track, though, and the only track to break the UK Top 20 as a single, was 'Modern Girl'. Finally, here was something that was grand and catchy enough to have fitted easily on *Bat* or *Dead*

Ringer. Unlike most of the rest of the album, with its now dated-sounding eighties' synth drums and every-trick-in-the-book spangled guitar, 'Modern Girl' sounded new and positive and as if it was actually going somewhere.

The album was recorded in London, and was his first attempt at a real 'band' album. But with Meat now in overall control of production, there were fights and delays. Paul Jacobs, in particular, had no time for co-producer Alan Shacklock, who was eventually fired. 'Take the "schlock" out of Shacklock and you get "hack",' as Jacobs put it at the time. He was replaced by German producer Reinhold Mack, who'd replaced Roy Thomas Baker as Queen's first-choice producer and knew exactly what a hit eighties' rock album should sound like.

They even wrapped the record in a semi-*Bat*-era sleeve – no winged gods or underdressed angels, but another motorcycle, ridden by the kind of junkyard kitten that might have been on a Whitesnake cover, atop a jumble of what looked like smashed and devoured cars. None of it was enough to save the album, though, which eventually sold more than *Midnight* but still came in nowhere fast in America. It did give Meat Loaf another Top 10 hit, briefly, in Britain, where he again returned to tour. Interviewing him while he was in London for three sold-out shows at the Hammersmith Odeon – a climb-down from his two sell-out shows at triple-the-size Wembley Arena on his previous visit – it was clear he was not happy. His band members seemed to tiptoe around him, his entourage of road managers and record company flunkies all happy to leave him be in his dressing room. I attempted a chat, a warm-up to the interview proper, whenever he deemed the time 'right'. But it was clear he didn't want to know. Not right then. Maybe later.

The show itself was strange. Like watching a once-successful star now in his cups, still sporting the big-stage motorcycle and the female accompanying singer – two blondes this time, in the enchanting forms of Doreen Chanter and Katie Mac – but with the feeling of everything having been reduced in size. It wasn't Meat Loaf that had got smaller, it was the pictures. The theatricality was there, even if the voice wasn't quite always. But instead of the days of wonder, when you peered at the big guy in the frilly shirt and braces and wondered what world he'd really come from, this was the monster let loose without cover.

During the tour, Leslie's health gave out. Meanwhile, the album's American release was delayed until April 1985, and featured a slightly different track list, as well as alternate mixes for some of the tracks. It didn't matter. Nobody was paying much attention any more. Once again, plans for a lengthy US tour were quietly dropped in favour of more shows back in Britain and Europe.

Meat Loaf's opening act on the UK tour was British hopefuls Terraplane (who would find chart success of their own a few years later renamed Thunder). They recall the tour now as being tense and often awkward. According to singer Danny Bowes, Meat Loaf was 'a total plonker. One night he came bursting into our dressing room in Newcastle, and the bass guitar was behind the door, and he slams the door right into it. The bass is smashed, fucking ruined. So I thought, "I'm gonna get you back – I don't care if it takes the whole tour." And sure enough, last date of the tour we're backstage and, as part of his rider Meat Loaf's got this massive buffet. So I thought, right.

'I get this salver with salad on it and I take it into our dressing room and do a massive shit right in the middle of it. And I've been drinking Guinness for days, right, so it's huge and totally black – it's a big black eel on the middle of this plate. So I put it back and arrange it with the salad and all that so that it looks lovely: a little bit of cucumber here, a sprig of parsley there. It looked delicious. So we go and do the gig, and when we come back the plate is empty – had it all been eaten?'

You might ask how far down could he possibly go?

The answer was: whether he actually ate the shit or not, Meat Loaf had a long way to go before he would ever be able to clean up again.

CHAPTER TWENTY

Love in the Dark

In 1986, Meat Loaf recorded and released *Blind Before I Stop*, and went on tour, just as he had with his previous two albums. Only this time there were no hits at all – anywhere. Not even in Britain, where the album spent one week dangling from the Number 28 spot. His confidence, always so fragile, began to crack and then shatter. He literally didn't know what to do next. The eighties were so different to the seventies. Hard-working guitarists and drummers had been replaced by stoic-faced synth players and no-faced drum machines. I ran into Meat Loaf a couple of times that year and he seemed lost, unsure of which role he should be playing. We did a bit on a cable TV show together and he was hung up on every little detail. He didn't seem able to relax. But he was willing to try anything, it seemed. He would happily play the buffoon if that's what was required. Or he could play the seen-it-all rock guy whose life was on the road, playing for all the good people. The only part he was absolutely not prepared to consider was that of the has-been rock star. Yet that's who he now most resembled both on and off the stage – and, most painfully of all, he knew it. Musically, without a permanent band, he was happy to work with anyone, anywhere, anytime – anyone who knew how to bring him another hit.

Apparently reconciled to establishing a fresh musical identity, untouched by Steinman-like flourishes or stylistic quirks, he placed himself entirely in the hands of the German producer-writer, Frank Farian. It was an astonishing move that reeked of desperation. Farian was the forty-five-year-old singer, writer and producer behind kitsch disco act Boney M. In the late seventies, Farian had led Boney M to eight Number 1 singles in Germany, three Number 1 hits in Britain, and dozens of Top 10 hits across Europe. But Boney M was considered an irrelevance, in rock circles, and Farian, now a multimillionaire, craved the credibility that working with an accepted album-artist like Meat Loaf might confer. Meat, meanwhile, was now desperate for a hit and Farian hadn't missed yet.

Recorded in 1986 at Farian's favoured studio in Munich, using his usual select session team of German and Scandinavian musicians and singers, the result was a truly bizarre collection of join-the-dots, made-in-the-shade-of-the-recording-console contrivances seemingly glued together by sheer force of will. Meat received a co-writing credit on three of the eleven tracks, including the excruciatingly over-the-top opening track, 'Execution Day', most of which belonged to Dick Wagner, minus his tough-love guitar, fed instead into the Farian sausage-machine of synths and indoor fireworks. Closer to home was the power ballad that Meat is credited with writing with his live band bassist John Golden, 'One More Kiss (Night Of The Soft Parade)', but the closest it came to emulating the glories achieved in the same department by Jim Steinman was the use of brackets in the title of the song. The title track was the worst of the three, co-written by the singer, with bassist Golden and another live band cohort Paul Christie. And of course there was the by now predictable duet with a fairly unknown female singer, in this case former Boney M backing vocalist Amy Goff, on the track 'A Man And A Woman'. Like some awful outtake from the *Top Gun* soundtrack, released the same year, that didn't make it because it wasn't as good as the Teena Marie track.

Smothered in Frank Farian's cluttered, what-does-this-button-do production, *Blind Before I Stop* became the runt of the Meat Loaf back catalogue, the air of desperation emanating from it was a million miles away from the daring, timeless qualities that made *Bat* and *Dead Ringer* (and *Bad For Good*) which made Meat Loaf such a deeply compelling proposition nearly ten years before.

What really summed up the whole sorry enterprise was the lead single, 'Rock'n'roll Mercenaries', which featured another power duet, this time with then briefly famous British singer John Parr, who had sung the title song to Brat Pack 'classic' movie *St Elmo's Fire* – and an American Number 1 – the previous year. (He had also written 'Cheating In Your Dreams' for *Bad Attitude*, but now he was famous and so qualified for co-billing.) If the title of the album, *Blind Before I Stop*, seemed horribly prophetic, in retrospect, the title of the single with Parr, 'Rock'n'roll Mercenaries', positively reeked of hubris. Written by Leo Sayer guitarist Al Hodge (and his little-known American co-writer Michael Dan Ehmig) if the song was trite (*'Money is power and power is fame!'* indeed) the video is testimony to just how low Meat Loaf was now stooping in order to save his dwindling recording career. A somewhat slimmed-down Meat, his hair slicked back and his face a mask of pretend intensity, plays a Union Jack guitar while Parr, his hair similarly slicked back, his face similarly distorted in mock anguish, plays a Stars and Stripes guitar – cos he's British and Meat is American, geddit? Then halfway through this excruciating spectacle, a young woman of no fixed purpose gets up and begins cavorting 'sexily' in front of them. She also has slicked-back hair and a very tight, short white skirt. She has also forgotten what it's like to smile. It's as if they've been so taken by the Robert Palmer video for 'Addicted To Love', released a few months before, they've decided to do their own version – that is, have some androgynous girls in the video, not all dressed in black like the Palmer classic, but in white. Oh wait, they had.

As far as anyone in the real world still cared, *Blind Before I Stop* became prima-facie evidence that Meat Loaf's once-extraordinary talents were now spent. That he had lost his way so thoroughly in the eighties there was simply no way back for him. The end point of a tawdry decade in which all the records he made without Jim Steinman were lame by comparison. There was always a reason for this, of course, at least to his mind: the producer was wrong, time ran out, and of course the ongoing background noise of the endless legal and financial wrangles he was forced to struggle against throughout this time.

There were now only straws to clutch at. A bit part as a bad guy gunrunner in the vigilante Edward Woodward TV vehicle, *The Equalizer*, small, offbeat parts in movies, including playing a dialogue-free mute in the movie *The Squeeze*, trying to both kill and make love to Rae Dawn Chong. 'My death scene is where I have my one line in the whole movie. I say: "I coulda loved ya." This after I've handcuffed her, thrown her around the room and sweated on her . . . it was wild!' Then there was *Out of Bounds*, another action thriller in which he played 'a pharmacist gone bad' who eventually 'got shot in the head in that one and blown up!' Not that he would do absolutely *anything*, turning down a part in *Texas Chainsaw Massacre II* because, he said: 'Rapists, someone who chainsaws people, I'm not gonna play that stuff. It's just stupid.' Yeah . . .

He claimed that he also turned down a guest part in the quintessentially eighties TV cop show, *Miami Vice* 'Twice!' The *Blind Before I Stop* track 'Standing On The Outside' – written by the songwriting team of Steve George, John Lang, Richard Page, who had just penned two US Number 1 singles the previous year for Mr. Mister – was featured during the third season of the show, during the episode titled 'Forgive Us Our Debts' (first aired 12 December 1986). *Blind Before I Stop* also became the first Meat

Loaf album officially released in the former USSR. But these were meagre comforts. The only song from the album that settled in the live show over the next five years was 'Masculine', a ZZ Top synth-guitar-style rocker co-written by gun-for-hire guitarist Rick Derringer, former Arrows guitarist Jake Hooker and lyricist Bernard Kenny. Once it dropped out of the set in 1992, though, it never reappeared.

Yet the more Meat Loaf fought to protect his name, continue his career, build something new, the quicker his luck seemed to be running out.

Back on tour, during the first of two nights at London's Wembley Arena, in March 1987, when he invited John Parr onstage to join him for 'Rock'n'roll Mercenaries', for some insane reason he forgot to actually introduce the singer. Parr stayed and sang the song, then stormed off. Despite endless phone calls and messages of apologies and deep regret, John Parr never spoke to Meat Loaf again.

While he was away touring, Leslie was at home trying to hold it all together. They separated briefly when he had a mad half-hour with a woman from Australia, but he realised he was just running away again, as he had done when his mother was ill, as he had done when fame first overtook him, and as he had now with his career crumbling around him. Leslie, an intelligent woman who wasn't about to quit now after all they'd been through together, agreed to a reconciliation.

And standing behind him, always in the shadows, would be Jim. As Meat Loaf spent the next five years stumbling around Europe in support of one limp album after another, Jim Steinman now bestrode America, raking in cash and acclaim. He revelled in his role, accepting that after the bruising experience of *Bad For Good*, this was what he was really born to do: writing sensational, inimitable songs and finding the right outlet for them. On both 'Total Eclipse' and 'Making Love . . .' he maintained control, using musicians he picked – Roy Bittan and Max Weinberg, Steve Buslowe on bass and Rick Derringer on guitar (the latter two were playing in Meat Loaf's touring band – who knew how he felt having guys on stage who were having the kind of charts hits he used to have but that now seemed as distant as a comet).

Jim worked piecemeal but he had a golden touch: he contributed another song called 'Faster Than The Speed Of Night' to Bonnie Tyler's album of the same name, and it quickly went platinum. In 1984, he wrote 'Holding Out For A Hero' for Tyler to sing for the *Footloose* soundtrack, and produced Billy Squier's double-platinum album *Signs of Life*. He worked briefly – and unsuccessfully – with Def Leppard on the *Hysteria* album. He wrote two songs for Walter Hill's film *Streets of Fire*, 'Tonight Is What It Means To Be Young', a quite monumental tune that opens with what appears to be about three choruses, and 'Nowhere Fast', both of which were sung by Holly Sherwood and mimed by the actors in the movie. (Jim thought the script was poor, and his opinion was borne out by weak box office returns.) Barry Manilow had a Top 20 US hit with 'Read 'Em And Weep', and Barbra Streisand recorded 'Left In The Dark' as the lead single from her multi-platinum 1984 record *Emotion*. Meat Loaf's new label Arista allowed him to record 'Nowhere Fast' and 'Surf's Up' for *Bad Attitude*, but the magic was missing, especially from 'Surf's Up', a song that would have been right in his wheelhouse before the vocal problems, the lawsuits, the bankruptcy, the broken relationships, before the whole fucking shithouse went up in flames.

Like dark twins, once they were separated, as one's star rose the other's had to fall . . . the power that they had wielded together not halved, not shared equally, but thrown into eternal imbalance. 'If my initial vision had been followed,' Steinman would later tell me, 'if it had just been left as Meat Loaf and Jim Steinman – I actually think it would be a total different history I'd be speaking about. I would have been thrilled to continue with Meat Loaf for twenty years possibly. I still would have done a few things with other artists, but mostly he would have been the mouthpiece for my songs.'

But now Meat Loaf was so far out of the loop there was no way back for him. Not unless Jimmy wanted there to be.

The lower Meat Loaf's stock fell in the eighties it seemed the higher Jim Steinman's climbed. He now thought of himself as omnipotent in the studio. The man who could take ashes and turn them into diamonds. He even wrote a theme tune for wrestler Hulk Hogan, then the biggest star of the squillion-dollar WWF franchise. What couldn't Jim do that wouldn't be just great?

He stumbled badly, though, when he agreed to produce a new album for young Brit-rock stars Def Leppard. The band's 1983 album *Pyromania* had sold over six million copies in America, only kept from the Number 1 spot there by Michael Jackson's *Thriller*. A year on they were ready to start work on the follow-up, for which even greater things were expected by their record company, Mercury. Only snag: Leppard's own superstar Svengali producer, Robert John 'Mutt' Lange – the South African ex-pat whose production genius had made stars of the Boomtown Rats, AC/DC and Foreigner (and these days is best known for his triumphs with Shania Twain, Lady Gaga and Maroon 5) – was unavailable, burned out after finishing work on The Cars' album *Heartbeat City*, destined to become his latest multimillion-selling success story.

Searching around for someone of equal stature to fill Mutt's shoes in the studio, Leppard hit on the idea of bringing in Jim Steinman. Like Mutt, Jim came with a reputation as a million-per-cent hit-maker with his own musical vision and unique way in a studio of bringing it about. Once they got in the same room, though, things almost immediately fell apart. 'I don't think he really had any idea what we were about as a band,' Leppard guitarist Phil Collen would tell me. 'It wasn't just the songs – we'd already fleshed out quite a few from doing some pre-production work at rehearsals with Mutt. Steinman just didn't seem to get our sound. I started to wonder if he'd even listened to any of our other records.' It was as if Jim felt the band should have been checking out *his* other records before beginning work with him, not the other way around. 'They'd look at you like these little puppies, "Oooh, what are we going to do?"' he later recalled, dismissively.

When I spoke to Leppard vocalist Joe Elliott, though, he was disdainful of Steinman's ability to control the sessions, hinting that perhaps Jim had grown too reliant in the past on his usual team of studio fixers like Todd Rundgren, Steve Margoshes and John Jansen, who would do the hard yards actually helping the artist lay down basic tracks. He talked of days where the band would be left to fend for themselves while Steinman sat in the studio imperiously waiting for them to get it together. 'All that Jim Steinman knew about the studio was that he didn't like the colour of the carpet.' There were also stories of Steinman hiring a taxi to take him from Amsterdam, where Leppard were recording, to Paris to his favourite restaurant because he was bored with the sessions, and another that he had the entire floor and lobby of his hotel redecorated at Leppard's expense because he didn't like the colour scheme.

Rumours that he bitterly refuted over the years. 'It was crazy! I'd love to know where this stuff comes from. The latest on the taxi story is that someone heard that it was really a plane I chartered! I said, great, I like that one. We'll say that's true . . .'

Eventually the band called time and Jim was fired. Joe Elliott told me that as far as he was concerned, working with Steinman had amounted to 'two months in wasted studio time'. Speaking five years later, Jim was still adamant that the fault was never his. 'It was a weird time.' He shrugged. 'I went to Dublin to meet the band, where they were living in tax exile. They're great kids, but they were like little boys lost . . . It's a very bizarre set-up there.

I got sick of it . . . Mutt did almost everything. He created them, and they were lost without him. I knew I was in trouble when we were in Amsterdam recording, and Joe comes in the studio going, "Hey, Jim! I saw a really fucking brilliant film last night, man." I asked what it was and he said, "Police *Academy III*." I said, "Oh, God. Great, was it, Joe?" and he said, "Oh yeah, much better than *Police Academy II*." Then it was just a question of – if I quit then I wouldn't get paid any money. So I held out until they canned me.'

The Def Leppard fiasco was quietly swept under the carpet while Jim went away and concentrated on repairing his reputation as a rock producer by working with American singer-guitarist Billy Squier on *Signs of Life*, ironically a job he was offered because Mutt Lange, originally hired for the job, was now busy working with Def Leppard again. This time, however, things worked as they were supposed to. The album yielded Squier's biggest US hit single, 'Rock Me Tonite' and the album sold a million copies. Life was good again. It was for Jim anyway.

CHAPTER TWENTY-ONE

I Would Do Anything

Jim Steinman's golden touch lasted until 1989, when he wrote and produced another complete album, *Original Sin*, for which he compiled a group of four female vocalists he called Pandora's Box. The record was lush and dark, a meditation on the dangers of sex in a post-HIV world, and it contained songs that would go on to be worldwide hits and sell in their millions, though not for Pandora's Box. Jim played up to the role of a modern-day Phil Spector, urging the girls – Elaine Caswell, Gina Taylor, Ellen Foley and Holly Sherwood – to the heights of excess and delirium while dressed head to toe in black, his now-silver mane halfway down his back, midnight sunglasses permanently on, and accompanied now by a pair of black leather gauntlets that he wore for almost every photo shoot, part Spector, part Helmut Newton.

Steinman primed the rock press with outlandish stories of how the album was inspired by the original myth of Pandora – first woman of the underworld, made by gods and Titans and armed with the gifts of beauty, persuasion, music and, above all, curiosity. Placed inside a jar (later mistranslated as a box) which once opened lay siege to mankind, which had previously lived in joyless, unharmed ignorance, Pandora was a punishment, a warning, an inescapable fate, the only ideal left inside the box after it was resealed being that of hope. Without hope, no dreams, no desires, no tomorrow.

Boy did this Pandora chick sound hot when Jimmy put it like that.

But of course the album was constructed from far more prosaic materials. Still alienated from Meat Loaf, gorged on having hits with other artists that were neither Meat nor himself, Jim still dreamed of having his name up in lights. Still yearned to make the perfect rock opera. Still had all these songs and words and ideas for shows that he wanted to make something of, come what may. He also really dug the idea of working exclusively with women singers. Not like Barbra Streisand, who'd had the big hit with 'Left Behind' but saw Steinman as just another grist-to-the-mill tunesmith out to make a dollar; nor Barry Manilow who had a hit with 'Read 'Em And Weep', but only after he'd smoothed it over with a verse or two of his own, nor even Bonnie Tyler, who owed her career to 'Total Eclipse Of The Heart' but now followed her own path. Jim wanted to put together his own girl vocal group, the way things used to be done in the old Teen Pan Alley days of Phil Spector and Burt Bacharach, Tamla Motown and the Brill Building. He wanted a musical force he could write for, sing and play for, produce, lead and *control*. 'I really wanted to do a girls' group very badly,' he explained at the time. 'Either that or I just wanted girls; I'm not sure which it was. But I was trying to combine professional and personal concerns.'

He said that he wanted to emulate sixties' gutter-pop sirens The Shangri-Las. 'They wore black leather, they had long black hair, they were really filthy, they came from Queens, New York. Everybody in Queens, New York, is really filthy, but not everyone in Queens, New York, wears leather. That's the reason they were stars and the other people from Queens, New York, are real schmucks.'

More seriously, he went on to explain how The Shangri-Las were the first self-styled bad girls in pop, the original Pop Pandoras, progenitors for every kohl-eyed, better-than-sex rock chick that followed, from Patti Smith and Debbie Harry to Chrissie Hynde and Courtney Love. Moreover, how influential The Shangri-Las were to Jim Steinman – and therefore Meat Loaf. Listen back to their hits, like 'Leader Of The Pack', with its revving motorcycle and tale of doomed teen love, or 'Remember (Walking In The Sand)', with its unusual-for-the-times bracketed title, and 'Give Him A Great Big Kiss', with its deliciously spoken word verses, all with their own sound effects and kaleidoscopic production by Shadow Morton. This was Phil Spector, but taken back to the street and left overnight in an alley to sweat.

The listed members of Pandora's Box, whose pictures were allowed on the album sleeve, were Elaine Caswell, whose working relationship with Jim went all the way back to *The Dream Engine*, and who Steinman claimed he had first spotted singing in a New York new-wave bar band where he was 'blown away' by her voice and 'the looks of an avenging angel'. Then Deliria Wilde, who'd most recently worked with Jim on the *Streets of Fire* soundtrack, and who Jim now described as a singer of 'Cuban, French, Italian and German descent, in that order' who was thrown out of a nunnery five years before 'for something so shocking I can't bring myself to tell you what it is'; Gina Taylor, a striking Canadian stage performer and future backing singer to Kelly Clarkson, then playing Tina Turner – 'as well as Tina ever did it!' – in a downtown production called *Beehive* – and Ellen Foley. Foley's solo career had stalled in 1983 when she released her final album for Epic, her part in the Meat Loaf story all but forgotten as first Karla DeVito stole her thunder, then those that had followed as Meat's 'love interest'. Since then she'd had bit parts in hit Hollywood movies, *Fatal Attraction*, *Cocktail* and *Married to the Mob*, and was playing the lead as Sally Smith in a modest stage production of *Me and my Girl* in New York. She leapt at the chance of working with Jim Steinman again. Also on the album, though not pictured, was Holly Sherwood, who'd been part of Steinman's dream team of vocalists, alongside Rory Dodd, since working with Bonnie Tyler; and Laura Theodore, a jazz-oriented singer also able to belt out rock classics. (She would later achieve a small measure of fame playing Janis Joplin in the 1994 stage musical *Love, Janis*.)

'I think rock music hasn't been reflecting current sexual attitudes,' Jim proclaimed grandly. 'Rockers are still coming out with the same macho, party-down bullshit. I wanted to write an album that sums up the last ten years. What I saw coming out of the AIDS epidemic, as with all plagues, was a plus side. This one is that it's restored sex as something dark and magical and terrible. I was a teenager right when sex was going from being overtly repressed in the early sixties to totally free in the seventies and it was very confusing. Shit, I remember shaking like a leaf the first time I was having sex. Terrified I was doing everything wrong, and a little bit horrified.'

Musically, alongside the collection of top-drawer NY session players, it was the usual suspects used by Steinman for the recording: Roy Bittan, Steve Buslowe, Steven Margoshes, Todd Rundgren, Rory Dodd . . . and the welcome return of the New York Philharmonic Orchestra, albeit in ghost form. The album seemed vastly overpopulated with singers and musicians, but it all made sense inside Jim Steinman's grey-haloed head. His strange genius was in evidence from the first line of the first song, 'Original Sin (The Natives Are Restless Tonight)', sung in her deep, sultry voice by Theodore over Jim's melodramatic piano chords: '*I've been looking for an original sin/One with a twist and a bit of a spin . . .*' From there the song starbursts into grand rock opera, the entire cast of singers flocking over the rumbling thunder of the music, as Foley and Taylor trade lead lines, six minutes of love and glory and blood and a broken porcelain moon.

The lead-off single was a grand, gothic ballad that dripped with heightened orchestrated sadness, called 'It's All Coming Back

To Me Now', breathtakingly sung by Caswell and featured in a video directed by Ken Russell (the filming of which went on for some days at Pinewood studios near London, with Jim cheerfully paying for the overtime from his own pocket). This was classic Steinman-as-latter-day-pop-saint, diviner of celestial melodies and complicated feelings you had to have lived long past midnight to have experienced first-hand: *'There were nights of sacred pleasure/ It was more than any laws allow!'*

In the same vein was the ironically titled 'Safe Sex', sung by Gina Taylor about a love made so far over the rainbow there isn't any way back. About what happens when innocence is gone and life is out of control and all you're left with is each other, for good or ill. 'I hate the term "safe sex",' Jim said. 'Sex has never been safe. It's about having the heart, the brain and the body totally exposed, and that's fucking dangerous. The girl in "Safe Sex" is saying, "You can't fool me. I don't believe in these absurd little fairy tales about love."'

'It Just Won't Quit', with Caswell taking the lead, is another heaven-and-hell ballad brought back from the edge of the world. Stunning and heartrending and as deliciously contrived as a big Hollywood ending – except the ending belonged to yet another love-times-death, black swans, green moons and deviant sex done with a tender smile master ballad, 'The Future Ain't What It Used To Be'. Stretched like bandages across ten bloodied but unbowed minutes of pomp and circumstance, as a show closer it's a peach. Just when you thought Steinman couldn't possibly shoot his spangled vision any further over the horizon, he takes it one giant leap further.

The rest of the tracks were equally stunning, though not nearly for the same reasons. An eclectic mix of cover versions – taking 'Twentieth Century Fox' by The Doors and transforming it into something three times as long and ten times as extravagant, replete with the bugling theme tune to Twentieth Century Fox films announcing its arrival for reasons that can only thought to be ridiculous; sampling Verdi's 'Requiem Mass' and simply re-titling it 'Requiem Metal', again for no particular reason anyone but Jim could think of; a dance-floor-thumping version of 'Little Red Book' by Burt Bacharach, based not on Burt's *What's New Pussycat* soundtrack original, but closer in style to Love's psyched-out 1966 version, except longer – obviously. And, finally, most shameless and defiant and delightfully unnecessary, 'The Opening Of The Box', which is literally a two-minute cut-and-paste of the latter half of Jim's Bernard Herrmann-inspired 'The Storm' from *Bad For Good*. Either Jim didn't care what people thought any more or he'd spent so much money hiring the New York Philharmonic to record the stirringly strident original, he felt he owed it to himself to at least give the old engine another spin. Few had bought *Bad For Good* anyway, so who would know? Or care? Then there was the obliquely titled 'Pray Lewd', a three-and-a-half-minute piano instrumental comprising Steve Margoshes reprising snatches of 'Original Sin', 'It's All Coming Back To Me Now' and 'It Just Won't Quit'. Self-indulgent to the point of sickly, so arch as to be hysterical, pointless yet brilliant, coming towards the end of the album it no longer mattered why. If you'd come this far everything made sense, nothing was real. Assuming you still even wanted it to be.

'Every time I finish a record, I always play it back to back with *Bat*,' Steinman revealed. 'This is certainly [my] most committed and unified [album] since *Bat*. It's also much darker than anything else I've done and it's very intimate. I think it's real smoky, a pagan album. I didn't want the girls to be hyperactive like all the girls in heavy metal bands. They look like they've got a ferret in their trousers, just trying to imitate guys. I wanted them to be real still and powerful, like ice goddesses.' He paused for effect, then added: 'There are so many girly girl singers now. I wanted this to be majestic and soaring.'

Of course, no Jim Steinman masterwork would be complete without its anthemic hymn to rock'n'roll dreams coming through on the back of flame-winged motorcycles. Here we had the ultimate in post-modern female empowerment anthem, flipping the switch on the boys: 'Good Girls Go To Heaven (Bad Girls Go Everywhere)' . . . 'Hey Johnny, Johnny . . . now you know what it's like to be damned.'

And of course there always had to be a grandiose monologue – though on this very special album there would be *three*. The first, which opens the album, titled 'The Invocation', spoken by Ellen Foley, is only twenty-one seconds long but speaks of the endless night and a lover who is 'darker than sin' – and is in fact a five-line scrap from Jim's lost but not forgotten *Neverland* musical. This segues noisily into the notional title track. 'I wrote the title track trying to cross the sixties' girl groups with Marlene Dietrich,' explained Jim. 'You know, platinum blonde hair and a long nightgown. From that it was an easy leap to The Shangri-Las. I wanted this project to be as though *Clockwork Orange* was about girls. The idea was never to have three back-up singers, but four girls, all singing.'

The second monologue, spoken this time by Jim himself, is a much more substantial piece titled 'I've Been Dreaming Up A Storm Lately'. This time it actually feels like a wavy line drawn straight from the subconscious, though of course it is as worked out in the minutest detail as everything Jim does. There's a lot of rambling about mirrors and their meaning, none of which made any sense – until nearly ten years later when the same monologue reappeared in an early draft of *Dance of the Vampires*, aka *Tanz der Vampire*, a musical remake of the 1967 Roman Polanski mock-horror movie of the same name. A future echo, perhaps? Maybe. But then Jim maintained that much of his thinking for the songs on *Original Sin* came from his morbid fascination with the undead and their burden of eternal love: another kind of

Neverland, where no one grows any older, just weird and weirder (and weirder).

The third monologue, again spoken, or rather yelled, by Foley, is another refugee from the orphaned *Neverland* stage show, re-configured here as 'The Want Ad'. This is the best of the three, though: incongruous, gory, lustful, funny, ashamed, demented, and eventually . . . polite. It's a tour de force, but how it is sup-posed to be received in this context is unclear. Except as a darkly comic stand-alone, which is more than enough.

Cut away the instrumentals, the monologues and provocative cover tunes and you were left with seven Steinman masterpieces – the same number as on *Bat Out of Hell*. And though no one had the insight or courage to say so at the time, *Original Sin* was a record that would ultimately stand alongside *Bat Out of Hell* as one of Jim Steinman's great achievements. And yet when it was released to great promotional fanfare in 1989, it flopped almost everywhere. As he told the writer Sylvie Simmons: 'When I was seven years old I had this fortune-teller who turned out to be a hooker disguised as a fortune-teller, so I don't know how valid it was – read my fortune in Times Square, New York. And she said I would spend my whole life in an ultimately self-destructive drive to astonish people. So every ambition I have is to keep astonish-ing and amplifying normal life . . .'

It was the kind of self-deluding, apologist rhetoric he'd been feeding himself since the days when so-called experts told him to abandon what he did and try to at least write a three-minute hit. In private, he was furious, thwarted, devastated. Jim had put everything into Pandora's Box, including a significant chunk of his sizeable fortune.

A ten-year journey that had begun in penury now ended in decadence for him. He would say that when he gave 'Making Love Out Of Nothing At All' to Air Supply (or 'two boring idiots from Australia', as he memorably described them) he did it because he needed the money in the post-*Bat* legal freeze, but there was something more interesting going on, too. Essentially Air Supply and Bonnie Tyler were underdogs, just like Meat Loaf. There was something in Jim, and in his songs, that made him and them work best when that dynamic was in play, when they were placed in the mouths of the unlikely and the unblessed, of the dumped and the passed-over.

They were heroic songs sung by losers. That was when they worked. That was how they worked.

It was as if Jim was writing for the part of him that found human contact difficult, who didn't look or sound like a cool kid or a potential star. He found the people who fit that notion and he gave them heartbreakingly beautiful, brilliantly bitter, wonderfully ornamented songs of revenge and lust and lost moments that struck deep chords with millions of people who felt all of those emotions echoing through their own lives. Ugly ducklings destined in their own hearts to become swans. Beasts turned improbably beautiful whom Jim Steinman had bestowed with powerful and mysterious gifts.

Why hadn't it worked with Pandora's Box? Because Pandora's Box was never seen as a group of underdogs, outsiders fighting for their lives. Quite the opposite, the band came wrapped in so much can't-possibly-fail, Steinman-as-messiah hyperbole the public was simply expected to roll over and lap it up. But the public choked. Too much sugar, too much muchness, it was like the *Bat* generation had grown out of their lost boys and golden girls selves and could no longer swallow whole Jim Steinman's vainglorious musical conceits.

The predictably excess-all-areas video for 'It's All Coming Back To Me Now' said it all. Directed by Ken Russell, creator of Oscar-winning films like *Women in Love*, *Tommy* and *Altered States*, and a man whose taste for mixing sex with fantasy, religion and death, whose filmic flamboyance was a match for Fellini, was exactly the kind of director Jim Steinman had wished for in his own various dream states. Visiting the set on a large soundstage at Pinewood Studios, the author Jon Hotten recalls dancers from the London production of *Cats* being, as he wrote: 'strapped into bondage gear at Russell's direction. Studded codpieces, tight leather jock-straps and dangerously spiked brassieres abound. Softened up by months of jumping around to Andrew Lloyd Webber, Ken and Jim have come as something of a shock to them.

'A complicated series of choreographed jumps are supposed to take them up to an imposing plinth, inset with powerful lights, where they're to surround Pandora's Box singer Elaine Caswell. Elaine, who is wrapped only in a thin gauze sheet, is suffering without complaint a painfully burned backside every time the plinth lights are switched on. She is due to be surrounded by the bondage-freak cats who, for the purposes of Steinman's script, are to kiss and caress her back from a self-imposed coma.

'Easy, eh? Apparently not. "For fuck's sake!" roars Ken, not happy. "Just cut this prancing around. I don't want that. Remember: only undulate on "Baby, baby." And . . . playback!" Now, just the motorcycle blazing on graveyard railings, a horse in a ring of fire and the snake crawling across the unfortunate Elaine's stomach remain to be shot from Steinman's typically lavish video script.'

But not even Ken Russell could find a plausible way to depict Steinman's original plan for the denouement. This called for a motorcycle to be ridden madly up a church bell tower until it reached the top and burst through a stained-glass turret window, Elaine still astride . . .

CHAPTER TWENTY-TWO

Shut Out The Night

From the jaw-droppingly hubristic notion of making a nearly eight-minute debut video in the here-today-gone-later-today age of quick-fire MTV vids, replete with sixty-second Steinman monologue (and moody rock-star pic) over the intro about 'horny angels' stalking the streets and motorcycles that 'reproduce in nocturnal allies groaning with greasy pleasure', to the conventional wisdom of ensuring that none of the female singers in the video – all in various leather pleasure outfits, bound, hanging, or stuck atop pedestals like erotic chess pieces – could possibly be described as ugly ducklings. This was Jim having his cake and shovelling it right down the audience's throats. Motorcycles on fire, with young women draped over them in a trance; muscled male sentinels drawing their gauntleted hands across the women's breasts and thighs; vipers, blood-letting, human sacrifice, lesbian orgies . . . Watching Meat Loaf forcing his tongue down Karla DeVito's throat in 1978 was a genuinely transgressive experience that said something about accepted (and unaccepted) sexual mores, about preconceptions, in rock'n'roll as in life. It didn't make you flinch so much as sit up and rethink your own position.

Ten years on, watching the Pandora's Box video was simply cringe-making. Like hooking up to an adult movie channel in an upscale hotel: expensive, improbable, soft porn for people who still thought reading *Playboy* was a dirty thing to do.

It served the song – which should have been a giant hit – not at all. It merely serviced Jim Steinman's now planet-sized ego. Everything louder than everything else! To the max! Until it just made you sick.

But while Jim was busy blowing himself up, Meat was simply blown away. For Meat Loaf the five years that followed *Blind Before I Stop* were a rapid and soul-destroying descent into the realms of has-been and once-upon-a-time. Arista had agreed to one last release, a double live album, offhandedly titled *Live at Wembley*, and taken from two shows at Wembley Arena in March 1987 – including the snafu involving John Parr. Made cheaply and produced by Meat Loaf's brother-in-law Tom Edmonds, less than half the album was made up of *Bat*-era songs, and it became the worst-selling of Meat Loaf's career, limping to Number 60 in the UK and exactly nowhere everywhere else.

He could still sell tickets to his shows in Britain and Germany, where he did a combined total of twenty-nine shows out of the thirty-four he undertook in 1987, but America had left him behind. He hadn't had a hit song on the radio there since 'You Took The Words Right Out My Mouth' ten years before. When he did finally perform in America again, in 1988, he was playing small nightclub joints like The Chance in Poughkeepsie (capacity: 1,000), The Chestnut Cabaret in Philadelphia (similar), The Stone Balloon in Newark (now an ale house serving 'meatloaf lollipops'). His biggest show back home was at The Ritz in New York, with a capacity of 1,500, but which he barely filled compared to the sold-out show just two weeks before by a new up-coming American band called Guns N' Roses. MTV had filmed the latter for a special. Meat Loaf couldn't even get his videos aired on the channel. A month after that, Meat Loaf was back in Britain, touring hotspots in Harrogate, Torquay, Newport and Bournemouth. He could still make a splash in London, but no longer at Wembley

Arena, instead he was relegated to the Hammersmith Odeon.

Leslie trained to be a travel agent, so they could save on travel expenses, and there were festival appearances to bolster the name, but even these occasions proved bittersweet, at best. Invited onto the bill for the Nelson Mandela 70th birthday tribute show at Wembley Stadium in June 1988, while still gargantuan acts like Dire Straits (featuring Eric Clapton), George Michael, the Bee Gees – and even ex-Spandau Ballet singer Tony Hadley – were given designated solo spots in which to perform, all Meat was offered was the opportunity to become one of a starry chorus comprising 'Little' Steven van Zandt, Simple Minds, Peter Gabriel, Jackson Browne, Youssou N'Dour and Daryl Hannah performing van Zandt's anti-apartheid anthem 'Sun City'. Meat Loaf's only other appearance that day was to introduce Salt-N-Pepa to the stage to sing their one and only hit so far, 'Push It'.

More ignominy was to follow just two months later when Meat Loaf played second on the bill to Saturday night headliners, Starship. The singer had never had much luck with British festivals. Unconsidered by Bob Geldof for Live Aid in July 1985, Meat Loaf had agreed to appear as special guest at the Knebworth Fair festival, three weeks earlier, headlined by the comeback line-up of Deep Purple. A day now fondly recalled by the 40,000 who were there (including this writer) as Mudworth, because it rained so hard that day, the crowd, even in the VIP area, was forced to wade through two-feet-deep mud just to get a peek of the stage. Having seen his mainstream pop career collapse without Jim Steinman to lift him, Meat Loaf had settled for trying to blend in with the emerging British heavy metal scene of the mid-eighties, as epitomised by Iron Maiden, Ozzy Osbourne and Motörhead. But the metalheads at Knebworth that year were not so easily fooled and they proceeded to rain down bottles and cans on the stage until Meat Loaf finally stormed off, to loud ironic cheers.

Three years on, at the Reading Festival, surely things would be different this time? In fact, they were even worse. The weather was again ominous; the sky knitted with grey thunderclouds. The hardcore metal crowd was antsy that the festival promoters had tried to broaden out the appeal of the show by including more pop, indie and soft rock acts like Run Rig, Deacon Blue, The Wonder Stuff and – heaven forfend! – Bonnie Tyler. The festival had started quietly enough, but midway through Saturday after-noon the crowd could stand it no more and began pelting Bonnie Tyler with bottles, many still full or half full. But Bonnie was the daughter of a Welsh coal miner who'd grown up on a hard-as-nails council estate. It would take more than a few English wank-ers chucking glass to deter her, and she battled through to the end of her set, leaving with a hard-won smile on her face and her dignity intact.

The crowd doubled their efforts for Meat Loaf, however, per-haps sensing weakness. This time he exited the stage after just twenty minutes when a two-litre cider bottle filled with piss hit him full in the face.

During this time there was only one new Meat Loaf track re-leased, a US-only single, 'A Time For Heroes', the official theme tune to the 1987 Special Olympics World Games, an international sporting competition for athletes with intellectual disabilities, held in America every four years. Sung by Meat with Queen guitarist Brian May playing lead, there was a concurrent instru-mental recording by Tangerine Dream of the same track on the B-side. It was precisely the kind of thing guaranteed to muddle the thinking on Meat Loaf in America still further. It was a great cause, a wonderful event, and a terribly cliché song.

By 1989, just as Jim Steinman was preparing to launch Pan-dora's Box onto a largely incredulous world, Meat Loaf looked like a down-and-out by comparison. Without a record deal, his career entirely without focus, he was reduced to taking bookings at such insalubrious venues as Katina's nightclub, in Hadley,

Massachusetts; Brassy's in Cocoa Beach, Florida; and the Bouck Gym, in Cobleskill, New York. The fact was he was not in a position to turn down work. The years of bankruptcy and lawsuits had taken their toll. 'Every time we'd get one case dismissed, they'd throw another one at me,' he recalled in 2003. 'And everybody thinks I had all this money but I didn't, because CBS did not pay my royalties until 1997. I got paid the royalties for *Bat Out of Hell* twenty years later.' No longer a prisoner to his addictions, he kept it together at home by coaching Little League baseball. He told the *Sunday Times* that he also made money from buying and selling property – 'I have a really good eye for doing up properties . . . I am very creative with interior design.'

In 1989, Epic did a deal with Telstar Records, a London-based telemarketing label that specialised in compilations, becoming the past and future home of such credibility-free musical acts as Ant & Dec, Victoria Beckham, Vinnie Jones, The Cheeky Girls and Jive Bunny, to name just a few. It was for a joint Meat Loaf/ Bonnie Tyler album, under the heading: *Heaven & Hell*: fourteen tracks, seven each from both artists, specifically from, in Meat's case, the albums *Bat, Dead Ringer* and *Midnight*; and Bonnie's, *Faster Than the Speed of Night* and *Secret Dreams and Forbidden Fire*. The main thing they had in common, of course, was that Jim Steinman had written ten of the tracks.

Backed by a matchlessly prosaic TV ad campaign, the album went platinum in the UK, hinged to the Top 10 for several weeks leading up to Christmas. For Tyler, this was a boon. Her own *Greatest Hits* had barely made the UK Top 30 three years before. As a career-reviving release for Meat Loaf, though, *Heaven & Hell* was a disaster; yet more proof that the singer was washed up, a has-been, living off the past, feeding on the scraps of dodgy moneymakers such as this. Certainly it did nothing for his touring profile. In 1990 he was back playing Finky's in Daytona Beach; The Moon in Tallahassee; and Pleasure Island in Orlando.

He was also putting himself out there as an opening act for now much bigger American bands like the Allman Brothers, who Meat Loaf supported at Madison Square Garden in New York in September. For a while he even tried stand-up comedy, appearing at small clubs in Connecticut and New York. But when your life has become a joke, it's hard to make fun of the rest of the world and he soon lost enthusiasm for the idea.

Meat Loaf was at home with Leslie and the kids during the Christmas holidays that year, looking forward to an almost empty diary for 1991, the only dates firmed up so far being an appearance at an annual bikers' bash at the Bindoon Rock Festival in Perth, Australia, in February, and more US club dates like a return to Toad's Place, in New Haven, the month after that, when he got an unexpected knock on the door. It was Jim.

Still licking his wounds from the commercial beating that Pandora's Box took, unable to accept that songs of his with the immense chart-owning potential of 'It's All Coming Back To Me Now' and 'Good Girls Go To Heaven (Bad Girls Go Everywhere)' had not been hits, Jim had come up with a new self-validating idea. What if he and Meat Loaf were to work together again? Not on the mean-spirited pro-rata basis they had existed on since *Bat Out of Hell* had shot them like rockets out of a bottle towards the stars all those years before, but, you know, as a team again? What if – and this was the crazy part – they got back together to finally make that sequel to *Bat* that Meat Loaf had apparently been so against the idea of back in 1979, still out of his gourd on booze and drugs and paranoia? The one that Jim stole back from him and tried to turn into a platform for his own career as singing star in his own right? Not *Bad For Good*. Not *Dead Ringer*. But . . . wait for it . . .

BAT OUT OF HELL II!

What would Meat Loaf say to that?

Meat laughed in his face. He thought Jimmy was joking, that

the whole thing was a joke. They couldn't do that? Could they? No! It was a joke! It had to be!

'There was no interest at all to begin with,' Steinman would recall for me. 'Even at MCA, where it ended up in America, it was referred to as a joke openly. It basically came from me – the concept – and Meat Loaf joined in, but at first even he said, "You're fucking crazy!" But I saw it as a cinematic series. Like I always enjoyed the second *Godfather* film more than the first, and the first was great, you know?'

Jim had shown up at Meat and Leslie's house in Connecticut clutching a bunch of songs in two beat-up Bloomingdales' carrier bags. But Meat was still sceptical. Too many years of being the whipped dog, the open joke, the dupe for every music-biz writer and producer looking for an easy payday, had left him cynical of so-called new opportunities. Guarded against his own desperate wish to rebuild his career through the good graces of yet another Svengali – even if this one had once been the source of all his dreams.

Jim Steinman was also nervous, although he would not say so out loud. Nervous that Meat Loaf might not let him through the door. Worried about what he might find left of the emotionally fraught neurotic he had walked out on once upon the long ago. Secretly panicked that perhaps he had lost his magic touch when it came to envisioning large-scale cinematic success. Arrived simply too late to rekindle the spark. Too late for the future, too far gone for the past . . .

The space between the two men had grown vaster than either could cope with, bigger even than success or failure. They didn't know where to begin. Then Jimmy suggested they simply sit at the piano and run through some of their old songs together from *Bat*, letting all of the bullshit – the lawsuits, the money, the bad albums, the bad choices and bad blood – fall away in the lines of the songs they had made so famous together. They realised right then that this was what it was all about. They realised that their names would always be joined together, so why not put them back together and in their original context, this time even bigger and badder than before?

When you said it like that it sounded easy. But they both knew it would not be. What other choice did they have, though, really?

The songs would be darker, the mood more sombre and bruised, a post-storm album for the apocalypse that they had lived through. One twin had risen; the other had endured a precipitous fall. It all came back to them now. If they could pull off a comeback together again, all would be forgiven, though never forgotten.

It was time, and they both felt it.

'I've always been convinced that his vocal chords are directly related to his id,' Jim reflected. 'I think they reflect a lot about what was going on. The weirdest thing is that I honestly said to people in '78, when things were falling apart, that I bet it takes at least a decade [for us to get back together]. To me, the timing of all of this has been so natural . . .'

But the state of Meat loaf's id, as the eighties had seeped like blood through a bandage into the nineties, was one of near total darkness. Resentful of what had happened: still angry, but with the help of Leslie he was accepting and ready to at least try to move on. The past shouldn't hold him back, he knew that. He knew he wanted to work with Jim, to do the thing that they did, however it went, however long it took. He knew that, too. But there were now certain things he wouldn't do.

'I can't sing unless there's a character,' he insisted to anyone that would listen. 'Because I don't sing. It's almost like being schizophrenic – I don't sing, the *character* sings. And if I'm not in touch with my characters on any given night – sort of like channeling – I can't sing.' Jim was amazed to discover that his old friend now forced himself to undergo certain rituals before allowing himself to even step on a stage or in front of a studio mic, with no one allowed to go near him. 'Going into Loafdom,' Leslie called it. 'It's not meditation,' he told the writer Lynn Barber, 'but it almost is. I start focusing. I start humming. I had a dream the other night that there was Bruce Springsteen, me, Freddie Mercury and Robert Palmer, and we're all backstage humming and having a discussion about how we warm up. "Oh I hum too!" It was a very funny little dream.'

And so at first it inched forwards, this raggedy, unforeseen coming together. Pinning Jim down had been difficult because he worked in his own way, like no one else. Sometimes it was difficult enough just finding him, let alone getting some work done. Just like *Bat Out of Hell*, the new record would take almost three years to make, soup to nuts. It began with Jim, as it always must. And once it was done, Jim described how it began this time.

'I started off this whole album with an image of Meat Loaf on stage,' he explained. 'For some reason, I started off with a live show image. "I'd Do Anything For Love (But I Won't Do That)" was the first song I wrote and it was definitely a *Beauty and the Beast* kind of story . . . What he "won't do" is said about six times in the song very specifically. It's sort of a little puzzle and I guess it goes by – but they're all great things. "I won't stop doing beautiful things and I won't do bad things." It's very noble. I'm very proud of that song because it's very much like out of the world of Excalibur. To me, it's like Sir Lancelot or something – very noble and chivalrous.'

But like Sir Lancelot in search of the Holy Grail, distracted by the earthly honours that would come from his knightly prowess, Meat Loaf would again be given only a glimpse of the future that he would spend his life in pursuit of.

For now, though, a glimpse would be more than enough.

CHAPTER TWENTY-THREE

Back Into Hell

'I always said I'd work with [Meat Loaf] again as soon as his voice was back, and he's singing real well now,' Jim Steinman said nonchalantly in an interview with the British writer Jon Hotten in 1990. 'I'm gonna write him the ultimate teenage car-crash death song, which will probably be called "Renegade Angel". It's gonna be wild!'

There goes Jim, I remember thinking. Still harping on about his lost masterpiece the way Captain Hook did his shark-eaten arm. Willing it to come back, against all the evidence to the contrary. As though wishes actually came true.

And yet, three years later, there it was. No, not *Renegade Angel*, the captain resigned finally, it seemed, to the hook, which both hampered him and gave him his death-rattling power. Instead . . .

It was promoted as the long-awaited follow-up. The one everybody had been waiting for, Meat Loaf's Second Coming. And in many ways that's what *Bat Out of Hell II: Back Into Hell*, as Jim grandiosely titled it, was. At least, to the same broadstream audience of moms and pops, kids and bigs, one-album-a-year buyers that had made *Bat Out of Hell* the global phenomenon it became. Just like its progenitor, *Bat II* would leave the avante-rock audience cold, befuddled, even offended by the sheer gall of it. The timing was equally ridiculous. The 1977 *Bat Out of Hell* had been released exactly one week before the zeitgeist-defining Sex Pistols album, *Never Mind the Bollocks . . .* The September 1993 release of *Bat II* came exactly one week ahead of the release of the third Nirvana album, *In Utero*. Like the Sex Pistols and the punk scene they single-handedly created, Nirvana's arrival had signalled what was seen to be a ground zero approach to rock, killing off the kind of ritualistic, richly layered, complex and stately musical manifesto that Meat Loaf and Jim Steinman espoused.

As Mark Cooper, reviewing *Bat II* in *Mojo* put it: 'Like most sequels, *Bat Out of Hell II* bumps up the volume and the budget; everything sounds enormous and lasts longer. More of the same only more so. It will run and run, even if it barely scrapes a mention on those critical histories. Think of it like the latest ride in a theme park and hold onto your stomach.' The two-out-of-five-star review in *Rolling Stone* was more typical of the dismissive attitude of most 'cutting-edge' music magazines: '*Bat II* is 75 minutes of the same harmless, low-octane operatic drivel. But this is the age of safe sex – no groping teens, please, not even a grunt. Just some insufferably long Steinman compositions with equally long names . . .'

The market *Bat II* was being pitched at, though, didn't read those magazines any more, didn't care about Nirvana or Metallica or whomever it was that the *NME* said was cool that week. They listened to the radio, watched TV. If they read music reviews at all any more it would be while browsing newspaper broadsheets or in magazines like *Time*, where they got the real lowdown: 'Anachronistic? Defiantly,' wrote *Time*'s critic Richard Corliss: 'The blood on these guitars is Chuck Berry red. The production reverbs with the heavenly choirs, sleigh bells and mausoleum echoes of Phil Spector's wailing Wall of Sound. The lyric lines are long and chatty, with more pomp to the bomp. *Bat II* is the fifties, sixties and seventies, packed in steel and wrapped in Mylar. Or go back even further. Meat Loaf is not quite Jussi Björling [aka the 'Swedish Caruso'], and Steinman ain't no Wagner, but in rock terms *Bat Out of Hell II* is a Gotterdammerung you can dance to.'

Exactly. What absolutely nobody from the critical elite picked up on, though, was how much *Bat II* represented a Jim Steinman greatest hits collection, more than a brand-new original work. Of the eleven tracks that filled the *Bat II* CD, eight are either new versions of existing Steinman songs or reconfigured ideas from existing Steinman tracks, including four from *Bad For Good*, the real, now lost follow-up to *Bat Out of Hell*. Even the ear-catching title of the album's cornerstone hit, 'I'd Do Anything For Love (But I Won't Do That)' was a recycled line from the Bonnie Tyler track, 'Getting So Excited', from *Faster Than the Speed of Night* – a cover of an obscure Lee Kosmin track from the seventies titled 'Getting So Exciting'. Steinman added one crucial extra component to this, though, on the later Tyler version when his voice breaks in at the end of the second verse, in imitation of the female protagonist, and croons: *'I'd do anything for love but I won't do that . . .'*

None of which took anything away from the gargantuan new Meat Loaf song which opened *Bat II*. Clocking in at twelve minutes dead, this was Meat doing what Jimmy did best, monumental, widescreen Little Wagner-esque rock with a capital 'R'. A dozen different verses, at least two different choruses, three parts to the song and, of course, featuring a duet with, in this case, an unnamed female singer, and not forgetting that riveting verse title, half of it in brackets. Steinman gold. Loaf luxury. Everything more and nothing less, forever and evermore . . .

Naturally the whole thing began with the sound of an over-heated electric guitar revving and roaring like a motorcycle – played by New York session wizard Eddie Martinez, David Lee Roth's original choice to replace Eddie Van Halen when he went solo, who'd also provided the raunchy, buzz-saw guitar to some of Robert Palmer's biggest hits in the eighties and had worked with Steinman on several projects already, including tracks for Bonnie

Tyler and Pandora's Box. In essence it's the 'Bolero' intro to 'Bat Out of Hell' all over again, right down to the gradual descent into a piano-led vocal. This time, though, Jim had an even better trick up his sleeve, by making Meat sing the opening lines as though it was the retrospective finale of the song; '... *and I would do an-y-thing for love* ...' Pulling the listener in before they even know they've been drowned in the riptide of the song.

The most astonishing thing about the intro to 'I'd Do Anything', though, is the sound of Meat Loaf's voice. It's the most beautiful and tender it has sounded since the days when he still had a fluent upper register on swooning, now almost forgotten classics like 'Two Out Three Ain't Bad'. Since the days before he had shredded his gorgeously operatic singing voice into mincemeat with all the booze and drugs and incessant touring. How was this achieved? In the days before pitch-tuning software and simple computerised modifications – common both in the studio and on the stage in today's touch-screen music world – the only way for Jim to have coaxed these performances out of Meat was to have had him sing and record them, verse by verse, line by line, word by word, if necessary, over and over, until made utterly perfect – a technique made familiar by the stunning work of producer Roy Thomas Baker with Freddie Mercury of Queen during their most commercially prolific period, but taken in excelsis here.

The rest of the track is a real rollercoaster ride, even in its drastically edited five-minute single form. Meat Loaf later claimed that while singing it he was inhabited by the spirit of a fifteen-year-old boy. But that's not what he sounds like when singing of not doing 'that' – a metaphorical blank the listener fills in for him with their own fevered imagination (although the specifics of what the singer won't do, if you read the lyrics, are made clear enough, i.e. '*I'd never lie to you* ...'). Meat Loaf sounds like he carries all the emotional pain of a person who has just, belatedly, tragically, discovered the real meaning of life, that sometimes going beyond what you thought possible is merely the start.

As if to illustrate the point still further, just when it seems the singer can add no more to a song already over-endowed with promises and wishes and hopes unfulfilled, comes the latest and perhaps greatest of the Meat Loaf/Jim Steinman female vocalists, Lorraine Crosby, with a whole slew of call-and-response verses of her own, which bring the song to an even more devastatingly desolate climax. *'I know the territory, I've been around,'* she sings with genuine anguish. *'Sooner or later you'll be screwing around . . .'* It's a vocal performance of such unexpected power and emotional accuracy that it finally lifts Meat Loaf out of the realm of rock opera tragi-comedy and into the beneath-decks world of real feelings, real doubt, real payback.

Cruelly, unforgivably, Crosby was not credited for her unsurpassable performance on 'I'd Do Anything', listed simply as 'Mrs Loud'. A British singer from Newcastle, she'd toured with several low-key outfits, both pop and cabaret, before sending Steinman some demos of songs she'd co-written with her multi-instrumentalist boyfriend Stuart Emerson. To her surprise, Jim liked what he heard so much he got in touch and invited Lorraine and Stuart to join him in Los Angeles, where he secured them a deal with MCA, the label that had just signed off on the *Bat II* deal with him and Meat Loaf. Asked by Jim originally to provide guide vocals for Meat Loaf, as he was putting down his first attempts to record his vocals for 'I'd Do Anything', Crosby heard no more until she discovered they had chosen her vocal over that of Cher, Melissa Etheridge and Bonnie Tyler for the duet role in the song. However, because she had technically recorded her parts as mere 'guide vocals' she was not entitled to a credit or even any royalties, despite the track going on to become the biggest-selling single of 1993, reaching Number 1 in twenty-eight different countries, including both Britain and America.

Adding insult to injury, she did not appear in the video for the track, where the model and budding actress Dana Patrick mimed her vocals. And when Meat Loaf promoted the single, making TV appearances all over the world, he did so with American singer Patti Russo performing Crosby's vocal parts. All in a day's work in showbiz, baby, as no doubt Ellen Foley, Karla DeVito and Kati Mac would attest. In a further bizarre twist, however, Crosby *was* credited on the album under her real name for her backing vocals on the tracks 'Life Is A Lemon And I Want My Money Back', 'Objects In The Rear View Mirror May Appear Closer Than They Are' and 'Everything Louder Than Everything Else'.

A minor recognition of sorts was finally afforded the young singer when Meat Loaf arranged for her to join him onstage in December that year, during his show at Whitley Bay Ice Rink, where she took Patti Russo's usual spot onstage for the performance of 'I'd Do Anything'. In years to come, Lorraine Crosby's career would enjoy a strange afterlife, as she performed the song regularly at holiday camp and social club engagements in England, culminating in 2005 when she sang a duet with Bonnie Tyler on the track 'I'll Stand By You' from Tyler's album *Wings*. The same year she appeared as a contestant on ITV's *The X Factor*, performing James Taylor's 'You've Got A Friend' and progressing to the second round before Simon Cowell called a halt, saying she 'lacked star quality'. Nevertheless, she released a solo album three years later, tellingly titled *Mrs Loud*, and in 2013 she appeared on the second series of *The Voice* but got no further than the audition stage after being rejected by all four coaches. Lorraine, it seems, would do anything for love, but she just couldn't quite do *that*.

The video they shot to accompany the 'I'd Do Anything' single was excessive even for those progressively over the top, MTV-dominated times. Directed by twenty-eight-year-old Michael Bay, a graduate of the Jerry Bruckheimer-Don Simpson school of production aesthetics and soon to become better known as the fast-cutting, style-over-substance, explosion-obsessed director of such 'high-concept' action movies as *Armageddon, Pearl Harbor* and the *Transformers* franchise, the seven-and-a-half-minute video for 'I'd Do Anything' perfectly mirrored the convoluted, death-or-glory romance of Steinman's music.

There were two versions of the video released – Bay's extravagant almost-eight-minute spectacular, and a shorter, MTV-friendly version. The concept is based squarely on a cross between the *Beauty and the Beast* story and that of *The Phantom of the Opera*. The full-length version begins with the noise of Eddie Martinez's motorcycle guitars, the words flashing across the screen, 'I Have Traveled Across The Universe Through The Years To Find Her . . .' and then we're off. A cloaked Meat-as-Beast-Phantom roaring towards the city limits on his customised Harley-Davidson pursued by cops on bikes, in cars and helicopters, the outlaw chasing his destiny. Finally he escapes into his mist-encrusted Gothic castle, past crosses and headstones, the cops mysteriously unable to follow up through the gates.

Cut to Meat-Beast-Phantom in profile, his face made up to look very much like a commander of the Klingon Empire, all warts and ridged forehead, as he croons the opening lovelorn lines of the song while regarding his long, werewolf-like fingernails. It's ludicrous, bombastic, laughable even, an overfamiliar, sick-making fairytale we already know the ending to – and that's just the first forty-five seconds.

After that Meat-Beast is back on his bike, riding straight through walls as grand chandeliers crash to the ground, vanquished cops scattered to the four winds as Meat-Beast leaves his bike and begins swinging through a dark forest like an overgrown Quasimodo. The queasy spell only broken by the appearance of the beautiful Dana Patrick, not so much miming to Lorraine Crosby's vocals as slinking around like the lead actress in a soft-porn *Playboy* shoot. At the video's long climax there is the moment when the goddess-like Patrick holds the beast in her tender embrace and – wait for it – he begins to turn human again. If only the beautiful princess had kissed the ugly frog, the way Karla DeVito had all those years before, the moment might have had at least a semblance of pathos. But she doesn't, of course, because that really would have scared the big kids who owned the playlists at MTV.

Filmed on location in LA County in July 1993, the opening chase was shot at Chávez Ravine, with the interior Gothic castle scenes filmed at Ned Doheny's famous old Greystone Mansion in Beverly Hills. The cinematography was by Daniel Pearl, best known for his work on *The Texas Chainsaw Massacre*, who described the video as 'one of my personal all-time favourite projects'. Meat's make-up took two hours a day to apply and was designed to be scary, yet 'with the ability to make him sympathetic'. Filmed over four days in 90-degree heat, naturally the whole thing went madly over budget. According to one executive, it 'probably had the budget of *Four Weddings and a Funeral*' – the hit movie being filmed at around the same time, which had a reported budget of $2.8 million.

The success of the single – and the album that followed in its wake – more than justified the outlay. Released in September 1993, 'I'd Do Anything For Love (But I Won't Do That)' went to Number 1 in almost every country in the world that bought pop singles – including spending seven weeks at Number 1 in Britain – and in the rest it went to Number 2. In January 1994, it won Meat Loaf a Grammy for Best Rock Vocal Performance, and is now remembered as one of the defining songs of a decade otherwise supposedly hung-up on grunge, Britpop, alternative rock, nu-metal and a dozen other sub-genres that meant nothing to most people. Most people may not have known much about the bleeding edge of popular culture, but they knew what they liked and suddenly they all liked Meat Loaf again.

When it reached Number 1 in America, even Jim Steinman had to admit he was impressed. Meat Loaf nearly went out of his mind again. In the sixteen years since his only previous hit single at home in the US, 'You Took The Words Right Out Of My Mouth', Meat Loaf had released twenty-seven singles – all flops. Now with the video in heavy monster rotation on MTV, the song all over every radio station nationwide, the biz was going crazy. Meat became the must-have guest on *The Tonight Show* with Jay Leno, *The Last Resort* with Jonathan Ross, he was asked to give and receive awards at various music, film and comedy shows. He was invited to sing 'The Star-Spangled Banner' at the Major League Baseball All-Star Game, which he breathlessly described as one of the biggest highlights of his career. Even Dana Patrick received several offers for solo record deals from overexcited executives who hadn't checked the small print and just assumed she was actually singing in the video.

After what felt like a lifetime of no one really seriously believing anything Meat Loaf did or said, now as the singer celebrated his forty-sixth birthday he had the whole world hanging on every word.

Sometimes, Meat Loaf told *Rolling Stone* in 1993, when he first heard Jim Steinman's lyrics, 'I think they're the funniest things I've ever heard.' Once he started singing them, though, they became as serious and unyielding as night. Because, he explained, he and Jimmy were more like an actor and playwright than a singer and songwriter. 'I play everything for real. That's the best comedy.' He wasn't a clown, though. He was a method actor. 'I'm different from Bette [Midler] or Cher or Sinatra,' he declared, as though there was some confusion on the matter. 'This might be a huge ego thing, but I tend to think of myself as the Robert De Niro of rock. I know that's absurd, but my idols are either sports figures or Robert De Niro.'

It was as if he couldn't stop looking in the mirror, asking fitfully as he flipped out his gun, 'You talkin' to me?'

And that the answer was and always would be: 'Well, who the hell else are you talkin' to?'

BAT THREE

In The Land Of The Pigs

CHAPTER TWENTY-FOUR

A Marriage Made In Hell

'What of Art? It is a malady. Love? An Illusion. Religion?
The fashionable substitute for Belief. You are a sceptic.
Never! Scepticism is the beginning of Faith. What are you
then? To define is to limit.'

–*The Picture of Dorian Gray*, Oscar Wilde

Even with the barrier-breaking success of *Bat Out of Hell II: Back Into Hell*, which followed the 'I'd Do Anything' single to the top of the charts in both Britain and America (and a dozen other countries), it took a while for critical perception of Meat Loaf to slowly turn on its axis. Never considered remotely cool even in the late seventies, when the original *Bat* broke the mould, the years since had seen Meat Loaf's artistic stature sink to the bottom of the ocean, his reputation become barnacled by a series of second- and third-rate albums and an ever-more-desperate willingness to do anything to keep himself in the game. Heavy hitting music mags like *Rolling Stone* and *Q* now offered major interview features to both the monster and his creator, though neither Meat nor Jim Steinman seemed fazed when giving almost entirely contradictory versions of how they had finally begun working together again. There appeared to be no discernible party line for them to follow. Or if there was, neither man seemed to have got the memo from the record company.

Discussing the involvement of Todd Rundgren, no longer in charge of production but hired to work on the extensive background vocal arrangements, Steinman was as effusive as ever. 'Todd Rundgren is one of the very few people I truly idolise,' he grandly claimed in Q. 'He's a genius and I don't use that word lightly.' While in the same interview, Meat fumed: 'I went to [Rundgren's] house to do background vocals and he was in such a foul mood I said, "Screw you!" and left. In a work situation he's the worst human being possible: he gets very abusive and I don't choose to be around it.'

Rundgren, though, played no favours in the studio. As he put it in the same interview: 'I have had a tendency to convey my feelings that the songs were unnecessarily long. Jim wants everything all the time and I run out of tricks after the first five minutes of a song.' The studio whizz who had played such a crucial part in making the original *Bat* such a huge success, also reflected on the heavy pressures the new *Bat* was made under. 'There'd been so much politics and legal wrangling that Jim wasn't in a jolly mood. The themes of the songs were darker because of the expectations this time around.' Then he admitted that he hadn't actually sat down and listened to the whole album yet.

Awright . . .

What the public banter concealed, though, was just how much bad blood had been stirred up again by revisiting the *Bat* story and trying to turn it, sixteen years later, into the start of a powerful new musical franchise. In his darker moments, Jim seethed that neither he nor Meat had been paid out any royalties from the original *Bat* album, 'since 1980' – the side effects of the years of lawsuits and countersuits. He claimed angrily that CBS had made $120 million from *Bat* and that Tommy Mottola, the label's pinky-ringed, shiny-suited maverick chief whose blinds in his 32nd-floor office were always tightly drawn, 'admits it's the most profitable record in the history of the industry, more so than *Thriller'*. A statement that caused Sony America, which CBS had long been amalgamated into, to issue the following statement: 'Sony has always accounted for sales to date and everyone at Sony, from Tommy Mottola down, is proud to be associated with this album.' The only significant figure from the original *Bat* album who wasn't still complaining, ironically, was the one whose barbed tongue had nearly driven Meat Loaf to suicide in 1977, Todd Rundgren. 'It makes a great annuity for me,' he said, when asked if he'd ever had any trouble being paid his royalties.

Meat Loaf, though, was the only one who had been forced to file for bankruptcy, something he was not going to allow any of them to forget. 'I was being sued for $85 million by Jim's manager,' he reminded the readers of *Q* in 1993. 'I spent $1 million on lawyers and was seeking protection from being sued again.' A toxic situation that led to the singer being advised, he now insisted, on not working with Steinman again.

A decade on, Meat now claimed that 'Jimmy never knew anything about' the vicious lawsuits that rained down in his name on his old partner's head. A convenient get-out clause for why they were working together again now – as if Meat Loaf really had any choice, then or now. Meat just kept telling himself that it wasn't Jim's fault that he went on to become so successful in the eighties while Meat's career withered on the vine. It must have been the fault of David Sonenberg, who had been managing both men when *Bat* hit so big. However, it was another strand of the retold story that conveniently overlooked the fact that it was Sonenberg – who still managed Jim – that Meat had approached in 1989, in a last-ditch effort to revive his career. At that time, though, said Sonenberg, 'Me and Jim didn't have the inclination to get re-involved. Later, when Meat still couldn't get a deal, his management asked if Jim would write and produce an album. He agreed and Meat asked me to get a deal, which I did for a fee. Why would he do that if I'm such a viper?'

The album, of course, was *Bat Out of Hell II*. Now on its way to selling 15 million copies worldwide, by the start of 1994 nobody wanted to rake through the dirt any more. In fact, neither Jim nor Meat wanted anybody looking too closely at anything other than the heavyweight numbers, the epic scale of the comeback, the reality-redefining dimensions of it all. Who cared that the album itself was little more than a best-of compendium of Steinman-penned hits-that-should-have-been-but-never-were?

One thing they did agree on was: 'Nobody writes like Jim Steinman,' Meat Loaf bellowed in *Rolling Stone*. 'All these things – bombastic, over the top, self-indulgent – all these things are positives.' 'Of course it's bombastic,' sighed Jim, who not only composed the songs but now took on the role of sole producer. 'I take that as a compliment. Rock'n'roll is the most bombastic form ever – heightened, oversized, gigantic, thrilling and silly.' By the laws of the second *Bat Out of Hell* album, rock'n'roll was also a free-for-all when it came to artistic ownership, musical identity, and a cuckoo's sense of commercial propriety.

As David Sonenberg mused at the time, 'If [Pandora's Box] had been successful there would have been no *Bat Out of Hell II*.' Jim did his best to deflect attention away from his other projects. Bonnie Tyler was really just 'a Welsh dairy maid with a lusty body.' Barbra Streisand had 'beautiful breasts'. Pandora's Box was a dream he'd had that turned into a nightmare. 'There have been very few cases where I've been interested in what the artist thinks,' he confessed.

The track selection on *Bat II*, though, showed just how little what the artist thought really mattered – to Jim Steinman or Meat Loaf's Steinman-rejuvenated audience. From *Bad For Good*, the original version of *Bat II* that Meat Loaf had railed against fifteen years before, he was now only too happy to record 'Rock And Roll Dreams Come Through', 'Out Of The Frying Pan (And Into The Fire)' and 'Lost Boys And Golden Girls' – all of which are like being given a privileged peek into some parallel-universe studio back in time where Meat is doing what he should have and singing the songs the way Steinman had intended, instead of leaving it to Jimmy to do. Not quite carbon copies, but with only the beefed-up voice and a decade's worth of enhanced technology separating them. From *Original Sin* came 'It Just Won't Quit' – another identikit version – and 'Good Girls Go To Heaven (Bad Girls Go Everywhere)', which does make a point of doing things somewhat differently, though depending on your taste, not necessarily better than the Holly Sherwood-sung original.

There was also the inevitable Steinman monologue 'Wasted Youth', which again had appeared in identical form on *Bad For Good*, although back then it was originally titled 'Love And Death And An American Guitar', Steinman repeating one of his most famous lines, *'I was barely seventeen and I once killed a boy with a Fender guitar'* (also used, obliquely, on a much-circulated Pandora's Box promotional video from four years before). There was more luxury padding in the instrumental track, the unnecessarily literally titled 'Back Into Hell', probably the least-interesting piece of last-minute thinking on any Steinman-related project, with all instruments programmed and performed by Jeff Bova. It's a Meat Loaf song without either Meat Loaf or Jim Steinman on it. Perhaps they went out for dinner while Jeff covered for them?

Indeed, of the eleven tracks on *Bat II*, only four were authentically new songs: the most important of which was the powerhouse single, 'I'd Do Anything For Love (But I Won't Do That)'. When Allen Kovac, one of the bosses at Meat Loaf's new management company Left Bank, told Jim, 'You've gotta cut nine minutes out of it, Jim . . . It'll never get played on radio,' Meat recalled: 'He was inconsolable, crying in front of everybody. *"It's my baby, you're butchering my baby . . ."* He was still fighting with Allen when it had been Number 1 for five weeks . . .'

Then there was the other universe-baiting ballad, and perhaps the most sober and reflective song Steinman has ever written, 'Objects In the Rear View Mirror May Appear Closer Than They Are' – a song about two best friends who lose each other tragically, where the singer forlornly repeats, *'It was long ago and far away'*, as though summoning up the lost spirit of 1977, echoing 'Paradise By The Dashboard Light', the vocal melody a tip of the hat to 'Surf's Up'. Those very personal in-references run alongside a lyric shot through with regret.

And there were two more upbeat originals, though no less complexly arranged and performed: the heavy-breathing 'Life Is a Lemon (And I Want My Money Back)' – which sounds uncannily like Def Leppard's giant worldwide hit single from 1988, 'Pour Some Sugar On Me', one of the tracks, in rough demo form, they would have been working on during their ill-fated time in the studio with Steinman – and 'Everything Louder Than Everything Else': big, vivid; Jim Loaf by numbers. Summed up in the song's big kiss-off line: *'A wasted youth is better by far than a wise and productive old age!'*

As Steinman would explain on his website, years later: ' . . . to me, the teenage aspect of everyone is the most attractive element. I mean, one of the lyrics I wrote on *Bat Out of Hell II* was actually very profoundly sincere, that a wasted youth is better by far than a wise and productive old age. And I really believe that. I mean, I'd rather be an eighteen-year-old wasted kid than Morley Safer any day' – referring to the staid figure of the longstanding US TV news reporter.

It seems Jim would will himself to stay young, at heart at least, even if, like Peter Pan, it meant falling back on his tried-and-trusted magic, holding tight to the impossible dream even as the rest of the world whizzed past him towards their own sunsets.

'The way Jim works on an album is this,' said Meat. 'First he recycles stuff that's either been lying around, or, often, songs he's used elsewhere in another form. He rerecords his songs with different people over the years until he finds the right place for them . . . Steinman regurgitates the older material, and then he writes three or four new songs, and that makes the album new.'

Well, yes, but this idea that Steinman's songs somehow exist in their own bubble just waiting for the right 'home' is disingenuous to say the least. That Jim Steinman had a magpie eye for his own material there is no question. But now, in his forties, he was also perhaps beginning to slow down in terms of the amount of top-drawer songs he could successfully complete without consciously repeating himself. It was one of the oldest tripwires in rock music – how much harder it was in middle age to rediscover the creative spark of your over-endowed musical youth.

From now on, the titanic songs would come less often and less quickly to Jim Steinman. Equally, however, Meat Loaf could – and did, when it suited him – claim that of those older songs, the tunes from *Bad For Good* were originally written for him to sing anyhow. He also reckoned that Jim had written 'It Just Won't Quit' for him before using it with Pandora's Box ('He put it on *Original Sin* without telling me. I could have strangled him,' Meat said – and it may even be true; unlike the other songs on *Original Sin*, a demo version sung by Rory Dodd exists).

'I'd have liked eleven new songs,' Jim admitted. But the truth was it really didn't matter to the millions who bought *Bat II*. 'Jim doesn't know this,' Meat confided in the British writer John Aizlewood, 'but a psychic told me that Jim has written his best stuff already and he'll never write like it again.' This was no longer music from the future, built from the top down. This was music – no matter how fantastical – of the bottom line: 'If this doesn't do three or four million,' said Meat, 'it'll be a cold day in hell before they let us do another.' Life, with its lemon-sharp taste for letting you down quickly, had taught Meat Loaf and Jim Steinman nothing if not that.

CHAPTER TWENTY-FIVE

All Coming Back

Meat's voice had changed, too, of course. It no longer had the elasticity of his youth, it had perhaps a harsher edge, but there was still something magical about him when he sang Jim's songs. The transformation still happened, just in a different way. Where he had once been the fat kid at the school dance, desperate to get inside a cheerleader's pants but destined to look on as the cool kids beat him to it, now he was older, wiser, sadder. When he sang 'I'd Do Anything For Love' it was as someone conscious that the years were passing by, that the happiness he thought would be his may now never come.

'It's amazing on an intuitive level, the fact just that he understands these songs,' said Jim. 'We have such different backgrounds, he and I. Such different lifestyles. We are totally different people – completely. But somehow, within the music, we connect on a level that's pretty strange – because we're so different . . . Meat is a performer serving a song and he'd be the first to say that. That's one of the reasons he's such a great performer. He does put the song, at his best, above his own personality or ego or anything.'

There were so many echoes of *Bat*. Although the money and the record deal were in place this time, they still felt like outsiders, older men in a musical landscape that had changed beyond recognition since 1977. Others of their generation were pushing nostalgia now, content with a life on the oldies circuit and the newly emerging classic rock radio stations in the US. Yet in the mid-nineties Jim Steinman and Meat Loaf would emerge unchanged and unapologetic, their music timeless in its own strange, repeat-to-fade way. As Terry Manzi of Meat Loaf's new management company Left Bank would say: 'The project was considered a joke as far as the industry was concerned. We were laughed at . . .'

Jim would laugh at the record company naysayers: 'I said, "Trust me, sixteen years is exactly the right interval. You guys put out records too fast."' Now, as before, the joke was on everyone else. The money they were both owed from *Bat Out of Hell*, ($120m according to Jim) was still sitting in a bank vault awaiting the resolution of their endless legal disputes, but the path ahead was suddenly clear. Again, like *Bat*, the millions upon millions that would buy *Bat Out of Hell II: Back Into Hell* were not the kind of people who cared what a few self-appointed arbiters in the music press or the record business thought.

So it wasn't cool. Well, who gave a shit? It sounded great, and it made everything else appear small and unambitious. This was Jim and Meat's great gift. And while Jim told everyone that the album had its title because it really was the 'true' follow-up to *Bat*, Meat came straight to the point: 'We called it *Bat Out of Hell II* cos that would help it sell shitloads . . .'

He was right.

It did.

It would be difficult to overstate what the success of *Bat Out of Hell II* did for Meat Loaf in the 1990s. The original 1977 *Bat* may have become a record-breaking sensation – spending more than five hundred consecutive weeks in the UK charts, going fifteen-times platinum in America, on its way to selling almost 45 million copies worldwide, making it the third-biggest-selling album of all time – but in reality it had been a slow burner, not reaching its sales peak until years after its initial release. By which time Meat Loaf himself was considered a relic from a bygone age, an anomaly in rock space and time, a dinosaur hurtling towards career extinction. There hadn't even been that one hit single from the original *Bat* that the whole world could sing.

The arrival sixteen years later of *Bat II* changed all that. It may have sold less than the original – if the word 'less' can reliably be applied to an album that sold nearly 20 million copies itself – but in 'I'd Do Anything For Love' it had gifted Meat Loaf with a signature song of a magnitude to stand alongside 'Stairway To Heaven' by Led Zeppelin, 'Maggie May' by Rod Stewart, 'Bridge Over Troubled Water' by Simon & Garfunkel, 'Life On Mars' by David Bowie . . . A musical calling card that would proudly announce his name whenever and wherever it was played anywhere in the world. Love it or hate it, *everybody* knew that song in the 1990s. Everybody still knows it now, though few could really hate it any more. It has transcended all human boundaries to become a musical monument. A sign of life on other dream worlds, where the hero is flawed, even disfigured, but still somehow gets the girl, the wondrous angel, the she-devil in disguise. Its endlessly repeated refrain (*'I would do an-y-thing . . .'*) burned into the minds of a generation, for good or ill.

For those of us whose memories were now growing longer than our hair, it was both a reminder of how undeniable Meat Loaf in harness with Jim Steinman really was, and a handy way of erasing the years of so-so albums and low-rent tours. For those new to the party it was a glorious introduction to the music of excess, of pop grandiosity and glamour at a time when the only other mainstream choices that year were the self-inflicted noise-pain of Nirvana, or the sweet-beyond-belief, modern, amazing grace of Whitney Houston.

Somehow Meat Loaf now encompassed both ends of that diaphanous spectrum. The mums and dads and little kids of pop suddenly loved him the way they loved Santa Claus. This big colourful guy who'd been around a thousand years but always showed up with a special present for everyone. The rockers paid fealty to the heavy bombast and epically proportioned, cloud-busting melodies and rhythm, the bikes riding through the flames. There was another, less obvious connection, too. In many ways 'I'd Do Anything For Love' was a song written specifically for the nineties, when the fears of a post-AIDS, pre-millennial generation that lacked the sexual freedom of the seventies and the financial free-for-all of the eighties was seeking its own salvation. What was it that he wouldn't do for love? Screw around. What was the message of *Beauty and the Beast*? Don't worry about the superficial. Love is everything – so do anything for it. It wasn't a fashionable rallying cry – this wasn't teen spirit that Meat Loaf was espousing but what comes long after it has evaporated – but it was something to cling to.

Speaking to Meat Loaf at the time, I mentioned how – unlike the punks, who considered the original *Bat* to be completely anti-thetical to what they were doing with their music – the leading grunge and rock stars of the early nineties were happy to admit their complete fascination with what Meat and Jim were cooking up together up there in that lightning-forked house on the hill.

'Right,' he said, nodding his head. 'What was interesting was people like Kurt Cobain in interviews would talk about *Bat Out of Hell*. A lot of the different grunge people would talk about *Bat Out of Hell*. So it must have had some influence on them somewhere. So to me it wasn't quite as strange [that they loved *Bat II*] because I just kept reading all these grunge [artists] out of Seattle talking about *Bat Out of Hell*. It was like really a weird combination but, you know, great, I loved it. Kurt Cobain, one of his favourite songs was "You Took The Words Right Out Of My Mouth" . . . And then you've got people like [Guns N' Roses singer] Axl Rose whose favourite song was "Two Out Of Three Ain't Bad" and wouldn't go onstage unless he heard "Two Out Of Three Ain't Bad" before he went on. Now you try and get your head behind that one, right?'

The important thing now was to try to keep the run going. Painfully aware of how easily he had allowed the momentum behind the original *Bat* to dissipate, Meat Loaf promised himself that history would not repeat itself, in that regard anyway.

The 'I'd Do Anything' single was still selling well around the world when they issued a second single from *Bat II* – the very track Jim Steinman had wanted them to release as the first single from the real *Bat II* back in 1979, and which he had instead found himself recording as the 'bonus' single on *Bad For Good*: 'Rock And Roll Dreams Come Through'. Accompanied by another whizz-bang video directed by Michael Bay – with Meat this time depicted as an oracle – albeit still riding around on his steel-horse motorcycle – saving the lives of such eternally damned figures as a runaway teenage girl (played by a then-unknown eighteen-year-old actress named Angelina Jolie) and an angry young boy about to join a street gang. With MTV now eager to rotate any-thing with Meat Loaf's name on it, the single became another big hit in Britain and America. At which point all Meat's previous labels began dusting down the archives, looking for ways to get in on the act. In the UK, the 'I'd Do Anything' single was still in the Top 10 when Sony rereleased 'Bat Out Of Hell' as a single in the run-up to Christmas – and were rewarded with another big chart hit, making Meat Loaf at that time the only artist to have two singles in the Top 10 simultaneously since The Beatles.

A third and final single from *Bat II* – 'Objects In The Rear View Mirror May Appear Closer Than They Are', edited down from its ten-minute-plus album length to a still enormous for daytime radio, nearly six-minute version – was released and again came with its own bespoke Michael Bay knobs-and-all video: this time a mini-movie featuring Robert Patrick, who'd recently found fame as the T-100 model liquid assassin in the *Terminator II* movie, amidst a fury of the kind of cataclysmic flying aircraft imagery that Bay would later use in the *Transformer* franchise. The single was another transatlantic hit, though not quite on the scale of its immediate predecessors. It didn't matter. Radios and MTV outlets around the world were still addicted to spinning 'I'd Do Anything For Love'. It was now official: Meat Loaf was for ever. The critics loved these videos and hated them in equal measure, but either way they were completely immune to their barbs. Here, echoes of the original *Bat* were uncanny: these were songs and videos that the people loved and that the people's love made bomb proof. Even more than the original, *Bat Out of Hell II* became *their* record.

In September 1993, during the week that separated the release of 'I'd Do Anything' and *Bat II*, Meat Loaf embarked on his first lengthy tour for five years with four nights at the Hudson Theatre, in New York. Though the return to large-scale arenas was still some months away, the Hudson was one of the oldest theatre venues on Broadway. It held less than a thousand people at full capacity, but for Meat Loaf these shows were like a homecoming. Of the fourteen songs he performed each night at the Hudson, all but one – the final encore of the night, a roistering version of 'Dead Ringer For Love' – came from the *Bat Out of Hell* albums, bookended between the opener 'I'd Do Anything For Love' and the set closer, 'Paradise By The Dashboard Light'. A tacit agreement that nothing of interest has really happened to him, musically, in the years he'd struggled alone without Jimmy's songs to guide him.

After that, everything got bigger than everything else. Meat Loaf went out on tour and stayed there for 215 shows that ran for almost a year. Australia, Canada, Britain . . . By February 1994 he was back in New York, at the 20,000-seater Madison Square Garden – this time as headliner.

'Yeah, he told me, 'It felt like a big comeback. It *was* a big comeback. But you have to figure I'd never been away. It wasn't like I'd been hiding. I'd been working the whole time. Getting better. Anyone paying attention knew that.'

Very few people had, though. Now it seemed like everybody was. Onstage, he had a new foil for the duets, Patti Russo, a New Jersey bombshell with a smoky, late-night voice and the where-withal to keep the slobbering Loaf at bay during his (character's) more lustful moments. She also had the chops to carry off 'I'd Do Anything For Love . . .' the pair extending the drama of the reveal, Russo dark and deliberate as she sang the *'sooner or later you'll be screwing around . . .'* line, Meat supplicant and trembling before her as the crowds shrieked and anticipated his reply.

Slightly sillier was the giant inflatable bat that emerged at the end of the show to hover over the stage, an idea Meat claimed came to him while he was watching *Spinal Tap*. The bat was worthy of the *Tap*, too – Meat thought it looked more like a chicken and gave it the nickname Happy Bob.

CHAPTER TWENTY-SIX

The Light of Darkness

The pressure was back on. But the singer, now in his mid-forties, had learned how to switch off once he'd left the stage for the night. He was no longer demonically possessed by Jim's songs once he'd sung them, no longer needed alcohol or anything else to protect him from fame. Indeed, as the years tumbled by he refused to admit that he'd ever had a problem with drink or drugs. 'At one point I had a nervous breakdown,' he allowed in a 2009 interview. He had never been a big drinker, he insisted. 'So when I started to drink, they said you're in trouble. That was a month maybe. It was short-lived. The godfather of my youngest daughter dragged me to a psychiatrist. Basically tied me up and set me in his office. So that worked out. It was fine. It was everything that had happened. The rejection, and then all of a sudden, after the rejection, you know, all the phoniness that comes out of it. "We believed in you the whole time," you know? One minute they are saying, "Get out of my office," and then patting me on the back, saying, "I knew you could do it." That kind of thing. It gets a little wacky.'

Yet he still felt as though Meat Loaf was somehow a character, a role, a persona he adopted to get the job done; still that strange hybrid between him and Jim and the music they produced. He knew that the managers and the record company suits weren't going to wait another four years for him or Jim to follow up a

Bat Out of Hell album with something new, but he chose to deflect that pressure by allowing Jimmy to call the shots this time – even though he knew, deep down inside, that the likelihood of Steinman coming up with an entire album's worth of brand new material on a par with his best work on both *Bats* was virtually nil.

Back in New York in October 1994, the only month off the singer had from touring that year, Meat and Jimmy met up a few times, not in a rehearsal room but for a few expensive dinners together around town. Steinman was pleased – and relieved – to find his old pal doing well under the circumstances. He was tired, under the cosh, but his voice was holding up pretty good. In the aftermath of *Bat II* he'd been determined to lose weight, even cut his hair. Anything to freshen up his image in the age of MTV. He'd been vegetarian for over ten years, then went on an all-protein diet, mostly meat, no carbs, supplemented by daily doses of Slimfast. The weight began to fall away to the point where, he claimed, 'I weigh less now than I did in the seventh grade.' Most impressive, he'd managed to keep the weight off. He would never be leading-man slim, he'd always be hoodlum large, but his general outlook was far removed from the days when he was serially threatening to kill himself. Meat was also suitably encouraged by these meetings, even if Jimmy did still insist on ordering several different starters and desserts – never a main course – which he would pick at with his long fingers.

The elephant in the room was whether they both really had it in them to go for *Bat Out of Hell III* – an idea they knew the record company, at least, would slaver like bone-hungry dogs to receive – or whether they should simply make another album together and call it something else. An idea they knew only they would be truly satisfied with.

'He was throwing out tempting song titles like "God Has Left The Building",' Meat Loaf would recall in his autobiography. 'Although I should have known better, we all started to believe he might actually have a whole album in embryo, tucked away in one of his ratty old shopping bags . . .'

A few more dinners, a few more evenings listening to Jimmy expound in a sort of stream of consciousness on the amazing ideas he had for the next album, and Meat began to realise that they were both dreaming. That Jimmy was simply opening the door to his inner universe, offering up his dream songs, his concepts, his mini-movies. Their physical realisation could be years away, decades, maybe never-never. Jim was older now, they both were, and the first youthful burst of their creativity was long over. Jim had only managed four original songs for *Bat II*. There was no possibility of him coming up with another seven or eight in the subsequent year and half. It wasn't the way he worked even when he could. There was also, buried in the background, the idea in Jim's mind that he still had other projects he wanted to see through. Andrew Lloyd Webber, the most successful British composer and theatrical impresario in recent times, with such global hits as *Cats* and *The Phantom of the Opera*, and whose career had taken off in 1971 with the original rock-opera production of *Jesus Christ Superstar*, had spoken openly of his admiration for Steinman as a writer of supremely theatrical music, and there were now whispers that the two might work together. With Jim still nursing the idea of one day staging his long-cherished *Neverland* musical, working with Webber was a prospect that far outweighed the possibility of repeating himself yet again with Meat Loaf.

None of which unduly bothered the singer – at least, not at first. Like an old married couple who now had eyes for other prizes, as well as keeping their own union intact, both Meat and Jim were happy to consider all possibilities.

Meat Loaf, who had kept up a steady if inconsistent career taking bit parts in films, had seen an upswing in his movie profile with his brief but hilarious appearance as the overcritical bouncer in the 1992 hit comedy, *Wayne's World*. Now with *Bat II* having restored his name in giant letters to the public, he wanted to explore the acting side of his career still further.

And although it hadn't really worked in the past, Meat saw some salvation in recording something that wasn't under Jim's imprint – it would free him of the Meat Loaf character for a while. Or at least that part of the character that Jim's songs owned. After the first *Bat*, Meat Loaf had stumbled into working with other people, other musicians and writers and producers and dream-makers, through necessity, because he had to, not because he wanted to – and the dire results spoke for themselves. Now, though, in the afterglow of *Bat II*, he began to wonder aloud if it might be possible for him to again work with other people – read: without Jim – but without throwing the baby-genius out with the rapidly cooling bathwater. Whether he might be able to have his cake and eat it – without everyone telling him he was a fat pig again?

Meat Loaf, whose appetites were never truly satiated, not for long, decided he could.

Once the decision was made that Meat Loaf would make his next album without Jim Steinman – and amicably agreed upon by the two principal actors – work progressed relatively quickly. This was not to be Meat Loaf looking for a whole new career, as most of his earlier albums without Jim had been, this was to be a best-of-both-worlds contrivance which played as closely to the singer's *Bat*-era strengths as possible.

Again, as with *Bat II*, the album would be propped up by two Steinman songs from the past – 'Left In The Dark', yet another musical refugee from *Bad For Good*, shorn this time, though, of its original 28-second Steinman monologue; and 'Original Sin', the title track and yet another hit-that-never-was from the Pandora's Box album.

But while both tracks had clear commercial potential as singles, ironically, the lead track from the album was an outright

Steinman-by-numbers copy, replete with bracketed title, written by Diane Warren, 'I'd Lie For You (And That's The Truth)'.

Warren was a professional American songwriter who had penned dozens of hits for everyone from Elton John, Tina Turner and Rod Stewart to Barbra Streisand, Aretha Franklin and Michael Bolton, to name just a few. These days she is better known for her hit-making skills with Beyoncé, Lady Gaga and Carrie Underwood, again to name just a few. Diane Warren is who you bring in when you need a cast-iron, radio-friendly, people-pleasing motherfucking hit – and that's the truth. And she did the job splendidly for Meat Loaf, not only giving him his second-biggest all-time hit after 'I'd Do Anything', but helping make the subsequent album it came from, *Welcome to the Neighbourhood,* become the best-selling of his career, after the *Bat* albums.

A pleasingly undulating ballad that hits the lights at all the crucial stops along the way, and a duet featuring the lush, chocolatey vocals of Patti Russo, it's as if Warren sat up all night listening to 'I'd Do Anything For Love' and 'It's All Coming Back To Me Now' and condensed them down into one delirious, quite superb Steinman-esque moment.

Not giving a fig who wrote it, the public lapped it up. Featuring the same Jim-team of Loaf-stars that had worked on both *Bats* – Rory Dodd, Jeff Bova, Kenny Aronoff, Eddie Martinez, Steve Buslowe, Kasim Sulton . . . the boys were back in town in force – 'I'd Lie For You' went to Number 2 in Britain and made Number 13 in the US. It was the same maintaining of a winning formula with the album, which also featured Paul Jacobs, Elaine Caswell – even Meat's now twenty-year-old daughter Pearl Aday joining in on backing vocals. Diane Warren also wrote the track that became the second single from the album, 'Not A Dry Eye In The House', another Steinman-esque power ballad that became a Top 10 hit in the UK, but barely sneaked into the US Top 100.

There had been plans to release the third and final

Warren-as-Steinman written track, another Patti Russo duet, 'If This Is The Last Kiss (Let's Make It Last All Night)', as a single, but with US ticket sales slowing to a crawl, it was decided Meat Loaf needed something more appealing to the (ticket-buying) hardcore rock audience. Hence the release of 'Runnin' For The Red Light (I've Gotta Life)', written by the Australian proven hit-making team of George Young and Harry Vanda, who'd made their multi-platinum bones guiding the career of AC/DC. (Although the credits on the album added the bylines of Meat, Russo and Sarah Durkee – Durkee last seen on a Meat Loaf album a decade before on *Bad Attitude*.)

The single was a flop everywhere except Britain, where it staggered to Number 21. It meant that while Meat Loaf could still tour Britain and Europe to packed arenas – he headlined London's 12,500-seater Wembley Arena four times on the *Welcome to the Neighbourhood* tour – his US tour profile had sunk below arena level once again. Indeed, he only performed in America five times that year, the highlight of which was a headline show at the 2,900-capacity Beacon Theatre in Manhattan.

In truth, *Welcome to the Neighbourhood* was a glorified stopgap, the weaker tracks not written by either Warren or Steinman bolstered by the same sort of padding Meat had brought to earlier duds like *Blind Before I Stop*. A cover of a Sammy Hagar-penned track, 'Amnesty Is Granted', with Meat duetting with the Van Halen singer: six minutes of guitar wank that Van Halen wouldn't have used as a B-side. A cover of the Tom Waits early classic, 'Martha', it lacks the authentic despair of the original and has none of the characterful charm of the Bette Midler version, which Meat had first seen her perform on an edition of *Saturday Night Live* back in 1979. It's just a . . . blank. A CD-filler. As for the minute-long track, '45 Seconds Of Ecstasy', sung for unexplained reasons by Susan Wood, and doesn't actually feature Meat Loaf – why?

Nevertheless, *Welcome to the Neighbourhood* was a better record than any Meat Loaf had made without Jim Steinman before, and his first significant hit without him. The success of *Bat II* meant that his labels, Virgin and MCA, were happy to invest in him knowing there was an almost-certain return, and he was surrounded by strong, commercially successful people. Rock-solid veteran producer Ron Nevison tooled the songs for radio. The album sleeve was a neat homage to fifties' pulp novels. It was a solid package, well written, in the main, well performed, certainly, and as credible as anything that stars of Meat Loaf's level were producing at the time. It sold over four million copies worldwide and it kept the show on the road, the money rolling in, and offered Meat some necessary respite from being at the beck and call of Jim's creative flow.

It was an old pro's job, a shelter in the storm. To the rest of the world it looked like business as usual. But to Meat Loaf at least, *Welcome to the Neighbourhood* finally proved that he had a career outside of being Jim Steinman's well-trained monkey-monster.

As the great Hunter S. Thompson once wrote: 'The music business is a cruel and shallow money trench, a long plastic hallway where thieves and pimps run free, and good men die like dogs. There's also a negative side.'

It was time, Meat Loaf decided, for him to show the world that Jim Steinman wasn't the only one who could do things without a giant pair of bat wings throwing their shadow over everything.

It was time to take the gloves off.

CHAPTER TWENTY-SEVEN
Fighting Talk

Chuck Palahniuk grew up with the story of his grandfather shooting his grandmother in an argument over a sewing machine and then turning the gun on himself, while Chuck's father, who was three years old, hid under his bed. Chuck went to the University of Oregon and qualified with a BA in journalism. He stayed in Portland and got a job on a local paper, but he didn't enjoy it so he ended up working as a diesel mechanic for Freightliner, where he wrote some of their instruction manuals as a sideline. He helped out at a local hospice, taking some of the terminally ill patients to their support groups. He joined a band of Dada-ist pranksters called the Cacophony Society, an uninhibited gathering of 'free spirits' started in 1986 by surviving members of the now-defunct Suicide Club of San Francisco. The Portland 'chapter' had officially opened in 1995 – the kind of anarchic gang of fuck-society mavericks Chuck could really relate to.

Once he got into a fight when he was camping, and when he went into work the next day with his face bruised and cut up, Chuck noticed how his co-workers avoided his gaze and pretended not to even see his injuries. Something that just confirmed for him his growing outsider status. He thought he'd like to try his hand at writing something other than instruction manuals, so he joined a workshop run by Tom Spanbauer, a writer whose work often explores issues of sexuality, race and the ties that bind disparate people together. Spanbauer was an advocate of a minimalist style called 'dangerous writing'. Chuck wrote a couple of short stories and a monster of a novel called *Insomnia: If You Lived Here, You'd Be Home Already*, a 700-page behemoth that wasn't particularly minimal but certainly encapsulated the spirit of dangerous writing. It was never published, though, as Chuck decided, finally, that it just wasn't good enough.

Chuck kept going and produced another manuscript called *Manifesto*, which became *Invisible Monsters* and was better, but was turned down by all of the publishers he sent it to, some, they said, because it was 'too scary'. That made him angry and so he decided he'd write something really transgressive and see what they made of that. He recalled the camping trip when he'd been in the fight, and the Cacophony Society, and the support groups for terminally ill people that he used to help at, and he set to it. He wrote whenever he could, at work in the garage, in the park in spare moments, listening to Nine Inch Nails and Radiohead. When he'd finished, he called the book *Fight Club*. He'd written it, in his words, 'to offend, to shock and to punish' those who had rejected him, and so he sent it to them all again.

An editor at WW Norton, called Gerry Howard, thought it was great and he kept on at his board to let him buy it, and after he persisted, they did. Even then nothing much happened: as with so many first-time authors, the book came out to a few reviews, modest sales and a couple of local awards, and that seemed to be that until 20th Century Fox began showing an interest in the film rights. Chuck got an agent, the Anglo-American actor-literary agent Edward Hibbert (who played the pompous, effete food critic on the hit TV show *Frasier*). Hibbert brokered the deal and Chuck ended up getting a cheque for $10,000 for the rights to his book. The Fox producer on the project, Ross Bell, hired Jim Uhls to write a script and started to think about directors. His first choice, future *Lord of the Rings* trilogy-maker Peter Jackson, was busy filming. His second choice, Bryan Singer, was sent the book but didn't read it, too busy getting ready to direct *X-Men*. British director Danny Boyle, still hot from his success with *Trainspotting*, read it but passed. David Fincher really liked the book – he'd pursued the rights before discovering they'd gone to Fox – but he'd had a bad experience making *Alien 3* for the studio and was initially reluctant.

Fincher eventually bit the bullet and signed up, though. Ross Bell approached Russell Crowe for the lead role, but Art Linson, who'd joined up as a producer and was senior to Bell, wanted Brad Pitt. In turn, Pitt was looking for something meaty and worthwhile after his most recent movie, *Meet Joe Black*, had not met his expectations at the US box office, despite doing well worldwide. He signed up. Then Edward Norton signed to play alongside him. This was how it went in Hollywood – comings and goings and no real certainty until all of the pieces fell into place, all the cheques got cut and someone finally shouted 'action'.

By the time all of that happened on *Fight Club*, Chuck had written two more books. But that was okay. Chuck was in good shape and he liked to fight. Turning *Fight Club* into a movie was some kind of dream. 'Every time I'd feel so good afterwards, being physically and emotionally exhausted, and being able to sleep so well,' he told the writer Robert Chalmers. '[There is] also the bond it created with people I'd previously hated – we would hash out our differences in a very physical, intense way, and after that we'd be best friends. I saw so much value in fighting. I still do. It's such a consensual act. The best fights don't occur between strangers. They occur between friends who trust each other.'

The plot of the novel picked up what he called the 'spiritual' element of two men beating the shit out of one another. 'It's sort of like church ...' Chuck said. Lifting parts of the novel from his earlier, unpublished *Insomnia* manuscript, *Fight Club* features an unnamed narrator who is suffering from insomnia and complains to his doctor, who advises him to go to a cancer patients' support group: 'To see what real suffering is.' At one such group he meets Big Bob, a former bodybuilder who juiced on dianabol (a powerful steroid popularly known among body-builders as D-Bol) and winstrol (a similarly powerful and popular muscleman steroid) – and ended up with testicular cancer for his trouble, and was now a squishy, flabby eunuch with 'bitch tits'; and Marla, a classic fuck-up who, it transpires, is a tourist to these places just like the narrator.

After an explosion destroys his condo, the narrator moves into an abandoned factory building ruled over by a mysterious an-archist named Tyler Durden. Tyler introduces him to Fight Club, an underground society of men who box one another under a strict set of rules, the first two of which are, 'You don't talk about Fight Club.' Fight Clubs spring up everywhere, and even Bob begins attending one – because of his 'bitch tits', he's the only Fight Club member who is allowed to keep his shirt on. Tyler starts 'Project Mayhem', an anti-consumerist organisation that commits acts of terrorism, and also starts an affair with Marla. After Bob is killed during one of Project Mayhem's operations, the narrator resolves to stop Tyler, only to learn that Tyler is simply a manifestation brought on by his insomnia, and that Fight Club and Project Mayhem are his own creations. He tries to kill 'Tyler' and himself in one final Project Mayhem explosion, but ends up in a psychi-atric unit looked after by former Project Mayhem members, who expect Tyler to come back one day.

It was a rich and layered book, full of ideas and anger, and it somehow chimed with the times. One of Chuck's themes seemed to be that masculinity was at a crossroads, and it wasn't being dis-cussed or written about. The book was also divisive and contro-versial, and became almost self-fulfilling when real Fight Clubs began to open. There were all sorts of theories about it: that it was a critique of emasculating consumerist culture; or that the fights between the narrator and Tyler were symbolic of the internal war that men fought with themselves, and so on. A professor in St Louis argued that Chuck used existentialism to smuggle in a subtext of romance and feminism. It was that sort of book: everyone who read it had a view, and maybe they were right.

All Chuck would say was that, 'all my books are about a lonely person looking for some way to connect with other people'.

Enter: Meat Loaf.

Once David Fincher had secured Brad Pitt for the role of Tyler (a happy reunion following a successful collaboration on the serial killer hit *Se7en*), Edward Norton for the narrator and Helena Bonham Carter for Marla, his next find was someone big enough, in every respect, to play Robert 'Big Bob' Paulson. Meat Loaf, who had once been Big Bob's size in real life, had spent the past decade losing weight. But he could act, and it was a considerable nod to his talent that he got the role. Bob is a supporting part, but he's crucial to the narrative drive of the film. He must be both repulsive and sympathetic, almost puppy-like in his devotion to the narrator but in touch enough with his previous life as a bodybuilder to come alive when he joins Fight Club. The audience has to root for him, because his death is a pivotal plot point. More than that, in one of the main departures that the script takes from the novel, in death, Bob becomes a source of inspiration for other Project Mayhem members, who chant 'My name is Robert Paulson' before they undertake their missions.

It would be a demanding role for a full-time screen actor, let alone a guy who spent most of his time singing for a living. Meat Loaf had done umpteen bit parts on screen; he carried the lead in his own videos, but he'd never done anything real like this. Not least experienced the demands that would be placed on him in the role, being able to hold his own when onscreen with Brad Pitt and Edward Norton without resorting to chewing the scenery. It was a mark of Meat Loaf's acting experience and talent that he became so integral to the movie. He suffered physically, too, spending hour upon hour inside a 40-kilogramme fat suit which was weighted down with rice and bird seed to make the skin sag convincingly, and which featured two unforgettably pendulous 'bitch' breasts that wobbled convincingly beneath his T-shirt. When he hugged Norton to those mighty jellies in one of the first cancer support group scenes it provided a blistering motif for the first act of the film.

It was an uncanny performance, but one that was more understandable when you remembered how Big Little Marvin had once felt. Meat knew how it was to be an outsider, and enough of Jim's characters were dogged beta-male losers for him to be able to tap back into that state of mind when he needed to.

And he loved working with David Fincher, who was establishing himself as one of America's most interesting filmmakers, fastidiously focused on the nuances of every frame of the rushes. 'I hardly spent any time in my trailer for almost ten months,' Meat said of the experience. 'I sat next to David the entire time. Well, not next to him – I would have driven him crazy – but close, like behind him, so I could see what was going on and what he was seeing. It got to the point, about four or five months into filming, that we'd break for lunch, and Fincher would call me into his trailer and say, "I want you to help me pick which one I should use." Of course, in my head I'm going, "What?" The first time he did that, I said, "I can't do that," and he goes, "Yeah, you can. You've been sitting next to me, so help me pick out the best one." His average take was forty-four, so we'd sit there and watch forty takes, and he'd go, "Which one did you like the best?" and I'd say something like, "Well, it's either twenty-four or twenty-six," and he'd say, "I agree with you, twenty-six."'

The film went on general release in October 1999 after screening at the Venice Film Festival. Its slick violence, up-close and upsetting, and the moral ambiguity of many of its messages confused the marketers, who had considered releasing it as an art film before it tested well with teenage audiences. They were pretty sure it was a film for men, even though Brad Pitt was in it, which usually drew a large female audience. The posters ended up with a pink bar of soap inscribed 'Fight Club', yet Tyler's soap-making (using fat discarded by a liposuction clinic) is a minor part of the plot. Fox ran TV trailers during WWE broadcasts, which David Fincher hated. Art Linson rightly described the marketing as 'ill-conceived and one-dimensional'. *Fight Club* had cost $63 million to make and took $37 million from its theatrical run in the US, a total bumped up to $100.9 million worldwide – which, given the marketing costs, meant it had probably just about made its money back.

None of which mattered to Meat Loaf. This wasn't about money. This was about acting credibility. Screen cojones. Hollywood hip. And proving to himself – and Jim Steinman and anyone else who wanted to mouth off – that Meat Loaf didn't need anybody to prop him up any more.

Wear your scars as a badge of honour – that was a lesson Meat Loaf had learned the hard way. He didn't need *Fight Club* to tell him that. Nevertheless, he basked in the controversy the movie stirred up among the critics, who took it all so seriously.

'For daring to imagine, *Fight Club* will take a few hits,' wrote *Rolling Stone* film critic Peter Travers. 'Fincher's film of Chuck Palahniuk's 1996 novel – with a high-voltage script by newcomer Jim Uhls – is already being misinterpreted as an "apology for fascism". One critic wondered whether Rupert Murdoch's Fox 2000, the company releasing *Fight Club*, "knew what it was doing" in spending $70 million on a movie that is "not only anti-capitalism but anti-society and, indeed, anti-God".' Travers went on: 'My take is that *Fight Club* is pro-thinking . . . And just wait until you see the raw wit and emotion Meat Loaf invests in his role . . .'

Meanwhile, one of America's most eminent movie critics,

Roger Ebert, of *At the Movies* fame, represented the red corner when he wrote: '*Fight Club* is the most frankly and cheerfully fascist big-star movie since *Death Wish*, a celebration of violence in which the heroes write themselves a license to drink, smoke, screw and beat one another up. Sometimes, for variety, they beat up themselves. It's macho porn – the sex movie Hollywood has been moving toward for years, in which eroticism between the sexes is replaced by all-guy locker-room fights.'

While here in the UK, the cudgel was taken up by Peter Bradshaw, who'd just become the chief film critic of the *Guardian*: 'Edward Norton gives a compulsively twitchy, nerdy, hollow-eyed performance . . . *Fight Club* has a classic scene where he turns up at a testicular cancer victims' group and the participants have to pair off, hugging, sobbing and letting it all out. He teams up with Robert – a cracking performance from the singer Meat Loaf (no kidding) – who has grown tits after his balls have been cut off. How pathetic is that? How metaphorical is that?'

How indeed?

Co-starring in *Fight Club* was the best thing that ever happened to Meat Loaf outside music, he later told me. He'd always been an outsider, even with his own touring rock'n'roll band. He was never a musician, not really a member of that club. Hence all the drinking and 'partying' in the early days: 'My attempt to fit into that whole stupid seventies' rock scene.'

Working with people like Edward Norton, he said, 'That's a whole other level of intelligence right there.' He went on: 'I would have to say that Edward Norton is without a doubt one of the most intelligent people I have ever met. His whole family are really talented. He can talk about any subject with great depth and knowledge. I remember I was hanging out with him and Kevin Spacey at one of the film screenings of *Fight Club*. Edward is going on about something or other, his face is all serious and focused. Suddenly, in the middle of this diatribe, Kevin Spacey blurts out: "Edward, what the fuck are you talking about?!" Ed looks up and, without missing a beat, just carries on from where he left off.'

Just as *Bat Out of Hell* had been in the late seventies, *Fight Club* was distrusted by the critics and underestimated in its appeal. *Bat* was too over the top and melodramatic, *Fight Club* was too violent and difficult. Both were heavily stylised and unlike anything else in the commercial mainstream. Neither were immediate hits. *Fight Club*'s second life began on DVD. As poorly marketed as some had felt the movie was, the DVD production was a master-stroke. Fincher took hold of it and ran with the freedom it offered him to complete the film on his terms and in line with his original vision. A single-disc version contained his commentary track, but it was the two-disc package that really took off and started the word-of-mouth running.

Fincher realised that the people who liked *Fight Club* really liked *Fight Club*, and they got everything – deleted scenes and outtakes, trailers, promos, the fake public-service announce-ments that Pitt and Norton had filmed for the movie advertising but which were discarded, storyboards, the works – all at a time before it became the industry standard thing to do. Fox's market-ing pitch was, 'The more you look at it, the more you'll get out of it,' and *Fight Club* was a film that rewarded repeated viewings, an immersive universe filled with cool weird people and off-the-wall ideas. Here, it found its real audience. In a way it *was* like a club – you either got it or you didn't, and if you got it, you were wel-comed in wholeheartedly. Cleverly, the DVD booklet reproduced every bad review the film had received; reinforcing the notion that it wasn't a club for everyone.

Over the next ten years, *Fight Club* would sell more than six million copies on DVD, in the process becoming one of those 'rites of passage' movies, like *Trainspotting* or *Apocalypse Now*, that a particular generation takes to its heart and regards as its own.

As *Newsweek* reported prophetically, it was a movie that would enjoy 'perennial fame'. Some of its original critics reappraised their view over the years as they had the chance to see *Fight Club* several times and rethink it in a different, less deadline-hungry knee-jerk light.

Its success had a darker side, too. Videos of kids fighting in real 'Fight Clubs' now appeared online. An American college student planted pipe bombs in various mailboxes in an attempt to make the film's 'smiley face' pattern on a map. A seventeen-year-old member of a 'Fight Club' in Manhattan detonated a homemade explosive device outside a Starbucks on the Upper East Side. Two employees at a day care centre in New Jersey were arrested and charged with staging 'Fight Club-style' brawls between four- to six-year-olds. A 'Fight Club' began at Princeton University.

The movie should have been a celebratory time in Chuck's life, but also in 1999, his father Fred, who had as a small child hidden under his bed while Chuck's grandfather shot and killed his grandmother, was in turn shot and killed along with his girlfriend Donna Fontaine, by Fontaine's former partner Dale Shackelford. Fred had not known Donna for long, having met her through a personal ad in the newspaper. It transpired that Shackelford, who at the time was imprisoned for sexual offences, had vowed to kill Fontaine upon his release. Chuck came to believe that Donna was seeking someone to protect her when she placed her lonely hearts ad, which was headed 'Kismet'.

Some people always took things just too damn far.

Others just didn't take them far enough.

Meat Loaf knew which camp he was in.

CHAPTER TWENTY-EIGHT

No Matter What

As an old decade turned into a new millennium, it was a time for taking stock. Meat Loaf was fifty-two years old. *Bat II* had made him rich – well, rich in terms of what most people thought of as rich, and certainly richer than when all of the legal shit from the first *Bat* was still flying about. He and Leslie had moved to California, although their marriage was now coming to an end, and they would divorce in 2001. They had been married for over twenty years. Leslie had been by Meat Loaf's side during the best and worst times in his life. Meat had stood by Leslie through the bad times just as she had stood by him. They still loved each other, he told friends, but the years away from home had taken their toll. Their eldest daughter, Pearl – keeping her father's original surname, Aday – now looked set for a singing career of her own, and the marriage had simply run its course. They would stay friends, but no longer lovers. Meanwhile, he had reunited with Jim and their fences had been mended. There was plenty left to do, and he didn't feel at all spent, but his definitive work was now behind him, as was Jim's. And they both knew it.

Yet that had its own pleasures. Meat Loaf could legitimately claim, with *Bat Out of Hell* and now *Fight Club*, that he had been involved in works of art in two fields, music and film. Not only that, but it was work that would endure and enjoy that fabled 'perennial fame'. Neither *Bat* nor *Fight Club* would lose their significance, because they were woven into the fabric of their times, they were remembered, exalted, and they were revered by their fans. Both were cultural events in their own strange way, and it was quite something for the lost boy from Texas to have achieved.

Similarly, Jim Steinman's career had also received a huge and unexpected boost following the success of 'I'd Do Anything'. His record working with artists other than Meat Loaf was spotted but generally good. Bonnie Tyler and Billy Squier had benefitted massively, Def Leppard had turned into a fiasco and his work with Brit-Goth-rockers The Sisters Of Mercy in 1990 had been only a qualified success. (Though, as always with Jim, the best of it – the eight-minute-plus 'More', which later achieved minor success as an edited-down single – would be recycled again and again: as a Gregorian chant, as a Brazilian heavy metal track, as a tremble-tremble NIN-style rocker for the 2003 MTV film version of *Wuthering Heights* (the latter produced by Steinman alongside his usual studio back-up team of Steven Rinkoff and Jeff Bova) – and finally, in 2016, on Meat Loaf's *Braver Than We Are* album.)

In 1994, as Meat Loaf was again knocking dead arena audiences around the world on the *Bat II* tour, Jim Steinman was back working with the 'Welsh milkmaid', producing new versions of 'Making Love Out Of Nothing At All' and, bizarrely, an eight-minute 'dance version' of 'Two Out Of Three Ain't Bad' for the Bonnie Tyler album, *Free Spirit*. (In a further bit of arm-twisting, Stuart Emerson, Jim's former protégé, and husband of Lorraine Crosby, who had sung on 'I'd Do Anything For Love', wrote three of the other tracks on the album.)

The same year Jim oversaw another cover version of 'Original Sin' – a full year before Meat recorded his version for *Welcome to the Neighbourhood* – this time as the theme tune for the hit movie, *The Shadow*, starring Alex Baldwin. Sung by the American singer and actress Taylor Dayne, to Meat Loaf's chagrin and

Jim's unambiguous glee, it is the best-known version of the song. Whatever the financial imperatives, Jim Steinman didn't want to be cornered into a double-act routine any more than Meat Loaf did. In 1995, while Meat Loaf was forging on without him on *Welcome to the Neighbourhood*, Jim was in the studio co-producing Take That's seventh UK Number 1 single and their last to feature Robbie Williams, 'Never Forget'.

While Meat Loaf was still selling millions of records, the singer had no problem with Jim Steinman's other, broader career. The last half of the nineties found the singer now fully focused on acting again. But if *Fight Club* had brought him to the attention of both serious-minded and high-fiving moviegoers everywhere, he was never quite able to parlay that newfound credibility into equally compelling roles. Before *Fight Club*, Meat was cool about playing such one-dimensional roles as the tour bus driver Dennis in *Spice World: The Movie* (1997), or Red the shady truck owner in the Patrick Swayze flop *Black Dog* (1998), or bottom of the bill parts like Floyd in *Outside Ozona* (1998), Iggy Lee in *The Mighty* (1998), and the comedy racist sheriff in *Crazy in Alabama* (1999).

Even when, in the wake of his success in *Fight Club*, Meat finally landed a lead role in a movie – the 2000 thriller *Blacktop* – it was as a trucker who turns out to be a serial killer. There were four more co-star roles in 2001, but none of these movies caught fire and Meat Loaf was back to playing fourth-on-the-bill roles like the Lizard in the weak British comedy-action thriller *The 51st State* (aka in the US as *Formula 51*). After that, he stopped using the name Meat Loaf in his movie roles, feeling it was unfairly bracketing him into 'specialised' roles, preferring to try to make it as plain old Michael Aday. The first movie he made under the new name was *Wishcraft*, a teen-horror flick in which 'Michael' played Detective Sparky Shaw.

After that it was a tsunami of bit parts, until, in 2003, Meat Loaf was 'tempted' back into recording a new album. In truth, his career badly needed the fillip that a *Bat III* would give him, but Jim Steinman wasn't ready for that yet.

Although Jim had openly flirted with the idea that he had a whole thread of songs just waiting for a third *Bat Out of Hell* album, he really didn't. While Meat got his film head on and the record company filled time by sticking out a Meat Loaf greatest hits album, *The Very Best of Meat Loaf,* by the early 2000s Jim was back working across a spectrum of musical projects that had at one end production work with a punk band called Iron Prostate (they split up while recording what would have been their second album – only one track, 'Bring Me The Head Of Jerry Garcia', survives) and exec-producing an album by the Ohio power-pop band Watershed. On the other end, reviving yet another Pandora's Box missed opportunity, this time with Céline Dion, when he (alongside Steven Rinkoff and Roy Bittan) produced a truly momentous new version of 'It's All Coming Back To Me Now'. Released in July 1996, it went to Number 2 in America, Number 3 in Britain and topped the charts in several other countries, selling three million copies along the way.

Jim Steinman was ecstatic. Meat Loaf was furious. He had wanted it for *Bat III*, went on record in several interviews claiming Steinman had actually written the song specifically for him, for the *Bat II* album, but that they had mutually agreed to keep it back for a future *Bat III*. The truth was the song actually dated back as far as 1986 and Jim had always held it back from Meat, declaring that a woman should only ever sing it. The fact that it not been a hit for Pandora's Box was taken as a personal insult by its composer. 'These songs are my children,' as he later told me. 'I want them all to do well and if they don't, I don't just give up on them.'

Meat understood all that but watching Jim pick up a belated BMI Song of the Year award for it in 1996 made his blood boil. It ended in court, with the singer petulantly trying to prove he had some element of dominion over the song. But Steinman won, and Meat was still furious about it for years afterwards. As Meat would tell me in 1998, 'Yeah, I felt like I'd been stabbed in the back when Jimmy gave that song away like that. That was supposed to be *my* song.' It only added salt to the wound, he said, when Andrew Lloyd Webber reportedly told Steinman he thought this song was 'the greatest love song ever written', that the Dion version 'will be the record of the millennium'.

Now, though, Lloyd Webber took his admiration for Steinman one step further, inviting him to help work on the music for his next stage production, a musical adaptation of a British film made in 1961 by Bryan Forbes called *Whistle Down the Wind*, about a girl who finds a murderer on the run hiding in a barn and believes that he is Jesus Christ. For that he needed lyrics of a darker, more Gothic hue. In Jim's hands, the action is transplanted to Louisiana, and the girl is now fifteen years old, allowing him to write about many of the things he always had done.

'I thought, God, how could that be a musical?' Jim said about the moment Lloyd Webber presented him with the original story. 'Then Andrew's next line was, "What do you think of setting it in America?" When he said that, it just clicked. Andrew was originally thinking more of a Midwestern setting, but to me it was immediately evoking the world of Faulkner and Tennessee Williams, that southern Gothic world. And that got me really excited.'

If Jim Steinman had spent his career almost exclusively specialising in unlikely partnerships, he still managed to surprise with this latest liaison: the eccentric, Jewish New Yorker with the penchant for leather jackets and skulls teaming up with the very British lord and purveyor of the world's favourite stage musicals. In truth, though, there was plenty of common ground. They were the same age, and Jim's background had been in musical theatre: at the time he was writing *The Dream Engine*, Lloyd Webber and the lyricist Tim Rice were writing *Joseph and the Amazing*

Technicolor Dreamcoat. As Jim and Meat worked on *More Than You Deserve*, Lloyd Webber and Rice produced *Jesus Christ Superstar*. Only then had their paths diverged (*Bat Out of Hell* came out a few months before the premiere of *Evita*).

As Jim joked in an interview with the *Sunday Times*: 'He's always envied my chart hits. And I've always envied his $800 million . . . I used to say to Andrew, "You took my career", and it's funny, because he said almost the same thing – shows you how the grass is always greener.'

Lloyd Webber and Rice had ended their partnership after *Evita*, and Lloyd Webber had since worked with Richard Stilgoe and Don Black on mega-hit projects like *Starlight Express*, *The Phantom of the Opera* and *Aspects of Love*. Now, with the creator of the *Bat Out of Hell* franchise alongside him, he looked to contemporise his next big project. 'It's a very collaborative effort,' Steinman insisted. 'We're involved in casting together and we work on the whole piece together. I never feel subservient. He's the boss in the sense that he's the producer, but I couldn't ask for a nicer collaborator, really. He's very demanding and intense – but then I am too.'

They may have looked an odd couple from the outside, the small almost-goblin figure of Lloyd Webber and Steinman, who, revelling in the publicity that they'd attracted, was camping it up in his usual leather biker jacket and gloves, even when appearing on breakfast TV shows. But they adored working together and hanging out. One night they would sit together and drink wine while listening to the works of Richard Rodgers, whose co-credits with first Lorenz Hart then later with Oscar Hammerstein, 'the greatest melodist of the 20th century', purred Jim, who had helped create no less than forty-three Broadway musicals, including such untouchable classics as *Pal Joey*, *Oklahoma!*, *South Pacific* and *The Sound of Music*. The next night they would go out together to watch kitsch former glam rock star (and future convicted child offender) Gary Glitter perform on what, though no one knew it yet, would be his final UK tour.

When Andrew first invited Jim over for dinner at his 4,000-acre estate in Sydmonton, it wasn't the collection of Picasso and Pre-Raphaelite paintings that impressed so much as the other guests seated round the table. Lloyd Webber had asked him which three people in Britain Steinman would most like to meet. Not taking the question seriously, Jim had laughed and said off the top of his head: Michael Broadbent, the wine critic, Beatles' producer George Martin and the beautiful actress Joanna Lumley. Lumley was away filming but the other two were happy to show up. Jim, an avowed Anglophile, was staggered.

Sadly, the show wasn't quite the overwhelming hit that two such box-office names might have expected. It premiered in Washington but didn't make Broadway after some poor reviews and problems with the book (the libretto), which was written by Lloyd Webber along with Patricia Knop and Gale Edwards. They revamped it and took it to London for a much more successful run, and it played for more than a thousand shows from 1998. It's since also enjoyed a couple of successful revivals under the theatre producer Bill Kenwright. Meat Loaf sang one of its Webber-Steinman songs 'A Kiss Is A Terrible Thing To Waste', a duet with Bonnie Tyler no less, on an album featuring various other 'big-name artists' including Tom Jones, Boy George and Donny Osmond, which covered *Whistle Down the Wind*'s songs, all produced by Jim. The hit from that, though, went to Irish boy band Boyzone, with 'No Matter What', a Number 1 in eighteen countries.

This was something else that Meat Loaf fumed about when we met the same year. 'This keeps happening to me,' he said, glaring out of the window of his top-floor hotel suite. 'I was supposed to be the one that recorded "No Matter What", not Boyzone! I mean, okay, they did a big hit version but come on, are you kidding? It was like . . . *nothing*. No body. No soul. Can you imagine what *I* would have done with that song?'

So why hadn't Steinman let him record it then? He frowned, puffed out his cheeks, glared some more. 'Because I guess they figure Boyzone are the bigger act at this time. Especially here in the UK. They wanted a big hit to launch the show in London and I guess they got it.' He shook his head again. 'But come on, can you imagine what that song might have been if I'd been allowed to kick it into shape?'

In fact, we wouldn't have to wait long to hear exactly what Meat Loaf would have done with 'No Matter What', his own eight-minute mini-opera version becoming the lead track on his own *Very Best Of* compilation album, which came out later that year. It was, as he had promised it would be, full of all the oomph he felt was missing from the hit Boyzone version. It was never released as a single, as it was, after all, the huge international hit that Boyzone had with the song that would go down in history.

There was also a third Steinman original recorded for the *Very Best Of* album, an offcut Jim had composed called 'Is Nothing Sacred?' with lyrics provided by one of Lloyd Webber's regular co-writers, Don Black. It was rerecorded as a duet featuring Patti Russo for its single release in 1999, reaching Number 15 in the UK but making zero impression anywhere else in the world. Scant compensation for missing out on 'No Matter What', but by then it hardly mattered. Once again, Meat Loaf was going to have to get used to living in a world where Jim Steinman was considered the really important one.

CHAPTER TWENTY-NINE

Only After Dark

In 1997, Jim Steinman got to fulfil yet another of his teenage fantasies when he was approached by Roman Polanski to work on a musical version of Polanski's 1967 film *Dance of the Vampires* (issued in the US under the title *The Fearless Vampire Killers*). It wasn't just his love for modern Polanski noirs like *Repulsion*, *Rosemary's Baby* and *Chinatown*, nor his obvious penchant for writing about vampires both real (in Jim's mind) and metaphorical, but the whole transgressive aura that hung over the French-Polish director. Polanski's pregnant actress wife Sharon Tate had infamously been stabbed to death in the Charlie Manson murders of the late sixties, the word PIG written in her blood over the door of the house where the grisly murder took place. But all sympathy for the director flew out the door eight years later when he fled America after being charged with – and pleading guilty to – the rape of a thirteen-year-old girl in LA during a photo session. Since then Polanski had worked exclusively in Europe, producing some of his best, and darkest work, including *Tess*, *Frantic* and *Bitter Moon*.

The *Vampire* stage show was to be a pan-European extravaganza that was first produced in Vienna, where it was known as *Tanz der Vampire* (the title it would use in other German-speaking territories). Jim was first hired to write the music, and later also wrote the book for the New York version of the show.

'I never write a song without first visualising the scenery,' Jim said. 'I step into another world and find a character and story for every single song. That's why I have been excited about getting the chance to write the music for *Vampire*. I saw the film in the sixties and have been a big Polanski fan since then.' He added gleefully: 'I once worked on the music for Murnau's famous *Nosferatu* and have always known that vampires would make an ideal subject for an opera or a musical. In fact, I wrote "Total Eclipse Of The Heart" – probably my most successful song ever – as a tribute to *Nosferatu*. That's why I had to include a new version of it in *Dance of the Vampires*, totally rewritten as a duet with German lyrics. The show is something pretty eclectic, a combination of savage rock sounds and opera.'

Tanz der Vampire was a considerable hit through Europe, although Polanski's reputation in America, where he remains to this day a fugitive from justice, impacted on the New York version, which had the book rewritten, much to Jim's disappointment, and led to a rupture between him and his long-time manager David Sonenberg, who was one of the producers of the show.

Again, Jim used versions of songs and melodies for different projects. During various stages of its different international productions, several old and soon-to-be new Meat Loaf songs emerged from Steinman's permissive pen, including 'God Has Left The Building', which he'd first discussed with Meat years before, renamed for the New York stage as 'God Is Dead', along with new versions of 'Total Eclipse', or 'Totale Finsternis' as it became in the original Vienna production, yet another version of 'Original Sin', and a number that Meat Loaf wouldn't record for another nearly twenty years called 'Braver Than We Are'.

As the new century unwound, Jim spent the first few years doing more of the same: he exec-produced an MTV movie of *Wuthering Heights* (he had long claimed that 'It's All Coming Back To Me Now' was inspired by the book), worked on another aborted musical, this time about Greta Garbo, and almost teamed up with Tim Burton for a stage version of the *Batman* film franchise. He and his production partner Steven Rinkoff staged a production of some songs from *The Dream Engine*. Ideas and projects swirled without any morphing into substantial hits.

And all the time, in the background, it was as if his past – and Meat Loaf's – was gathering in, rushing to catch up and overtake them as *Bat Out of Hell* had its twentieth and then twenty-fifth anniversary. Yet still the principal actors in this real-life on- and off-stage musical drama resisted the pull of the inevitable. Meat continued to tour, able to pack them into Wembley Arena and various Stadhalles in Germany. But in America he had fallen off the arena circuit again, doing the rounds instead of endless theatres and entertainment centres. In 2001 he took part as a featured artist in the European Night of the Proms tour, an evening of rock music woven around classical music, that took in twenty-two shows in Belgium at the Sportspaleis in Antwerp, twelve in Holland at the Ahoy in Rotterdam, and thirteen at various venues around in Germany. He spent most of the tour in rented luxury apartments, doing his handful of songs each night and being paid handsomely for his time. Yet still he wanted more. He and Jim had both always wanted more. It was the chief thing they had in common. Too much was never enough.

It seemed like some kind of immutable law. They worked together, had a huge hit, then had a sort of semi-separation during which Meat may record some of Jim's older songs, before making a record that didn't involve Jim at all and somehow seemed to be doomed because of it.

Although Meat called *Couldn't Have Said it Better*, his seventh studio album and the third without any Steinman songs, 'the most perfect album I did since *Bat Out of Hell*', it wasn't, of course. He had one Diane Warren song, another sing-it-from-the-hilltops power ballad, 'You're Right, I Was Wrong', but this time it wasn't considered strong enough to be a single. A misstep, in retrospect, perhaps, as the track that was chosen in its stead, the ponderously longwinded and artificially upbeat 'Did I Say That?', written by the album's co-producer James Michael, missed the charts by miles. There were four other tracks also co-written by Michael, with Mötley Crüe bassist Nikki Sixx – the two played together in Sixx's side band, the only modestly successful Sixx:A.M. – along with a handful of off-the-peg numbers written by little-known hacks. They all faced the same problem that everyone collaborating with Meat Loaf who wasn't Jim Steinman faced – they weren't Jim.

Steinman had proven that his writing was in some way inimitable, not that it stopped them trying. The title song was probably the best, and it was greatly enlivened by Patti Russo, who sang a tremendous counter-melody during the duet section, but much of the rest was pretty lame filler stuff. Meat struggled for an identity beyond Jim's characters, perhaps because he'd been possessed so profoundly by them over the years, and found it harder to get as intense with less good and less evocative songs.

The problem was compounded because Meat was providing his side of the deal. He was a part of Jim's songs and it was very hard to divide him out of them and put that essence into something else. Released in September 2003, *Couldn't Have Said it Better* didn't quite bomb, but it was restricted by a deal that saw it recorded for Universal Germany and then licensed to Mercury in the UK and the indie label Sanctuary in the US. It went Top 10 in Germany and Top Five in the UK, did pretty well across Europe, but sank almost without trace in America, where Sanctuary failed to get it away (although it is perfectly possible no one could have muscled it much higher than the Number 85 it hit on the Billboard Hot 100 it was destined to become).

The accompanying tour was a greater success. Meat Loaf fans knew what they were going to get when they bought a ticket. He always played the hits and he always put on a show, and whatever album he had out at the time wasn't going to change that. The age of self-styled 'classic rock' acts going out there and putting on a jukebox of their biggest hits was upon us and nobody begrudged these artists their seeming inability to add anything truly worthwhile to the canon.

Meat toured long and hard once again, throwing everything into it. Now, though, for the first time his health – his physical health – gave way. On stage at Wembley Arena in November 2003 he collapsed and was diagnosed with a heart condition known as Wolff-Parkinson-White syndrome, which was corrected by surgery (it was a condition often associated with elite endurance athletes – his doctor joked that he should be flattered to have it). It wasn't going to stop him, he said, but he knew he had to dial it back, and he did: his insurers made it conditional that no show now last longer than an hour and forty-five minutes. He played another 160 shows, and during his run in Australia was accompanied for two shows by the Melbourne Symphony Orchestra, which were recorded for the album *Bat Out of Hell Live*.

Towards the end of the tour he introduced a new song into the set, trailing it as one that formed part of a proposed *Bat Out of Hell III*. It was called 'Only When I Feel'. It was to prove absurdly optimistic . . .

If *Bat Out of Hell III* ever truly existed, it was surely only in Jim Steinman's mind, where anything still felt possible. And we know how things could exist there, in that enchanted realm, part Neverland, part teenage Wagner, part apocalyptic wasteland of the heart . . . If *Bat III* existed in that place, it sounded huge yet distant, bruised by the passing years, a more reflective, darker, colder record in the way that some of Jim's songs had been going. The future just ain't what it used to be, as he had warned us all those years before on the Pandora's Box album, if only anybody had actually listened to it.

But if Meat Loaf was now trying to will it into existence, there were still many obstacles in the way. And yet they'd done it before, together, conjured something into life with the old magic. A decade on from *Bat II*, the time seemed right. Didn't it? And they were coming to an age where they had to acknowledge that time was in some way running out. They were both now pushing sixty and their bodies were more vulnerable, their creative impulses slightly dimmer. One by one the lights were going out. It was only natural but that didn't make it good. And perhaps it would have all seemed less imperative, less pressing, if they didn't depend so much on one another. They had known each other for more than forty years, and yet they had produced just two albums in full partnership. It wasn't a high strike rate, and how many more chances might they get?

Jim Steinman, though, still felt time was somehow on his side. He had proved he could have mega-hits without Meat. Meat could make records and films and tour without Jim. But they were locked together by *Bat Out of Hell*, locked together for life, which was strange when you remembered the arguments about the original sleeve and how people would be confused by the fact that there were two of them. Now that was what people *wanted* – the two of them, Jim doing his thing and Meat doing his and making the sounds that they could only make together.

But Jim didn't live in the real world and had no intention of starting now. Meat Loaf wasn't the only one likely to keel over when the pressure got too much. Where once his dark moods waxed and waned with the moon, Steinman confessed in public now that there was more to it than that. That maybe it wasn't that he had been the one chasing the darkness all this many lifetimes, but the darkness that had found him – and would no longer let him go. He'd been living by night for so long, he could no longer live any other way. He would often go weeks at a time without seeing another soul. With the advent of email and the

Internet, he didn't even have to speak to anyone any more if he didn't want to, and more and more as the years passed he felt less inclined to.

None of which actually brought him peace. 'My brain never stops,' he complained, 'it's so hard for me even to sleep.' Confessing to one interviewer: 'I am not happy much. I get really depressed, unbelievably depressed. This is hard to articulate. I don't find being incredibly depressed depressing, if that makes any sense.'

He was now taking aspirin every four hours to ease the constant pain he claimed he still endured from his long-ago dental disaster following his near-fatal duel with that lady biker. 'I am conscious of pain a lot,' he explained. 'I've lived with it since that operation. I don't know how that affects me. I don't want to sound morbid about it – people live with a lot worse – but I think it has affected me in some ways quite deeply.'

He still liked to go out with guests for dinner – though for him dinner meant breakfast, still ordering almost everything on the menu, some in double portions, which he would invite everyone to share – as long as they didn't mind him eating with his fingers. He would talk with his mouth full about how gluttonous he was. But his real addiction was to the night. And to the strange and interesting things the night could do to you – if you let it.

The years were now flashing past like the lights of a night train. Maybe that's what got to him, made him impatient. Maybe that's what led to everything that happened next . . .

They had first started talking tentatively about it in 2001, though they had both played hard to get, to begin with. Nothing much happened and they did other things and then once Meat was off the road, they started again. But as Meat would explain, Jim got ill, seriously ill, and Meat Loaf decided to go ahead with *Bat Out of Hell III* without him. 'It was absolutely selfish on my part,' he said. 'He had a heart attack and two strokes; his health was the main concern for me. It was a hard decision to make, but he had had a second stroke, and ... I didn't think he was physically ready to do it, to commit to that kind of work. And I was afraid we'd be in and out of the studio for five years ... and I'm not exactly the youngest chicken in the pen either. And so I needed to move.'

Move he did. He had a bunch of Jim's songs that he'd never recorded. He found a producer in Desmond Child, a brilliant, nailed-on hit maker whose catalogue as a songwriter included 'Livin' On A Prayer' and 'You Give Love A Bad Name' for Bon Jovi, 'Dude Looks Like A Lady' for Aerosmith, 'I Was Made For Loving You' for Kiss, 'We All Sleep Alone' for Cher, 'Livin' la Vida Loca' for Ricky Martin and at least a dozen more built-for-speed hit singles. Meat was initially set on Child as the other main writer on the project and using Michael Beinhorn to produce, but when he sat next to Child at the sound desk 'it was like I was talking to Steinman'.

Together they had some serious clout: they pulled in Queen guitarist Brian May, former Frank Zappa and David Lee Roth uber-guitarist Steve Vai, then gold-plated session man John Shanks, a glorious vocalist called Marion Raven to sing with Meat Loaf on Jim's 'It's All Coming Back To Me Now' (a song Meat would finally get to record even though he would be the last to the party, but which he'd try to enliven the prospect of by insisting he'd 'always heard it as a duet'), and the breaking star Jennifer Hudson on another Steinman song, 'The Future Ain't What It Used To Be', both from Pandora's Box. May appeared on 'Bad For Good' (the same track Meat had dismissed years before as 'too much like Springsteen ... all right but not great') and they recorded a few other of Jim's songs, 'If It Ain't Broke, Break It', which was a rewrite of 'Only When I Feel', the song Meat had introduced from the stage as part of *Bat III* during his last tour, plus 'In The Land Of The Pig, The Butcher Is King', 'Cry To Heaven' and 'Seize The Night', all of which Jim had been working on since the aborted *Batman* project with Tim Burton.

Desmond Child was one of the few songwriters who could write convincingly in Steinman's style, and he produced an absolute doozy in 'Blind As A Bat', one of the strongest songs on the album and a tune almost indistinguishable from one of Jim's.

Bat III was a long album, and in the absence of anything else, they went to the edge, to the max, with dense, cacophonous sounds, vast orchestral moments and maximum drama from note one. It was subtitled *The Monster is Loose* and that's what it was, a real Frankenstein job, with a bolt through its neck and electricity coursing through its veins while it lumbered along on somebody else's legs . . .

CHAPTER THIRTY

Hell's Bells

But wait – did you say *Bat Out of Hell III*? When did that happen? I remember asking myself these questions when the *Bat III* album was released in October 2006. Unlike *Bat II*, with its huge trailblazing lead single, 'I'd Do Anything For Love', and the massive, industrial-strength publicity machine behind its launch, with Meat and Jim jetting around the world to promote it, the arrival of *Bat III* was so anticlimactic it almost didn't register. The 'It's All Coming Back To Me Now' single, with Marion Raven, released three months before, had hardly registered either, squeezing into the UK and German Top 10s but making no impression whatsoever in the US. The only country where it went to Number 1 was in Norway.

Yet here we were, just Meat Loaf and I, sitting in another £2,000-a-night hotel suite, this time at the Mandarin Oriental in Hyde Park. Him grumpy as I fiddled with my recorder, his breakfast plate of porridge going cold on a nearby table, me still wondering how the hell he could really call his new album *Bat Out of Hell III* when Jim Steinman's involvement seemed so . . . minimal? Not a word one would ever have used normally in regards to anything Steinman had done. Indeed, it seemed sacrilegious almost to see not the tag line 'Songs by Jim Steinman' on the cover, as it had been on *Bat I* and *II*, but, somewhat gallingly, 'Songs by Jim Steinman *and* Desmond Child'.

My first question should have been, 'What the fuck?' Instead I opted for asking when the idea for a *Bat III* had first come up, as far back as *Bat II*, maybe?

'Oh, before that.'

Really? So this was always the plan?

'Yeah.'

How far back, not as far back as *Bat I*, surely?

'Well, Jim may have mentioned it back then, it could have been in Jim's head as far back as . . . well, it wouldn't have been when we were recording *Bat I* because we didn't know that we were ever going to get to record again. But back in the mid-eighties, when we started talking about doing *Bat II*, there's always been the talk of *Bat III*.'

So what took so long? We're now talking almost as long between *Bat II* and *III* as *Bat I* and *II* . . .

'Well, first of all you got . . . well, this wouldn't have been *Bat III* if I didn't think it was right. I mean they – record companies and people – tried to do *Welcome to the Neighbourhood* as *Bat III*, and I fought 'em. You have no idea the huge arguments that I had over that. I said, no, this is not a *Bat Out of Hell* record. This is not even close to a *Bat Out of Hell* record. It's a fine record, it's good and you can put it out, it's got songs on it that are good. But it's not a *Bat Out of Hell* record. There's just something very different about *Bat Out of Hell* records. They're just bigger. They're renegades. When you get an album that's a renegade, it's not like anything else. In '77, *Bat Out of Hell* wasn't like anything that was out there – nothing! There was nothing like *Bat Out of Hell*, not even close. In '93, there was nothing like *Bat Out of Hell II* . . .'

He was in full media blunderbuss mode. I tried to focus him a little more. 'You say the *Bat* albums are a very specific thing and yet this one is a little different . . .'

'Yeah, well . . . See, it started out that we were doing *Bat III* with Jim, and . . . and, he just wasn't able to do it.'

'Why not?'

'Okay, this is what happened. He had told me he was ill, he had strokes, which he did, and that he wasn't . . . he couldn't start right away because of his health. Since then he's denied that, so I don't know what to tell you on that. All I know is that when we were getting close, the contract was to be signed for him to do it, he didn't want to sign the contract because, I don't know why, but I know that two days prior to this time he was telling me that he needed six months' rehabilitation because he couldn't play the piano with his hands. So if that wasn't true, then that wasn't true, but that's what he said to me. So that's what I know.'

Had he actually written any new songs before this? I asked.

'Well, he had written some stuff. He had sent me . . . just like he did on *Bat II* where we used a lot of his old stuff and four new things, that's how I got what I got . . . he had sent me, oh, I don't know, fifteen songs, and I was talking to him, saying, "I don't think these are right for a *Bat III* record. They're fine but they're not right for *Bat III*."'

He fidgeted, wanting to get past the whole Jim thing. It was obvious something serious had gone down, but getting Meat to say what that was was not going to be easy. I waited for him to arrange his thoughts. Eventually . . .

'The bottom line to it was – and I've spent a lot of time thinking about it, and I'm not saying anything negative about Jim, I'm just kind of giving you a history of it – the bottom line was I think his health was an issue to him. He wanted to do it but it was gonna take a very long time for him to complete the project. And when . . . basically, I decided that I wouldn't wait for him. And that's when it became kind of ugly.

'Because I just didn't have it in me to sit and wait for four years . . . It still took two years from that time to do it. But you've got to go all the way forward. Desmond Child did a beyond amazing job. I mean, truly. I'm not gifted enough in the English language to convey in words the job that Desmond Child did. Excellent, unbelievable, bombastic . . . I don't know. There's better adjectives that I can come up with. All I know is that Desmond Child gave his heart and soul to this project. I think he believes he came close to giving his life to it.

'But the true story is that three days ago now, Jim and Desmond talked for over an hour. I would imagine they've probably talked again since then. They had been passing emails back in May [2006] about different lyrics in different songs and what was going on. Jim was actually blown away by the record and talking to Desmond about when we go in to do the box set – we plan to do a box set in three or four years' time. Jim was saying that when we go in to do that he wanted Desmond to produce but that he really wanted to sit with him when we are doing it. Because . . . I could be wrong, I just think Jim's health is an issue even though he doesn't want the public to know, so maybe we shouldn't talk about it.'

There were certainly lots of aspects to the new record that were, uh, quite surprising, I said.

'Yeah, well, that's good. Because that's a *Bat Out of Hell* record.'

At the same time, was it part of Desmond's job to take on board that this was number three in a line and that you needed something you could recognisably trace from one and two?

'Yeah, you have to have that. You need the line you can trace. But also that can be a micro-line.'

Cos some of the stuff kind of breaks that line, don't you think?

'In a sense [it does]. In [another] sense it doesn't. If you go to "The Monster Is Loose", well, it breaks it but it stays right with it.'

It's certainly big . . .

'Well, what line did *Bat Out of Hell* have? You know, you can't go back and say, well, you've gotta have this because that happened. Well, before that happened there was nothing. So there was no line for *Bat Out of Hell*. There was no . . . if you wanna say, "formula". There was no formula, there was no line. So as far as I'm going, yeah, there's elements of Todd's background, there's elements of piano, but at the same time there's elements of being totally different.'

And you wanted that?

'Yeah, yeah. That's what *Bat* was. *Bat* was totally different. So I wanted surprises, I wanted people to go, "Wow, that's not what I was expecting!" Yeah, absolutely. So "Monster Is Loose", "Land Of The Pig", things like that, people aren't expecting that from this. But they're dead-on *Bat Out of Hell*.'

Hmm. Whose idea was it to bring in people like Marilyn Manson guitarist John 5?

'Well, that was . . . I gave Desmond the song title, "The Monster Is Loose", and that came from baseball. From what one guy used to say to another guy . . . his name was John Sterns and he said it to Mike Piazza in '99 . . .'

I tuned out. I am not an American baseball fan and had no idea who he was talking about. What struck me was how reluctant he was to discuss why John 5 was on his album. Maybe he didn't know. Finally, he got back to talking about *Bat Out of Hell III*.

'It covers a whole lot of ground. You know, I wasn't convinced until April [2006] that this was a *Bat Out of Hell III*. Because, I just didn't know . . . I could hear what we were doing and I could see what we were doing but . . . um . . . when you don't have Jim and you're working with somebody else that's not Jim then, yeah, you have to doubt that. Um . . . so . . . yeah, up until April. Everybody kept saying, *Bat Out of Hell III*, *Bat Out of Hell III* . . . We were working on a CD cover [and] we were doing everything and I wasn't saying to anybody, well, okay . . . I mean, they were all planning *Bat Out of Hell III* and in my mind I was planning a record and if it's *Bat Out of Hell III*, great.'

It sounded like an afterthought. What was it that finally made up his mind? 'I think it's when I did the vocal on "Land Of The Pig" and I realised what I was dealing with here. I love that song! It's so . . . Steinman loves it. Steinman loved the [he goes to say "original"] . . . Because if you were to hear it as the Steinman demo you would be going, "How did he get that out of that? How in the hell did anybody get that out of that?" Because the Steinman version is *very* West End-Broadway. I mean, so *Oklahoma!* that it's ridiculous – and sung really legit. But I loved the song from the first time I ever heard it because I liked what it was saying. It's kind of, never really written a protest song. I flipped some lyrics in there so it wasn't so . . . so it can remain timeless. Because there were some lyrics in there that would have taken it away from being timeless, and I made sure we stayed in that thing that *Bat Out of Hell* records also have to have, which is where they can be played anytime, it doesn't make a difference what year, and still work.'

What made him go back and do 'Bad For Good'?

'Oh, I had done everything else on that record except for the ones I don't like . . .

'It's like, *Bat II, Bat I,* yeah, they're in the same line but they're not . . . you know, they're opposites of each other. And then *Bat III* is the same but completely different. And being, thirteen, fourteen years apart is a good thing. First of all, I don't know how it is thirteen years, I haven't figured that out yet but it was.'

They go quicker as you get older.

'Yeah, they go quicker and you just don't get it.'

So why did you do the song 'Bad For Good' this time?

'Yeah, I just thought it was a good one to do. We did "Rock And Roll Dreams", and I did "Left In The Dark" and I did "Lost Boys". And I'd done "Surf's Up" back in '85. I've done all the ones that I've liked. The ones that drove me crazy . . . you won't ever hear me do "Dance In My Pants" or you won't hear me do "Stark Raving Love" . . .'

I had interviewed Meat many times over the years. I'd seen him in good moods, bad moods, exhausted after a show and on top of the world after an album. But I had never seen him so on the defensive before. Did he even know why the hell he was making another *Bat* record, other than for the money? Which is not a bad reason to do anything, it was just wearing to find him trying to reconcile the harsh business realities of his decisions now to the romance that used to surround the title *Bat Out of Hell*. It had slipped under the radar in 1977 until it became such an overwhelming sales success that the gargantuan tunes within it became simply undeniable. In 1993 it had exploded back into life with such fire and passion that it had brought his career back to life from the dead. Now this. What was this meant to be? Did he even know any more?

'So here we are,' I said, '*Bat Out of Hell III*. It's the twenty-first century, we can do everything – DVDs, West End shows, computer games – what are you gonna do with this "franchise" now?'

Ah, that was easier. He replied that he would begin by touring it in the conventional sense, there was a massive world tour planned to run for two years, twenty-one shows then two weeks off, to be repeated ... The show would not feature any material from any of the other albums, not even 'Dead Ringer For Love', just all material from the three *Bat* albums. Plus a 'new musical element which will make it be different in the first ten seconds' that he won't tell me about 'because then there wouldn't be surprises'.

The live show won't be *too* theatrical, though. 'I'm more an improv kind of guy and I would get bored too easily if we had to stick to the same rules every night, in terms of theatrical effects and all that stuff. All I really know at this point is how we're gonna start the show – but I'm not gonna tell you that either. You can come back and we can talk about it again after the show.'

What about the rumours of a *Bat Out of Hell* movie – were they true? He nodded enthusiastically. 'There is a guy writing a script and I keep forgetting his name. I feel completely insane and completely embarrassed that I can't remember his name. It's right on the tip of my brain but I just can't find it.' I give him the name: Australian filmmaker Stuart Beattie, whose major claim to fame at the time was directing *The Curse of the Black Pearl*, the then most recent movie in the Johnny Depp-led *Pirates of the Caribbean* franchise.

'Yeah,' he said doubtfully. 'Is it gonna be a movie, though? Well, like I say, they're working on a script. I've been in forty-three movies now and been asked to be in seventy. So, you never know . . .' He sighed. 'If everybody would just stay out of the way and let it happen, it would happen. The problem you've got is you've got so many people in the middle of it. You've heard the old saying "too many cooks spoil the broth". If everybody would sit back and let a writer write, let a director direct, let actors act, then you might have something. But it's everybody's need to be in control of something that will screw up everything all the time.

'Like *Bat I*, I never tried to be in control. *Bat II*, never tried to be in control. I'd put my two cents in and back off. *Bat III*, I don't try to be in control. You hire. We hired Todd Rundgren, he was hired to make this a record. When we do the box set and I put on the original demos of *Bat Out of Hell* everybody's gonna sit around and go, "Oh my! Wow! What Todd did is amazing!" And if we put in the original demos we had for *Bat III*, or even for *Bat II*, everybody's gonna sit around going, "Wow, Jim did great!" But he came in and got out of the way and let Roy Bittan do a lot of work on *Bat II*. Desmond – you're gonna go, "Desmond? Really? Wow! That's interesting! How did he get 'Land Of The Pig' to sound like that?" Or even "If It Ain't Broke", because Jim told him he didn't think you could make a song out of "If It Ain't Broke" but Desmond did. He went way past it.

'So that was really good. I think everything worked out like it was supposed to. And I believe that in life, too. That *Bat II* came out at the right time. *Bat III* will come out when it's supposed to. Whether it's the right time or not, it will come out when it was supposed to. I'm one of those master-plan guys. I believe in fate. Like, once you take that pathway you have to work on that. You have to clear the path, you have to make the grass grow, you have to fix your path. If you don't, your path remains rocky and nothing ever gets done. But once you choose the path you have to work on it. And I worked harder on this record than anything I've ever worked on in my life. I'm telling you the truth. We were doing vocals and Desmond was asking an old dog to do new tricks.'

He talked about how Desmond kept pushing him – forcing him 'to get away from the style I've done the last five records with' until he became despairing. '"You've got to be rockier, you've got to be more street." He was giving me notes and I couldn't do 'em.' Eventually, for the first time ever, Meat got a vocal coach in and that did the trick, he said, to the point where he was now considering having the coach come out on the road with him for this tour.

So was this it now? The end of the line for *Bat Out of Hell*, or were there already plans for *Bat IV*?

'Oh, God, I don't know. People keep going what about *Bat IV* but I'm going, "I don't have enough time in my life for that." All you gotta do is add fourteen years to how old I am now and that's the end of that. I don't even need to say no there won't.'

CHAPTER THIRTY-ONE

Erections of the Heart

Some months after I interviewed Meat Loaf about *Bat Out of Hell III*, I spoke to Jim Steinman. More reclusive than ever, he was no longer leaving the house. Therefore I would have to phone him. No problem. But could I make it, say, around 5.00am, Connecticut time? Well, of course. You don't plan on interviewing the vampire then complain that he stays up late.

It was ostensibly for a lifestyle article but within minutes we had left that subject behind and begun talking about what was really on Jim's mind, the same thing that had preoccupied him throughout his career. I later chiselled a short thousand-word piece out of it for *Classic Rock* magazine, but the rest of our two-hour conversation remained untranscribed – until now. By the end of the conversation we had talked about working on a book together about Jim's life. He seemed excited. Gave me all his details. But when I emailed him and called back a few days later to follow up, he never replied. I didn't know it then but a lot of his plans were about to unravel. They would later come back together, but by then years had passed and the interview remained in my archive.

It began when I asked simply why he hadn't really been involved in *Bat Out of Hell III*? 'How much time do you have?' he chuckled darkly. 'There's no way to put it simply, I'm sorry . . .'

He didn't want to get into the excruciating detail, he said, but it did prompt him to reflect more deeply, for the record, than he had before. He sounded almost wistful. At least, to begin with . . .

'You keep re-evaluating what you do,' he sighed. Back when he wrote the songs for the first *Bat* album, he said, 'I didn't really know what I was doing. I knew I wanted them to be cinematic but I never thought of them as show tunes. Such a dirty term now, though really some of the great pop songs of all time are really show tunes.'

As the years – and the *Bat* albums – flew by, though, the critics had caught up with him. 'I just read a review, I think in *Q* magazine, where it said I proved that it was really only a skip and a jump from hard rock to show tunes. Well, to me it's a really powerful skip and a jump – if that can be true that a skip can be powerful. The jump from rock'n'roll to show tunes is not in the scheme of the world and landscape of music. But to me it's not a big step. That for me goes for all kinds of arts and creative work. Like it's not a big skip to go from Hitchcock to Jean Renoir or Orson Welles, Carol Reid, or any other great filmmaker if you really narrow it down to what's making it great. That's basically how I reacted when it came to writing my songs. I just know I like songs to be cinematic. Being cinematic, they have to include a stage language because that's part of cinema.'

What about musically? 'Musically, it was just whatever I could come up with. I didn't at the time sit down and say, okay, I'm gonna write these Wagnerian epics. I mean, you don't use language like that. It was basically sweating, thinking, "Holy shit, I hope I can come up with something!" which I think is what everyone basically thinks.'

Did he still have the taste for listening to rock music and opera?

'I've been listening to tons of rock'n'roll and opera. Through my whole life that's been true, since I was six years old. It's that combination without separation – they were the two musical forms that I'm most attracted to. I think the common denominator of both of them was they are both simultaneously thrilling and ecstatic as well as ridiculous and absurd. And I like that combination. That's one of the reasons why a 350-pound guy named Meat Loaf wasn't weird to me. It took me about half a beat to say, "Okay, Meat . . ." I had no sense that this was such a strange name – because to me it wasn't. I grew up with Kirsten Flagstad' – the highly regarded Norwegian singer of Wagnerian opera – 'and Wolfgang Windgassen,' a famed German singer, again of Wagnerian opera.

'I mean, those names sound *totally* made up, like something out of George Lucas. I was already living in a sort of fantasy world and Meat Loaf was a perfect Wagnerian element. So when I tried to write the music my heart was really exploring the world I was being led to by the light of Wagner. In my heart I wanted to have the effect that Wagner does. More so even than rock'n'roll because I didn't really know how to do it as well in rock'n'roll. I was just totally taken with the fact he could sing that way, he had obviously still to be worked on, but he had genuine presence and charisma and acting ability. And he had a great upper Heldentenor voice. He had a really great operatic voice.'

He said his 'best memories of Meat Loaf' now all went back to their earliest days together. 'To me, the public discovered him from 1977 on, *after* his best years. I can't say he's like Maria Callas who really was most famous after her best years but it's that I just don't think anyone could understand the true thrill it was for me to be alone in a room that could only hold a piano and like a few people, day after day, for like two years, where we'd go to rehearse – and to hear his voice in those surroundings where the actual room would shake and the piano would seem possessed and epileptic. It was the *physical* sensation of *physically* registering his voice that was special. You'd never find it much these days and you didn't much those days.'

The huge late-seventies success had been a double-edged sword, he said. Even Meat Loaf acknowledged that now.

'It's true literally that he went out one way and came back

another way. He transformed completely. There were a lot of components to that. But I know Meat Loaf himself refers to it as being "The Success" having changed him. I don't necessarily buy it to be that simple. It was everything. I mean, I'm speaking about him so I can't really say. I'm doing a third-party observation. But to me it was like the perfect storm of destructive elements.'

In retrospect, everything else that immediately followed was a mistake, he said. His mind drifted back to *Bad For Good*. 'It was supposed to be his record but I did it because there was a complicated legal thing. The record company was demanding something. He wasn't close. So I . . . most of the vocals on there were reference vocals for demos for Meat Loaf. The damn thing is about an octave higher than I sing. So it was incredibly diffi-cult for me to sing it at all.' Meat Loaf's subsequent claim that he didn't make the record because he had qualms about a lot of material on it was merely a smokescreen, he suggested, adding that Sonenberg, who didn't manage Jim as well until 1980, 'didn't help. It was just a mess.'

Looking back now, he said, the reason he and Meat didn't con-tinue working together 'was simply . . . it can be blamed on us but primarily it was other people. Meat Loaf and I agree about that. It was a constant litany of get-the-new-album-out, new product, new product, new product! It was a screaming, keening, insidi-ous mob in my mind. New product! It was like a horrible beast in slow motion, "noooo product!!!" It just never stopped. And Meat really did not have the strength to articulate what was bad about that. Whereas I can over-articulate anything. So I would constantly fight back.'

Had the fuck-ups not occurred, had his 'initial vision' been followed – that he and Meat would be an equal partnership – Jim would still have worked in theatre and films, and, as he put it, 'I would have been able to do it all. I would have been able to do what Roger Waters has been able to do.'

He was referring to the spectacular *The Dark Side of the Moon* touring show that Waters had turned into the biggest dollar-grossing show on Earth that year, with receipts in excess of $400 million. 'Roger Waters has enough of an anchor with Pink Floyd that allows him to navigate from that anchor. Whereas, Meat Loaf began as my anchor but quickly disappeared in about a year.'

He said he was 'extremely proud of that record', meaning 'Total Eclipse Of The Heart', and insisted it was never intended for Meat Loaf, as the singer often claimed it had been. 'I didn't write it for anyone but Bonnie. It's funny because [the record company people] expected me to give them another sort of "It's A Heartache" country record. But I just met this Bonnie Tyler and I thought, all I can see her as . . . and this is another example of how I work. I have to have a vision of someone as a performer, on a bare stage, with great lighting in a pin spot in the middle of the stage. I have to see that, it's an image from opera, basically, that I grew up with. I have to envision them in that moment, about to sing the song, and know what the song's gonna be. There is a fair comparison to musicals but it's because that's my world to set up something. It's the womb from which these babies are born, so to speak. So [with Bonnie] I had to envision a situation where a Joan Sutherland is on a stage backed up by The Who and Phil Spector's group – and then I could go ahead. I couldn't write like opera composers but I was going for the same effect for "Total Eclipse".'

It was different with Pandora's Box, though. 'I knew when I wrote for Pandora's Box that I'd written songs that I would have written for *Bat Out of Hell*. I knew when they came out that they were *Bat Out of Hell* songs. And I was very pissed off that Pandora's Box hadn't made it. I'm still very pissed off. I *adore* Pandora's Box. I'm as proud of that as anything I've ever done and they never even got released in America. To me that's disgusting and I can't forget it. Because they didn't make it in the UK they didn't put the record out in America. Everyone likes to say their stuff is ahead of its time but to me that was a kind of Spice Girls' setting but six years before the Spice Girls. The idea was to be the ultimate girls' group, and they wouldn't release it in America and then I had no choice. One of those bad things about show business.'

So when it came to *Bat II*, he was like, I'll show them. This would be Jim's revenge on the music biz, he confessed, not Meat's. 'I was really pissed about Pandora's Box and it really hurt me, and my instinct was, as they say, to get back on the horse and show 'em, you know? You fuckers, you missed it! This was brilliant, Pandora's Box. I'm gonna make it so you *can't* ignore it. So I decided to do another Meat Loaf, album, which seemed suicidal in terms of a career, so to speak. But I didn't give a shit about that. I was just proving something to myself, I guess, ultimately. I knew that the music style hadn't changed for me and I always believed in my heart that if I liked it the audience will. It's probably one of the most basic things you have to believe, and one of the most difficult things. It's very complex, I think. But I believe that.

'I had the same feeling about *Bat II* as I had about the second *Godfather* movie. I thought, as long as I make it better than the first *Bat* album, it'll be good.' Another dry chuckle: 'And I have that feeling about it to this day on. But I didn't get to complete it, which is frustrating.

'I felt bad for Meat Loaf. He was wandering around touring, not doing well.' Once they got together again around the piano, 'He sounded so good. It was like he was going through a phase where his voice was really good again and I knew he just needed me to work with him and he could sound great. It wasn't easy. We did a lot of takes but I had the song "Anything For Love" and that was my opening movie, like the *Psycho* moment. I thought it was a good companion piece to [the track] "Bat Out of Hell". I felt that too about "Bad For Good". I mean, rather than write hit singles my obsession was always writing these epics, writing sweeping, cinematic journeys that were also, to use my phrase at the time, erections of the heart – which is what I define all songs as. And that's what I was aiming for: that same erection of the heart, the same jugular, urgent feeling.'

Meat's career 'was in bad shape', he admitted, when they did *Bat II*. But that just spurred him on, he said. 'There was no interest at all. It was so hard to get record companies interested. No one came to us. It came from us. It basically came from me. Not the idea of doing another record so much as it was me who said it *has* to be called *Bat Out of Hell II*. Meat Loaf didn't want that pressure but I was the one who was obsessed with that. I was thinking of *The Ring* by Wagner. One *Bat Out of Hell* seemed paltry to me. I was thinking more like three for four.

'That had been true of Bonnie, too – you know, "Total Eclipse Of The Heart", one of my most jugular erections-of-the-heart songs. Bonnie was a brilliant artist to work with for that. That had a central image of a person on the stage. It was Bonnie in a white satin nightgown with blood all over her dress and a knife in her hand.' To write the song, 'I had to be able to visualise that dramatically. With Meat Loaf, I had to await different visualisations. "Anything For Love" I always saw like the video. It always to me was a Beauty and the Beast kind of situation. It's always simmering under the surface with Meat anyway. But to me it was very explicit in this one – the beauty, and the beast holding her by some power – and that was the initial scene of the video and the song.'

I explained how when I'd spoken to Meat just a few months before he'd told me there had always been a plan for a *Bat Out of Hell III*. Was that how Jim remembered it too?

'Yes, it is. In my mind it was at least three. It was more like a *Lord of the Rings*. I mean, I wish *Godfather IV* would happen because I don't think *Godfather III* worked.'

An interesting parallel, I pointed out, as *Bat III* was clearly the weakest of the trilogy – with the obvious missing piece being Jim himself.

'Yeah, I know, so it's very difficult for me to comment. But I miss the aspects of it without criticising it.' On *Bat III*, 'I miss thunderous piano. I miss the dynamics of my work, which are very extreme. And I miss the operatic – *real* operatic – textures. And I really miss humour and I miss that aspect of personality and sense of wonder. Those are the main things that are missing and that I really worked hard, intuitively, getting into the other two *Bat Out of Hells*. I think it's a great Meat Loaf record. I'm speaking in terms of it being called *Bat Out of Hell III*. I think it lacks something and I think many people won't articulate it. But it does have to do with very specific technical points. One of which is, "Anything For Love", if you actually take it and use a metronome, so to speak, listening, there's something like thirty-five tempo changes. It's *constantly* changing. Every section changes. It was the same with [the track] "Bat Out of Hell". And Roy Bittan, who's a genius and played the piano on both, he was so against that aspect. He is a great, strict theorist. He believes everything should be subject to the theory that tempo is non-changeable. That it has to have a groove that doesn't change. And he'd always fight me on this. And Roy was one of the few geniuses I've met. But that in fact was the thing that Lou Reed complimented me about in an article. He loved "Anything For Love" and [the tempo changes] was what he loved. He said the future of rock'n'roll was in playing with the supple ability to change like an orchestra does with a conductor. That never occurred but that was a great vision and a great way of reading why that was a great record.'

Was there, though, an easy way of explaining why he hadn't been involved with *Bat III*? 'There's no real easy way. It's a combination of factors. A very *big* combination of a *lot* of factors, you know? I wish I had been involved but it didn't work out.'

He tried to say something more. Then changed his mind. It was only later I really understood why.

CHAPTER THIRTY-TWO

The Monster Let Loose

With Meat Loaf back on tour throughout almost all of 2007, pushing *Bat Out of Hell III* as somehow even better than the real thing, the one question that followed him everywhere he went was why Jim Steinman wasn't on *Bat III* too? He gave the world the story he had given me, inferring that Jimmy was simply too unwell to take part. Dropping occasional mentions that Jim had a problem with his face following a stroke, which is why he didn't show up to the press launch in New York, though never sounding entirely certain. How he would love to have Jim back and involved at some stage, though, if possible . . .

'This is like first-time artist stuff here,' Meat complained. 'Because all you got on a *Bat Out of Hell III* album is doubters. People get excited at the initial concept. And then they go, "Hmmm, I don't know. It's just a marketing tool." Well, yeah, it is. I mean, record companies see the title *Bat Out of Hell III*, you bet it's a marketing tool for them! But it still has to deliver. Take a Harry Potter. If the next Harry Potter movie doesn't deliver, the one after that, forget it. People are not stupid. So you can call it what you want, but if it's not in the grooves then you don't have anything.'

This was never really about Jim Steinman's health, though.

Now that all parties have clammed up on the subject, it is hard to establish a precise chronology for the legal nightmare that was about to break out. What's certain is that Jim Steinman had registered the phrase 'Bat Out of Hell' as a trademark in 1995. (Here we make an important distinction between a trademark and a copyright – you cannot copyright a title.) Having *Bat Out of Hell* as his trademark meant that Jim could theoretically control its application in the commercial arena. He was at liberty to allow anyone to use it, and for the decade since he'd taken out the mark he'd been happy for Meat Loaf to do so on various tours, a *Best Of* record and a live album. At some point in the months before the release of *Bat Out of Hell III: The Monster Is Loose*, however, his lawyers informed Meat Loaf's lawyers, management and record companies that they were withholding permission in this case.

That left Meat with two choices: bin the album or sue. He sued. He filed a complaint on 28 May 2006 in the Los Angeles Federal District Court against Jim Steinman and David Sonenberg for the sum of $50m.

The complaint was revealing, the best documentary evidence available on what was really going on. It alleged that Steinman wrongfully registered the phrase as his trademark in 1995. 'Meat Loaf has used the phrase "bat out of hell" extensively for the past 29 years in connection with his recordings, videos, tours and merchandise,' it went on. It claimed that Steinman had not used the mark, but nonetheless registered it in 1995 as owned by Steinman's Bat Out of Hell Inc. with the US Trademark Office, and never objected to Meat Loaf using the phrase 'until a recent falling out'.

Meat Loaf's lawyers also claimed that Steinman had been offered a contract to produce *Bat III*, which executive producer Winston Simone said was, 'by far the best producer agreement that we had ever seen. Unfortunately, Jim decided not to sign the agreement or accept the very substantial advance.' Steinman and Sonenberg had, it alleged, then used the trademark rights 'as the basis of a campaign to undermine and interfere with' Meat Loaf's concert, album, tour and contracts with others.

As a Contact Music press report had it: 'The suit asks the court to declare who owns trademark rights, seeks damages in excess of $50 million for interfering with Meat Loaf's contractual relationships with his labels and for an injunction stopping further use of the mark by Steinman. "Meat Loaf will not be bullied by anyone. He will continue to use the title 'Bat Out of Hell' in any way he wants," says his attorney Louis "Skip" Miller.'

Perhaps there was a hint as to where the problems began in one of David Sonenberg's rare public thoughts on the matter, given to *Billboard* once the battle was over and the record was out: 'Jim's health is excellent. That's not the reason he didn't participate in [*Bat III*]. He had some meaningful health problems about four years ago, but he's been totally healthy the last couple of years. His health in no way impacted on his involvement in the *Bat Out of Hell* project.'

It also emerged amidst the legal detritus that Steinman was working on a new project, a group with Steven Rinkoff called The Dream Engine – yet another echo from the past that Jim was simply not ready to let go. It was rumoured that the first Dream Engine album was to be called *Bat Out of Hell, A New Generation*, with a 2006 release. And that this is what really prompted the case over who owned the rights to the title Bat Out of Hell. It was also rumoured that the singer's legal team had filed papers claiming Meat had actually written the songs on *Bat* and *Bat II*. But no one really believed Meat Loaf was that delusional. It was all press politicking. The kind of bullshit you find yourself wading through when opposing lawyers begin chewing over $50-million lawsuits.

Ultimately the row was resolved out of court. Jim was awarded profit points on the album and in return granted the use of the trademark and of the songs of his that Meat Loaf had recorded. As the record company that would release the album, Virgin commented: 'The two came to an amicable agreement that ensured that Jim Steinman's music would be a continuing part of the *Bat Out of Hell* legacy.'

'You know, it's funny, to me it was never a love and hate thing,' Jim would say years later. 'I mean, my memory of it with Meat Loaf is it was always very much two guys working together, we were never incredibly close, but on a personal level I think I can honestly say, with maybe one or two tiny exceptions over thirty years, I never even had a huge problem with Meat Loaf person-ally. The real problems came, the problems he had with his voice or with problems with management, lawyers – that I stayed away from. I just didn't get involved.'

Which was probably true.

'It resolved itself very quickly because neither one of us wanted to argue,' Meat Loaf told Reuters after news of the lawsuit finally broke. 'We're not going to have a knock-down brawl. We just have too much history . . . There's a mutual love and respect there,' he said. 'Sometimes there's just disagreements that in business two people can't settle, so you just need to involve other people . . . You always hate to see it get to that.' Meat also hated seeing it get as far as the press. In mollifying mood, he declared: 'If it was not for Jim Steinman and his brilliance and his ability to turn a phrase and his concepts, we wouldn't be here tonight.'

Meat Loaf was speaking in a New York nightclub in a con-verted church lit by candles, at a party to celebrate the album's success. He insisted that Jim, 'really liked the record, that's really important to me. We tried to show him as much respect and loy-alty as we could.' Adding, 'It's his concept to do *Bat Out of Hell III*.' Which was the truth, strictly speaking. Just not the version Meat Loaf was now peddling . . .

'I knew I would have to shoot for the moon or the end of the universe if I was going to do *Bat Out of Hell III*,' Meat Loaf told Reuters in New York. 'The *Bat* just has a life of its own, so you can't say you're gonna top it or you're gonna beat it, you just have to try to do something special because lots of the songs on those other records hit a real emotional chord in people. So this time, I wanted to make that kind of connection with every song.'

Pressed on the elements missing from the album – the very things Steinman had complained to me about – he faced the criticism down. 'Overall, I wanted this to be edgier and rockier than the other two *Bats*,' he deadpanned. '*Bats* are typically piano-based, and we still have plenty of piano, but I have a lot of guitar-based stuff as well. I've always been mentally more hard rock than I've shown on records before, and I think the concerts tend to be where that's come across. So I've pushed that this time. I was like, "Hey, let's rock this sucker." So, we did, and it scared the hell out of me.'

And of course he had nothing but praise for Jim's replacement at the controls, Desmond Child. 'I thought Jim Steinman was tough and wants everything perfect. Well, Desmond wants it even more perfect and I didn't think that was possible. I've never worked so hard. I got a vocal coach for about four months and I've never done that before. But all the work really paid off because the vocals all sound great. It was never like a studio record. Everyone was playing like they were in a band and it was a band project with Desmond Child as the leader. People's emotions were showing and it was fabulous to watch.'

Asked in other interviews on tour if it was true that there was a *Bat Out of Hell* stage musical in the works, Meat would frown and put the whole idea down as 'impossible. You can't make a stage show out of *Bat Out of Hell*. It wouldn't work.' Then the whole thing was allowed to drop as word spread that Steinman was, in fact, now involved in a new 'dark, anime-like' show for Disney's new 'hipper' JET-X TV channel, to be called *Bikers of the Round Table*, for which he would reportedly write a song a week and executive-produce. There was even a new Steinman quote doing the rounds, apparently in support of the story: 'The first thing in my mind before I wrote *Bat* was the image of a motorcycle doing a pirouette. Now we'll see it . . .'

Actually, no, we wouldn't – or certainly not in that context. A decade on the official word is that the project is still 'on hold'.

It was as if the sins of the past were rising up again, at their heart the endless little mystery of what *Bat* was and who it be-longed to – a part of Jim and a part of Meat, indivisible by the name on the album sleeve or the writs of the lawyers. It was a truth understood best by the pair of them, and they would prob-ably both agree that it could never really be settled. Too much had happened. It had been going on for a year shy of forty, and it would never be resolved.

Speaking to an Asian news outlet around the same time, Meat said, 'I consider [Jim] to be one of my best friends but the real thing is about managers: I think Steinman's manager is the devil and Steinman feels the same way about my manager. So we had to communicate through managers and he refused to sign some papers that would have allowed for the recording of *Bat Out of Hell III* without a hitch. So, really, I didn't sue Jim Steinman. I sued his manager.'

The real sadness was not that they used one another, but that *Bat III* didn't happen in the way it was meant to. Like *Renegade Angel, Bad For Good* and *Dead Ringer*, it had fallen into the great chasm that the other two *Bat* records had created, just another of their lost boys, never to be heard as they heard it, never to be heard as they meant it.

The press, of course, had a field day. *Rolling Stone* came straight to the point. 'A lawsuit settlement prevents Jim Stein-man from commenting on *Bat Out of Hell III* in a "derogatory" manner, so this review will speak on his behalf: *Bat III* is a thrown-together mix of Steinman scraps – twenty-year-old songs and pieces from [the past]. Producer Desmond Child and a team of other songwriters try their damnedest to recreate the bombast and grandiosity of Steinman's arena-opera epics, but their efforts fall short.'

'Meat claims that *III* will be the last of the *Bats*, so, fittingly, it's the most ludicrous of all,' wrote Caroline Sullivan in the *Guardian*. 'Following a copyright lawsuit, this is the first album on which writer/producer Jim Steinman has played no active part. The whole thing is, of course, ridiculous.' Or as the review in *Entertainment Weekly* neatly nutshelled it: 'For the attentive, there's one other clue that Meat Loaf's signature classic-rock sound is being re-created by talented scabs: the lack of cheekiness. With Steinman at the helm, keen humour helped leaven the hugeness. Without that wit, *III* still produces scattershot cheap thrills . . . But to pretend that this follow-up really belongs to the *Bat Out of Hell* lineage? I would do anything for my love of the original LP, but I won't do that.'

Ten years later, Meat Loaf would finally confess in *Rolling Stone* what he really thought about *Bat Out of Hell III*. 'I'm not gonna get into the political aspects of *Bat Out of Hell III*. I wanted to strangle somebody, but not Jimmy, trust me. There is no *Bat Out of Hell III*. That should have never happened. To me, that record is non-existent. It doesn't exist.'

If only that were true.

CHAPTER THIRTY-THREE
Dissentience

After all of the trouble, all of the strife, *Bat III* sold strongly out
of the box – reaching Number 6 in the UK album charts and
Number 8 in the US, where his last record had barely cracked the
Top 100. It was testament to the power of the name, the pull it
exerted on the imagination, but the album had nothing to power
it onwards in the way that word of mouth had done for *Bat*, or
that 'I'd Do Anything For Love' had for *Bat II*, and it fizzled rather
than sparked. He went out on the road in stages, a brief US and
European tour on release of the album, and then something
bigger and more ambitious, the *Seize the Night* tour, in 2007.
Here the years of toil began to catch up with him, the thousands
of shows getting into character and testing his voice to the limit
finally taking their real toll.

In April Meat had to cancel a run of shows through illness.
He was back out in May, and through the summer, a relentless
run through the UK, Ireland, Sweden, Denmark, Germany,
Switzerland, Holland, back to England, back to America, back to
Germany, then to Scotland, alighting on Halloween at the Metro
Arena in Newcastle upon Tyne, where after an hour and eighteen
minutes of the show, and as he began to sing 'Paradise By The
Dashboard Light' for the many thousandth time, he just stopped
and said to the audience: 'Ladies and gentlemen I love you, thank
you for coming, but I can no longer continue – this may be the

last show I ever do in my life,' and he walked off to sit in his dressing room, utterly exhausted, fully cooked.

Meat Loaf was sixty years old and he'd been doing it all for far too long. He apologised to his promoter, Andrew Miller, who said soon afterwards, 'I've spoken to his doctor, and it's clear it's just exhaustion and stress. He'll be fine. We hope that twenty-four hours' rest will get him better.'

Spoken like a true promoter.

The next two shows were cancelled and then common sense prevailed, along with the diagnosis of a cyst between his vocal chords, and the rest of the tour was pulled. He was back out six months later for another summer in Europe, twenty shows and each night a seventeen-song set, and then back to America for another six shows. At the end of it all, he'd been the subject of a documentary, *Meat Loaf: In Search Of Paradise*, which was directed by Bruce David Klein and won selection to the Montreal World Film Festival. The poster was a black-and-white profile shot of him, head in hand, and although he spent much of it in rambunctious form, was a reflection on age and the growing price it was extracting. The *New York Times* review of the film ran, in part: 'The director, Bruce David Klein, portrays his subject – who was 59 during shooting – as an obsessive, self-punishing performer, striving in vain to put on a live show that matches the visions in his head.'

The newspaper's headline was just as telling: 'The Dashboard Light Now Casts Its Glow On Nostalgia'.

Having declared he had played his last show, Meat Loaf was back in the summer of 2008 playing festivals and one-off shows in Britain and Europe, returning to America for six shows at the end of the year, a mop-up from the abbreviated 2007 tour. But the hoped-for *Bat Out of Hell III* bonanza never really got off the ground. Yes, it did better than any album he'd released since *Bat II*, but in the scheme of things that wasn't saying a hell of a lot any more. He finished the year with a nearly sold-out show at the

3,000-capacity United Palace theatre in New York, performing the big hits from both *Bat* albums, along with a couple from *Bat III*, which pointedly had not been hits, 'Blind Like A Bat' and 'If It Ain't Broke, Break It'. Bizarrely, he began the show with two covers: Fleetwood Mac's 'Oh Well' and – huh? – 'I Want You So Hard (Boys Bad News)' by the Eagles of Death Metal, which barely anyone in the audience recognised, or particularly liked. The encores were 'Roadhouse Blues' by The Doors, which seemed . . . odd. But not as weird as when he segued it into 'Why Don't We Do It In The Road?' by The Beatles. There was also a lengthy instrumental section in the middle of the show, given the title of 'Dissentience' – a derivative of the Latin for 'dissent'.

The show had become like a metaphor for his career: no one quite knew what was going on any more – and Meat Loaf didn't care! Something drove Meat Loaf on, though. What was it? Depending on what figures you liked, *Bat Out of Hell* was now either the third- or the fifth-biggest-selling album of all time. He was right up there with anyone who'd ever done this for a living. He'd sold millions of copies of his other records, too, and played thousands of shows from dirt-box clubs to international stadiums. Others of his ilk lived a stately semi-retirement, their commercial moves made on the timescales of large corporations. Why not kick back in Calabasas with his new wife, Deborah Gillespie? They had been introduced by mutual friends and married in 2007. A pretty, slim blonde, some years younger than he, Deborah would accompany Meat Loaf wherever he went, on tour and off. So why not spend some time off-book with his new wife, enjoy the stuff he enjoyed doing – playing in his baseball fantasy leagues, collecting memorabilia, going to ball games? Instead of that, he took a few months off and began making another record, a record he knew Jim would again have no part in. He'd been punishing his voice and his body for decades with show after show and still he didn't back off.

Was it Marvin that drove him forward, the needs created in childhood? He could change the name to Michael but was that really enough? Or was it Meat Loaf, the character he had assumed, created for and by Jim's songs, a monster that needed to be fed? He remembered years ago, after *Bat II*, going back to Dallas for a show, and inviting loads of his high school and college friends. His father Orvis had died back in 1974, and though Meat now claimed he'd forgiven his father, he'd been in the ground a long time before the singer really felt that. Instead he wondered if Billy Slocum was going to come. He did, but it was different. Billy, the guy he'd thought was the coolest kid in high school, looked at him as if he was from another planet. 'You're a legend,' Billy had said. 'Meat Loaf, the guy who used to fix motorcycles with him, was gone. I was no longer there. In his mind, I'd just vanished,' he recalled.

Maybe it was better to just keep on running, keep going, don't stand still because if you stand still, you may have to think about all of this stuff, and who wants to do that?

There may have been another path open to him, an alternative universe that began with *Fight Club* but even that avenue now appeared closed to him. In the six years since, he'd appeared in another fourteen movies on top of everything else. He'd starred in *Blacktop*, a thriller with Kristin Davis that got good reviews but didn't fly. He'd been in *Focus*, the film of an Arthur Miller novel, with William H Macy and Laura Dern. He was in *The 51ˢᵗ State* with Samuel L. Jackson and Robert Carlyle. He was in comedies and dramas and action flicks. He played Jack Black's father in the Tenacious D movie, *Pick of Destiny*. Maybe, had he not had albums to make and tours to fulfil, he might have become the great character actor he proved he could be in *Fight Club*. After all, he'd been acting as long as he'd been singing, and it was easier on the body and probably on the psyche, too. Filmmaking was a shared responsibility. But it wasn't his path, wasn't his way.

Something drove Meat Loaf on, for all of these years, and he wasn't going to stop now – with or without Jimmy in his corner. He liked to go to a writers and actors card game when he was at home in LA. They'd meet once a month; play cards and shoot the shit. One night his friend Kilian Kerwin, who'd worked with the English director Tony Scott and wrote for most of the big studios, said, 'I got a story of a guy dying and his life's flashing forwards not backwards . . .'

Meat had been sent a song called 'Peace On Earth' by a songwriter named Rick Brantley and the first line went something like, 'Goodbye my friends, it was good to know you'. Somehow, he wasn't sure from where, he had an image of a soldier going to war. He called Kilian and asked him if he'd done anything with the storyline yet. Kilian didn't even remember it at first but they got talking and they worked on the image, a soldier sitting next to his dead friend, images of a life he might have flashing by. Kilian went off and wrote and Meat went off and started putting songs together, thinking, as he always did, about the character. After a month they met and the basis for a record was there, concept and storyline.

This was how Meat worked now. This was what he did. If you tried to explain to someone what his role in the creation of everything was, it would be difficult to understand. He didn't necessarily write the lyrics or the music, he didn't come up with the original idea, but somehow he inhabited it, he found a way to bring all of these disparate things together into something meaningful, and something entirely different to the thing they had been when they were alone. It was creativity – the subconscious function of the brain that made magic things happen, and it couldn't always be defined by a writing credit. That's how Meat Loaf saw it.

'It's a story of a non-specific soldier in a non-specific war who has been wounded on the battlefield,' he explained of the concept that would become his eleventh studio album, *Hang Cool Teddy Bear*, released in 2010. 'He's with his friend and his friend has been killed. It's all very edgy and very graphic. He sees his own blood across the dirt. He's sitting there seeing his friend dying, he's been hit with shrapnel.'

He went on, breathlessly. 'The opening line talks about how much it hurts. It hurts in a way he never imagined. He sees his own mortality so he thinks he is going to die. And at that moment, instead of his life flashing backwards, which is what he has always been told is going to happen when you die, his life flashes forward. So initially he's back in his hometown and he's back with his girlfriend only his girlfriend is a different girl . . .'

He had a new slate of writers. Desmond Child contributed one song, Rick Brantley three. Justin Hawkins of The Darkness chipped in, as did James Michael, Jon Foreman, Marsha Mamalet, Liz Vidal and the *American Idol* judge Kara DioGuardi. The producer was Rob Cavallo who had a golden touch, especially for the nouveau fake 'punk' that had been clogging the charts: he'd gone multi-platinum with Green Day and the Goo Goo Dolls, and with plastic goth-teenies My Chemical Romance. But he'd also worked with Phil Collins and Fleetwood Mac. He understood songs and sound making, and when Meat Loaf played him the initial repertoire, Cavallo listened to them, and to his ideas. 'I had nineteen songs,' Meat recalled, 'and three of them made the record. Rob said, "Look, these other songs are for a different album than the one we're making."'

Like the brilliant actor he was, he allowed the director to have the final say. At the same time, he said he felt that Cavallo was able to put his ego aside in a way that Jim and Todd and Desmond Child weren't, and as a result the finished record was more 'his' than some of the others. 'Every other producer I've ever worked with has put his ego into it,' he told the music website The Quietus, once *Hang Cool Teddy Bear* was out. 'So, you had my ego, you had Steinman's ego, and you had Todd's ego on *Bat Out of Hell*. That was a good combination. It worked; everybody was willing to go. "Okay, I'll do that." "But wait I'll do this." "Okay, I'll give you that and I'll take this." That was a good combination; we worked really well together on that record.

'Desmond Child's ego is really strong, he doesn't play well with others. Rob Cavallo has an ego as a producer but it never comes into play. With him it's about the artist. It's about making Meat Loaf's album Meat Loaf's album. You have all these other people around you, these incredible musicians and engineers. And you know I didn't know this about myself, believe me, basically what I did is my vision, how I wanted it to sound. What I wanted to sing, and how I wanted to move it forward. So that's the thing, nobody messed with it, for the first time ever.'

The results were more streamlined – this was now mainstream rock with a capital 'R' – than even *Bat III*, and as the *Guardian*'s Caroline Sullivan noted, 'It desperately needs a ballad.' Cavallo produced a slick modern rock record that was generally applauded by the critics as one of the best of Meat's non-Jim albums. It didn't sell, though. Not like the old days. Top 30 in the US, Top Five in the UK and Germany, but at a time when the record industry had tanked and even Number 1 records didn't sell a tenth of what they had done in the past.

But it boosted Meat's confidence as an artist. He felt like he finally wholly owned something he was offering to the world. Even if almost nobody that bought either of the first two *Bat* albums would ever listen to it. Maybe the soldier idea had bubbled from his subconscious because that was in a way how he saw himself, an old warrior who had been battling it out for a long time now, weary but unbowed, still doing it long after the others had fallen.

'I am the original fighter,' he said. 'I've been in this business for forty years. And you know, some people get lucky. Some people just walk this golden path. I've walked the dirt road with a lot of rocks on it and with a lot of rabbit holes.'

He toured once more, spending July and August travelling America, playing casinos and theatres, arts centres and 'events venues', all B-market territory, no NY or LA, no SF or any of the big payday cities like Detroit and Chicago. Fun family dates. Big hats and bigger smiles, howdy-doody ma and pa shows. There were some Christmas dates in the UK to end the year, but only one Wembley Arena. Tinsel and tears; fake snow and strange set lists. Five of the songs he performed came from *Hang Cool Teddy Bear*. Five came from *Bat Out of Hell*, three from *Bat II*, one from *Bat III*. But if his professional life had settled into the lucrative but mundane treadmill of the classic rock circuit, his personal life had bounced back. He was more settled, married now to Deborah Gillespie, and watching his stepdaughter Pearl make a career as a singer (Pearl would also marry into the music business – her partner is Anthrax guitarist Scott Ian) and his daughter Amanda embark on life as an actor.

He made another record in 2011, *Hell in a Handbasket*, again without a single Steinman song, although he had hinted that there was a possibility one would appear on later versions of the album (it didn't). There was a mad cover of 'California Dreaming' and a guest rap by Chuck D – evidence that in Jim's absence, and without the conceptual ideas he'd found for *Hang Cool Teddy Bear*, Meat Loaf was once again resorting to throwing the kitchen sink at the wall to see what stuck.

The *AV Club* review cut to the heart of it: 'Too much of *Hell in a Handbasket* is just generic songwriter-mill fodder, over-cranked and over-sung. The heart is there; with Meat Loaf, the heart is *always* there. But the skin is synthetic, and not in any kind of super-cool or ironic way. This album is neither fun enough nor weird enough to demand the kind of obsessive replaying of Meat Loaf's best.'

He toured it wholeheartedly as usual, but the hound dogs were on his trail now, close enough for him to feel their breath. He had a nightmare in Australia, where he was asked to provide the half-time entertainment at the AFL Grand Final, an occasion as momentous Down Under as the Super Bowl is in America. Perched on a small stage set in one of the stands, something went catastrophically wrong and stayed that way during the excruciating fifteen-minute set. The band sounded okay and Patti Russo held things together as best she could, but Meat was dreadful, wandering in and out of tune, his diction, which was becoming problematic the older he got, moving between the lyrics in continuous sounds, rending them amorphous and indistinct. Fan videos were immediately uploaded on YouTube and went viral, and he compounded all of the brickbats by calling the critics, 'butt-smellers' and lashing out at the AFL, who had paid him a reported half a million dollars to perform.

As the respected Melbourne newspaper the *Age* rather uncharitably put it: 'At times he seemed to sing in keys previously unknown to mankind, and deep in the fifth set of "Bat Out of Hell" he sounded not unlike some larger form of sea mammal in considerable pain and/or distress. Part of the sport in watching the extravaganza became trying to guess which extremely familiar piece of pop history the Loafster was currently strangling.'

He hadn't been good, but he didn't deserve that. From now on, though, Meat Loaf found himself consigned to the has-been hell of TV reality shows like the US version of *Celebrity Apprentice* where, in 2011, he had the ignominy of being fired by Donald Trump – for being 'too emotional'. The result of an onscreen explosion in which Meat accused actor and fellow Texan Gary Busey of stealing his paints during an art project, calling him a 'motherfucker' several times and threatening to kill him. 'You look in my eyes,' Meat screamed at Busey. 'I am the last fucking person in the world you ever want to fuck with!' Then was physically restrained from attacking the bemused actor.

Two minutes later the bag Meat Loaf had actually put his paints in was discovered hidden under some towels. He continued to curse Busey but by now the singer was fooling no one. He had to go.

Quickly.

CHAPTER THIRTY-FOUR

What Part of My Body Hurts Most?

There was only one move left. They'd fucked up *Bat III*, and they both knew it. Meat Loaf and Jim Steinman were both sixty-six years old in 2013, when they began emailing each other again without needing their lawyers or managers to intercede. How many more chances would they get? It was apparent that Jim probably didn't have another album of material in him. It was the natural way of things. Very few musical artists on Earth were more productive in their sixties than they were in their twenties – Leonard Cohen, Lou Reed and David Bowie had seemingly managed the impossible and saved their best work for their last. But they were the exceptions that proved the rule. Richard Wagner's late dramas may be considered his masterpieces but Phil Spector and Paul McCartney hadn't done anything since the pop world was still new. Jim Steinman may have fallen somewhere between the two as a modern composer with classical influences, but even his great engine of creativity was slowing, no longer fuelled by the same flow of energy. Jim's writing was probably in the same sort of state as Meat's voice, still standing, but like a glorious ruin. Time was forcing them to face one another's frailties. With it came the realisation that they would have to answer some fundamental questions.

What happened to Meat when Jim's creativity slowed down?
What happened to Jim when Meat's voice went quiet?

As young men they had created a thing called Meat Loaf on a record called *Bat Out of Hell*. Who or what 'Meat Loaf' actually is was a question that had dogged them ever since the first arguments about whether or not Jim's name should be on the album sleeve. It had shadowed their careers, and there was still no answer.

Apart they were one thing and together they were another.

But the thing that they were together – that version of Meat Loaf – was weakening now, as they grew older.

In 2013, Meat Loaf told the British chat show host Jonathan Ross that, 'We've been communicating back and forth for the last six months every day by email. We've cut three tracks, we're getting ready to cut three more, and then we'll hopefully cut three with Steinman.'

One last album together then, seemed to be the plan. Would it be called *Bat Out of Hell IV*, though? No, age and too many lawsuits, too much life and death had passed to play that game again. They thought it would take two years to make the album, in the end it took three. The title changed from *Brave and Crazy* to *Braver Than We Are*. The latter was the title of the song Jim had written for *Tanz der Vampire* – in turn he rewrote that into 'Going All The Way (A Song In Six Movements)'. And he wrote another, 'Speaking In Tongues'. Meat also recorded the first two songs Jim had ever written, 'Who Needs The Young' and 'Skull Of Your Country', as well as other old compositions – 'More' which Jim had written for Sisters Of Mercy, 'Loving You Is A Dirty Job (But Someone's Got To Do It)', which had been recorded by Bonnie Tyler in 1985 . . .

This time, though, they weren't being cynical, they weren't fighting one another, or trying to bolster album sales, or arguing over whom exactly Jim had written the songs for. They were using what little they had left to give, the last gas in the tank. All parts of the buffalo. Even Ellen Foley and Karla DeVito came and sang on it. When they were done, Meat said, 'It's a tribute to Jim Steinman really. It's a tribute to both of us and our work together.'

Jim also issued a beautiful and mad screed about what *Braver Than We Are* meant to him: 'Hearing it in its entirety – I can honestly say it's one of the GREATEST works of ART I've ever been involved in! Nothing amazes me more than to end up with a record that, for me, stands with the top ten recordings of ALL TIME!!' And he said something else, perhaps the best thing he could say: 'Meat is heroic in his ravaged voice, tragically, inspiringly heroic.'

They had spun full circle, as far as Jim could see. Forty years before, Meat Loaf was tragic and inspiring because he was a fat loser inhabiting songs about a fat loser's improbable dreams of what he might be, and in doing that he struck a chord with almost everyone, because almost everyone had felt that way at one time or another. Now, as Jim saw and heard, Meat couldn't sing like that any more. He was heroic in a different way. He answered the bell. He stepped up to the plate. He returned the call and – as always – gave it everything he had. This time, though, what he had was ravaged by the years, it was old and broken, yet magnificent and unbeaten. What's more it *couldn't* be beaten. Jim understood that. He understood that as long as Meat Loaf answered the bell, his spirit would never break, even though his body was already beginning to. Released in September 2016, *Braver Than We Are* could never sound like *Bat Out of Hell*, or 'I'd Do Anything For Love'. It could never be what they heard in their heads, what they wanted it to be. The years had taken that away from them for ever. Instead, it wasn't a great record. It wasn't even a particularly good one. But it was a noble one, a proud one, a brave one. In that regard, it was their best.

Some of the critics viewed the enterprise kindly. 'A mad, florid knockout,' *Classic Rock* magazine cooed. 'Strength through absurdity.' Some, though, did not. 'The album, vocally is questionable to say the least,' announced the *Daily Telegraph*, 'with even diehard Meat Loaf fans saying the singer struggles to keep up with Steinman's compositions – but that's how he does it these days.'

In fact, most of the media attention drummed up by the release of Meat Loaf's thirteenth album was focused on his health. He was playing live in Edmonton in June 2016. He'd just started 'I'd Do Anything For Love' when he slumped to the floor, unconscious. Amateur footage showed that his vocals carried on for a line after he'd fallen, making it look very much like there was some sort of backing tape playing, but he would deny that once he'd recovered.

'We weren't sure at first whether it was part of the act or it was something for real,' said Lindsay Sundmark, who watched it happen. Five years before, he had fainted during a gig in Pittsburgh. But wild rumours that he had died circulated, and the tour was cut short. A couple of months later, once he'd recovered, he told the *Guardian*: 'I hit the highest note in "I'd Do Anything For Love" and just felt really dizzy. I thought I'd finish the song sitting down, and as I started to sit down I passed out. We did another seven gigs, but by the time we got to Moose Jaw in Canada I felt like I was dying.'

The rest of the shows were pulled, and as he admitted in the same interview, he thought that he might never appear live again. 'Does it feel strange that you may have played your last ever show in a place called Moose Jaw?' he was asked.

'It does feel strange,' he replied. But feeling strange had never stopped him before. Why should it now? By then he was doing promo for *Braver Than We Are*. The same *Guardian* writer, Dave Simpson, noted at the start of his piece that Meat was 'sounding slightly slurred'. The slurring was also apparent when he did the rounds of UK TV and radio that month. Appearing on the lunchtime talk show *Loose Women*, he appeared to have trouble pronouncing some words. He told them: 'My assistant said, "Don't talk about this . . ." but I went to a doctor the other night and he told me that my tongue was swollen. And I have no idea why. It was causing me to talk slower than normal. Cos I saw myself on TV and I freaked out. I'm going, "I look like I'm drunk . . ."' He also told the show: 'I have a pinched nerve in my back. When I stand up to walk, it feels like I have Norman Bates from *Psycho* stabbing me in the back, and it hurts like hell.' Asked about performing again one day, he admitted: 'Oh, I can't. I can't stand up longer than five minutes . . .. The back thing came out of nowhere. I woke up one morning and I fell down. Growing old is not for wusses . . .'

That appearance came in September. In November he was back in the UK, and had to use a cane when he collected an award from *Q* magazine on stage at the Roundhouse. On the same trip he appeared on the national TV breakfast programme *This Morning*, again speaking about his back issues and again causing alarm among some viewers, who noted how pale and frail he seemed.

Meat Loaf like the rest of us was entitled to handle matters of his health however he wanted, but one thing was sure: his touring days were done. It seemed inconceivable, as he approached his seventieth birthday, that his voice or his back could stand up to the rigours of it.

It was over and this time it wouldn't be coming back. He knew that.

I also spoke to Meat Loaf at the end of 2016. He was back at home in LA, still doing his best to sell his new album, doing his best to conceal the fact that he was now so ill the right side of his face looked like that of a recovering stroke victim. He couldn't stand without his cane, found it hard to walk even with it. And his voice was unmistakably slurred. But his spirit was still high. He remained, as ever, defiant, the old actor still hungering for the spotlight of centre stage.

The man himself was determined to play down rumours of his imminent demise, and do what he could to promote what he proudly, if somewhat wincingly, insisted on telling me was 'The *real Bat Out of Hell.*' It wasn't, of course. But, as he well knows through often painful experience, the mere mention of the word 'Bat' in connection with any of his albums is enough on its own to force a more considered appreciation – and much greater sales potential – of what, in reality, he readily conceded, was going to be 'The last album I will make. This is it.'

Indeed, *Braver Than We Are* positively reeked of last-calls, with many of the key components of the original 43-million-selling *Bat Out of Hell* temporarily reuniting. Not least, Jim Steinman, who wrote the songs, though most of them were originally penned at other times for different reasons.

Talking to Meat Loaf now, though, he freely admitted the new album was his last hurrah. 'I can't talk about why,' he said, 'but I can tell you I've got a couple more [Steinman] songs I'm gonna record, then that's it for me.'

He was still explaining away the walking stick that he is now forced to walk with as the consequence of the 'pinched nerve in my back' line. The slurred vowels and blinking right eye, how-ever, go unmentioned, at least in his presence.

Having interviewed Meat Loaf many times since we'd first met decades before, I had over the years grown used to being received as a recognised ally. But Meat Loaf no longer knows who I am. No more so than when we last met a few years before, in London, when he was in such poor health he was reportedly 'taken ill' in the green room of the *Loose Women* TV studio and had to be hurriedly ushered away just minutes before he was due to appear before the watching millions.

He had also acquired a much more benign take on his off-on relationship with Steinman: one that both men had consistently presented to me over the years as 'ambiguous', to say the least.

Now, though, Meat Loaf insisted that, 'Jimmy and I have never had an argument. Never!'

Meanwhile, 2017 looked certain to be a defining moment for both men. In October it would be exactly forty years since the release of *Bat Out of Hell*. An event that insiders reliably informed me would almost certainly spark a 'deluxe' reissue, with those two extra new Steinman-penned tracks Meat told me about, and a farewell tour by the singer – another big reason why his health issues were being played down in public.

Writing this now, though, six months later, I am told that behind the scenes the likelihood of Meat Loaf ever performing on stage again are extremely slim indeed.

The fact remains, Meat Loaf, who is seventy this year, is on his last go-round. It seems the Meat Loaf phenomenon – 75 million albums sold worldwide, including over 19 platinum albums in the UK, 30 platinum albums in Australia, and 20 platinum albums in the US – is now finally coming to an end.

CHAPTER THIRTY-FIVE

Jim Steinman's Dream

In February 2017, Meat Loaf was back in London. The reason, he said, was to lend support 'for Jim's dream of forty years'.

In 1977, a few weeks after the release of *Bat Out of Hell*, Meat recalled saying to Jim that they could finally make a musical based on the *Bat* songs, now that they were out there on vinyl. It wouldn't have been at all a strange notion given that Jim had just written *The Dream Engine* and *More Than You Deserve*. And it wasn't as though the opportunity hadn't arisen since – Jim had written lyrics for *Whistle Down the Wind*, music for *Tanz der Vampire* and toyed with the *Batman* idea.

But in the way that their entire careers were ones of timing – good for bad, bad for good – the time had never been quite right. In the intervening years, the jukebox musical had assumed a major role in theatres, pulling in punters that wouldn't ordinarily consider a night out there. Perhaps it began with ABBA's *Mamma Mia!*. Queen had made a considerable fortune from *We Will Rock You*. Everyone from Rod Stewart (*Tonight's the Night*) to Green Day (*American Idiot*) had now had a go. The formula was to concoct a story around the hits and let a big song-and-dance cast loose on material that the audience already knew and loved intimately.

With *Bat* ready to mark its fortieth anniversary, and Jim and Meat probably at the end of their creative partnership after *Braver*

Than We Are, nothing now stood in the way. And, whether knowingly or not, *Bat Out of Hell: The Musical* had a built-in advantage over most jukebox shows: Steinman was a theatrical writer who had always written with a story in mind, and Meat Loaf had characterised the songs rather than just sung them. Nostalgia meant that the original fans of the record saw the material through the glow of youth, and for them it was moving and transformative.

When the director, Jay Scheib, studied the material he saw that: 'More or less, it is like real rock and roll. It is about growing up without ever getting old, it is about refusing to grow up because it is just too painful sometimes, it is about falling in love and not being able to stop yourself, even falling in love knowing your heart is going to be broken again. So somehow I'd like to think that the fountain of youth founded the soundtrack of *Bat Out of Hell*.'

When I had spoken to Jim Steinman about a *Bat* stage show some ten years before he had been very emphatic over exactly what kind of show it would be. The plan, he said, even back then, was for him to put on 'a very good epic in London. It will open in London. It's going to have its own theatre built for it – and that's *Bat Out of Hell*. A musical, yes. I hate calling it that but, yeah, a musical, but of a new kind.'

And would Meat Loaf star in it or take any part? 'Not Meat Loaf, no. He isn't involved at all. This is my *Bat Out of Hell*. It's my attempt to tell the actual story of the *Bat Out of Hell* series that I did, and give it real power. Basically, it's doing *Mamma Mia!* but hopefully differently and better. It makes all the songs make sense. It enacts the songs. It involves a great creative team. A lot of dance. Gerald Scarfe is doing all the animation and production work, and it's gonna be in 3D, which is a first, I think, for musical theatre.'

It sounded amazing. What else could he tell me? 'They are going to build a theatre, that's the plan. There are producers and the thing is in place. The idea is to build our own theatre designed around the show. Cirque du Soleil have done it many times in Las Vegas. It just has almost never been done for commercial theatre, in any kind of conventional way. But it was deemed by the producers, who are extremely good, that that's the way to go with this, that it's ultimately better to build your own theatre and do whatever you want.'

I asked for a date and he said: 'Probably we're talking about London in the fall of 2008.' First, in 2007, there would be 'about four months somewhere else, yet to be determined. Unfortunately, everyone tells me Ireland can't support a long run, so we're looking for places to do about four months where we preview, basically, and try it out. But it's very complex. It's gonna involve a lot of real motorcycles, motorcycle stunts, skateboard stunts, jousting . . . a lot of visual spectacle and action, gymnastics of every kind. Recreating the techniques of great movies like *Crouching Tiger* or *Hero*, you know, wires, try to recreate all that and yet have a really good story. I mean, that's my hope. That all this spectacle and 3D is amazing but that the story hopefully, at the end you actually cry at. That's the story that I took as the basis, the impetus to write all the songs that I wrote for *Bat Out of Hell I* and *II* – and including a couple from *Bat Out of Hell III* that just happened to end up there. But it's basically *Bat Out of Hell I* and *II*.'

He said that the only two songs from *Bat III* 'that I think I need are "It's All Coming Back To Me Now" and "In The Land Of The Pig" . . . "Land Of The Pig" is a song I love and that's perfect for a moment in the show. And it is a show based on, basically, the Peter Pan myth – but so was *Bat Out of Hell*. It just has to be seen. And I think it's a great solving of a mystery, you know? I mean, it's not a great mystery, it's not like finding out what Shakespeare had in mind, it's just me.'

What else could he tell me? 'I don't want to talk about it too specifically but at one point there's a mention that "this is no bloody jukebox musical!"' he laughed. 'Instantly that's said the largest jukebox ever created rises up on the stage. Like a *monster* jukebox, it's fabulous . . . like the Stonehenge of jukeboxes. And it has all the titles of all the possible songs rotating in lights around the whole jukebox. We're not gonna print in the programme what songs or what order the show is in, so you're just seeing the jukebox with rotating lights of various song titles. You just never know which one it's gonna stop on, it's just gonna land on it . . . I hope it's great, and it is all based on the Peter Pan story and [whatever] I'm allowed to put in. Just treating it as Peter Pan if he was really eighteen years old and my whole point always with Peter Pan that I wanted to tell in the film was that it's science-fiction. In my version, the Lost Boys become genetically frozen and can't age. I was totally intrigued in sci-fi terms, what would happen if you were eighteen years old for your eighty-five, or hundred years or more? I mean, I've always found that interesting from a sci-fi point of view. I mean, what does that mean, if you're eighteen for sixty years, do you experience any change at all? Does experience change you or do you have to genetically develop? So if you have a physical condition that keeps you at eighteen could you possibly change enough just from experience? Or even would that contradict the fact that you're still eighteen genetically?'

It was certainly an interesting conundrum. 'I think it's at the heart of Peter Pan, though. Barrie never dealt with it [in the original book] but that's what I'm trying to deal with, the idea of taking Peter Pan seriously as sci-fi and as eroticism in rock'n'roll. Because it's the ultimate rock'n'roll myth, you've got to admit. I mean, James Barrie might not have known about the Stones, The Beatles, or The Who, but he sure wrote the ultimate myth for them. I mean, The Who – who could have possibly come up with a better aphoristic, brilliant description of a generation than "I hope I die before I get old"? Which is Peter Pan! JM Barrie! Which is the Lost Boys! It's the ultimate rock'n'roll futuristic wasteland, in my version. And so to me it's fascinating, because to me Peter would become a kind of Caligula. He'd be so mad! That's my image. After being eighteen for forty years, how mad would you be? When you're eighteen every moment is life and death. Every moment is jugular, to use my phrase that I always use. But if you're eighteen for sixty years, wouldn't that make you totally insane? Having to create new sensation, new excitement *every hour*. You'd be so exhausted and to me it would turn you into a madman, this sort of Caligula-like figure. But I think pervading that or overruling that is the romanticism of the piece. And to me the greatest story I can imagine about love is Wendy and Peter. With Peter never growing at all and Wendy just growing old the way human beings do, and it becomes the ultimate May-to-December romance . . . tragedy, actually, because she moves forward and he doesn't, and that's exciting too, to me. A love story in terms of eroticism, in terms of a whole visionary world.'

A decade on, now that the show is finally here, not quite everything that Jim Steinman had originally envisaged had come to pass, but by God, it was close. No Gerald Scarfe, not really in 3D, but the set for the show was still incredibly detailed and ambitious. Designed by Jon Bausor, whose previous work includes *Bugsy Malone*, it includes full-scale escalators, three levels and a number of motorcycles. There are also cameras mounted on props and the actors to beam different perspectives of the action onto big screens to create an immersive experience and bring the audience close to the action. Speaking now in soundbites, Jim told the press: 'It's a story about kids who never grow up, and who fight authority . . .'

The show opened in Manchester in February 2017, with plans for it to transfer to London in the summer. It was launched to the press outside the London Coliseum, the stage where the show would receive its world premiere in June. Meat Loaf walked on stage with his cane. Jim was too ill to travel. Meat took the microphone and said to the crowd: 'This has been Jim Steinman's dream for fifty years, and for my friend of forty-two years and somebody who I love dearly to see his dream finally come true is remarkable. Thank you for making *Bat Out of Hell* what it was – without England it wouldn't exist.'

Forty years, fifty years, who knew? Who cared? This was now Jim's world. We were all just living in it, looking at it through Meat Loaf's eyes.

They were not together, and yet they had come full circle, from the stage of the Public Theater where they had first laid eyes on one another to the stage of the London Coliseum, where the years had kept them apart, two kids, one fat, one thin, one rich, one poor, an odd couple who'd lived strange lives together and apart, joined forever by this. And now, bizarrely, poignantly, tellingly perhaps, looking more like each other than ever before: both portly, both battling the after-effects of ill health. Jim still dressed like the rock star he never was; Meat now dressed as the home-loving family man he'd wished his own father had been.

If Meat looked up at the banner flying proudly from the building's exterior, he didn't say, but his thoughts would be interesting.

Above the image of the flaming bike, in a huge gothic font was: *Jim Steinman's Bat Out of Hell: The Musical.*

The words 'Meat Loaf' nowhere to be seen.

NOTES AND SOURCES

The foundations of this book are based on my own original investigations and archives, beginning with interviews and conversations over the years with Meat Loaf and Jim Steinman. (The most recent with Meat Loaf in 2016.)

I have also spent a great deal of time compiling as much background material as possible from as much published – and, in a few cases, unpublished – material as there is available, including books, magazine and newspaper articles, websites, TV and radio shows, DVDs, demo-tapes, bootleg CDs and any other form of media that contained useful information, the most important of which I have listed here.

However, extra special mention should also go to a handful of sources that proved especially helpful, in terms of adding to my own insights and investigations. First and foremost to the official Meat Loaf autobiography, *To Hell And Back*, the Virgin new edition paperback of 2000. Co-written by Meat and the always-excellent David Dalton, it is a wonderful work, which I urge readers to investigate. Also, Sandy Robertson's superb original Meat Loaf and Jim Steinman biography, *The Phenomenology Of Excess*, first published by Omnibus Press in 1981. I was lucky enough to know Sandy in those years when he wrote it, and it was through his fascination and deep insight into the Meat Loaf/Jim Steinman phenomenon that I also became a lifelong observer. Through his book and also his numerous brilliant pieces for *Sounds* magazine. Jim Steinman still loves that book so much the last time we spoke he told me the reason he had never done a book of his own was because he would never be able to come up with a better title than Sandy's. Again, I strongly urge you to seek it out.

Another wonderful source of information was Jim Steinman's official website, www.jimsteinman.com. Dedicated to Sandy Robertson, it is a brilliantly comprehensive, and marvellously frank guide, particularly to the earlier years of this genius songwriter's life and career. Check it out.

There were also occasional one-off pieces, which were so exceptional they forced me to rethink several parts of the overall story: Dave Dickson's several insightful pieces for *Kerrang!* in the 1980s; Lynn Barber's typically pin sharp piece in *The Guardian* in 2003; the excellent John Aizlewood in *Q*, 1993; Chuck Palahniuk's brilliant books, *Fight Club* and *Stranger Than Fiction*; and Jeff Maysh's brilliant piece in *Narratively*, 2014; Chris Munday in *Rolling Stone*, 1993.

Other sources deserving of heartfelt thanks and praise include: *Classic Rock, Mojo, Uncut, The Scene, BMI MusicWorld, Associated Press, BBC Radio One, AV Club, Billboard, Sunday Times, Melody Maker, NME, Circus, The Independent, The Mirror, RAW, Mail On Sunday, bullz-eye.com, Playbill, Contact Music, Reuters*, the Virgin promo disc for *Pandora's Box, Classic Albums DVD, Channel News Asia, The Quietus, The Guardian, The Times, LA Times* and the *New York Times*.

INDEX